THE
VISION OF
JUDAISM

VISIONS OF REALITY

A Series on Religions as Worldviews

Series Editor: Roger Corless, Duke University, Emeritus

A common assumption behind many surveys of religions is that there is something called "religion" which is a uniquely classifiable phenomenon and which may be dealt with and written about according to recognized and agreed upon subdivisions. Systems identified as religions are then fitted into a prescribed format without considering whether the format is suited to the particular system under consideration.

This series is motivated by the awareness that, rather than there being something called "religion," there are many *religions*, and the more they are studied, the more each one manifests itself as equally profound, nontrivial, and adequate unto itself. Each volume will be an attempt to take each religion on its own terms. Comparison may be made with other religious traditions, but there will be no attempt to impose a single methodology in order to reduce the plurality to one basic scheme.

Published Volumes in the Visions of Reality Series:

THE VISION OF BUDDHISM
Roger Corless

THE VISION OF ISLAM
Sachiko Murata and William Chittick

THE VISION OF JUDAISM
Dan Cohn-Sherbok

THE VISION OF JUDAISM

WRESTLING WITH GOD

by Dan Cohn-Sherbok

Paragon House
St. Paul, Minnesota

Published in the United States by
Paragon House
2285 University Avenue West
St. Paul, MN 55114

Cover image "Battle of Jacob and an Angel" by Jan Spychalski courtesy of the
National Museum of Poznan, Poland.

Library of Congress Cataloging-in-Publication Data

Cohn-Sherbok, Dan.
The vision of Judaism : wrestling with God / by Dan Cohn-Sherbok.—1st ed.
p. cm.—(Visions of reality)
Includes bibliographical references.
ISBN 1-55778-808-1 (pbk. : alk. paper)
1. Judaism—History. 2. Reform Judaism. I. Title. II. Series.
BM155.3.C64 2004
296.3—dc22
2004000377

Manufactured in the United States of America

The paper used in this publication meets the minimum requirements of American
National Standard for Information Sciences—Permanence of Paper for Printed
Library Materials, ANSIZ39.48-1984.

10 9 8 7 6 5 4 3 2 1

For current information about all releases from Paragon House,
visit the web site at http://www.paragonhouse.com

For Lavinia

CONTENTS

Editor's Note

By choosing to present a unified vision of Judaism through the metaphor of *wrestling*, Rabbi Cohn-Sherbok has put much of himself into this book. As a Jew he is part of the wrestling, the history of debate and controversy, which he describes. Judaism is for him a living tradition which looks to the future as much as to the past. At times this wrestling leads him to move from descriptive to prescriptive language as he strongly recommends how the wrestling should proceed. Readers who do not agree with the recommendations may wish to use them as a focus for discussion and as a way of entering into the wrestling themselves.

Roger Corless
Series Editor

Acknowledgments

I would like to acknowledge my indebtedness to a number of important books that provided information and source material for this study: Louis Jacobs, *A Jewish Theology* (London; Darton, Longman and Todd, 1973) and *Principles of the Jewish Faith* (Northvale, New Jersey; Jason Aronson, 1988); John Polkinhorne, *Science and Christian Belief* (London, Society for the Promotion of Christian Knowledge, 1994); Paul Badham, "The Implications of John Hick's Theodicy for Christian Faith and Practice," Paul Weingartener, ed., *The Problem of Evil in the World* (Peter Lang, Frankfort, 2004); I would also like to thank Roger Corless for his support, and Rosemary Byrne Yokoi and her staff at Paragon House for their help.

Preface

Throughout the history of the Jewish nation, Jews have piously kept the covenant. Dedicated to God, they have seen themselves as his chosen people. Yet, from biblical times they have also challenged God. The tradition of wrestling with God begins with Jacob's confrontation with a divine messenger at the ford of the Jabbok river. According to the Book of Genesis, Jacob was left alone, and an angel battled with him until the break of day:

> When the man saw that he did not prevail against Jacob, he touched the hollow of his thigh; and Jacob's thigh was put out of joint as he wrestled with him. Then he said, "Let me go, for the day is breaking." But Jacob said, "I will not let you go, unless you bless me." And he said to him, "What is your name?" And he said, "Jacob." Then he said, "Your name shall no more

be called Jacob, but Israel, for you have striven with God and
with me, and have prevailed." Then Jacob asked him, "Tell me,
I pray, your name." But he said, "Why is it that you ask my
name?" And there he blessed him. So Jacob called the name
of the place Peniel, saying, "For I have seen God face to face,
and yet my life is preserved." (Gen. 32: 25–30)

Here Jacob struggled with God, and thereby became Israel.
Later the name Israel was applied to the nation as a whole. The
Jewish people collectively are Israel (meaning "he who wrestles
with God"): unlike other religions, which elevate submission to
God as a cardinal principle, Judaism encourages critical reflection. From biblical times to the present, religious Jews have
struggled to make sense of God's nature and action in light of
their contemporary knowledge. This volume, which presents a
new vision of Judaism for the twenty-first century, stands in this
tradition. The theme of Jacob struggling with God's messenger
is the dominant motif throughout. As I will seek to show, the
true Israel can only prevail if it continues to wrestle with God.
The patriarch Jacob himself knew this all those years ago. As he
limped away from the encounter, he declared, "I have seen God
face to face and still my life is preserved."

The book is in four parts. Part I, Wrestling with Myself, begins with an autobiographical account of my experiences as an
American Reform Jew. The narrative continues with my exposure to the perplexities and problems of the Reform rabbinate,
and focuses on my shift in theological perspective, which serves
as the basis for my reinterpretation of the Jewish tradition.

Part II, Wrestling with the Message, outlines the central
tenets of Judaism: the existence of God, divine omnipotence
and omniscience, creation, providence, revelation, Torah and
mitzvah, sin and repentance, the chosen people, the promised
land, the Messiah, and the hereafter. In all cases, I describe my
own exposure to these doctrines, present their development in
the tradition, and conclude with a critical evaluation. The chapters in this part are designed to introduce readers to the basic

principles of the Jewish faith as it has developed through the centuries, as well as to provide a critical assessment of traditional Jewish belief.

Part III, Wrestling with the World, is concerned with Jewish practice and includes Sabbath, pilgrim festivals, New Year, Day of Atonement, days of joy, life-cycle events, marriage and divorce, the home, and death and mourning. Again, each chapter starts on a personal note, continues with a depiction of these practices in the tradition, and then offers a critical analysis of their place in modern Jewish life.

Part IV, Wrestling with the Vision, is an examination of Jewish belief and practice in the modern world, emphasizing the need for Jews to adopt a more tolerant stance.

PART I

WRESTLING WITH MYSELF

Chapter 1.

WRESTLING WITH MYSELF

Growing up in the leafy suburbs of Denver, Colorado, I had a typical Jewish education at the local Reform Temple. At the age of eight I was sent to the Temple summer camp located in the Rocky Mountains about fifty miles from Denver. I remember sleeping in a wood cabin by a mountain stream with a group of other boys. One day the rabbi came up from Denver to visit the camp. After lunch, he came to inspect our cabin. Accompanied by the Camp Director, he stopped by my bed and asked my name. "Dan Cohn-Sherbok," I replied. He looked me over. "That bed is a mess," he said. "And you look a mess. You're a messy little kid."

This unpromising beginning was followed by years of religious education at the Temple Sunday school. Jewish boys and girls from throughout the city were taken by their parents on Sunday to the Temple, located in an affluent part of the city. Surrounded by a gigantic parking lot, the Temple loomed over the neighbouring suburban houses. The stained-glass windows of the sanctuary—in abstract designs—dominated the building. At nine o'clock cars arrived, children were unloaded, and more than a hundred children streamed into the building. The bells then rang, and we went to our classes.

For two hours, our teachers attempted to impart knowledge of Judaism to unwilling students. Most had no interest in the tradition. Instead of listening, they made paper airplanes, threw spit balls, and giggled throughout the lesson. On one occasion, a trouble-maker in my class jumped out of the ground-floor window and ran away. On another Sunday a substitute teacher struggled to restore order. The students took no notice. She told them to shut up. They stuck out their tongues. When she said they would never learn about their heritage, they yawned. Eventually a fight broke out between two boys, cheered on by the girls. "Come on, Max," some of the girls screamed. "Punch him in the face." Blood was dripping from the smaller of the two when the Principal arrived, and sent all of us home.

After class each Sunday, we flooded into the sanctuary for a worship service. The rabbi, robed in black, recited the prayers, read from the Torah, and preached a sermon. The teachers walked up and down the aisles to ensure that there was no commotion. Few paid any attention to what was going on. The girls continued to giggle. The boys poked each other, exchanged baseball cards, and drew pictures in the prayer book. Only a few students showed any interest. They were the odd-balls, the out-casts who were avoided by cliques of students who knew each other from ordinary school.

Despite such disdain for the Jewish heritage, most boys had bar mitzvahs at the age of thirteen. Hebrew teachers taught them the alphabet. The boys memorized their Torah portion by listening to a tape recorder. Over and over they played it, attempting, parrot-like, to mimic the words. In addition, they learned a short speech usually written by their parents. On the day of their bar mitzvah, they mechanically went through the motions as anxious mothers and fathers looked on in the presence of friends and relatives. When the service ended, there was a small celebration in the Temple hall, and then most families arranged a lavish party.

At my bar mitzvah reception, the tables groaned with food. In the center was a huge swan carved in ice; from its beak, drops of water dripped on the table. There were piles of chopped liver, mounds of smoked salmon, stacks of knishes and oceans of cocktail dips. I sat with my parents. Guests came up to our table and congratulated me. From this vantage point, I surveyed the crowd. Plates piled high, they were having a splendid time.

During the years in religion school, I attended dozens of bar mitzvah parties. Some were held in private cinemas. Others took place in the evening with bands and dancing. For most bar mitzvah boys, the most important aspect of this event was the presents. I must have had hundreds.

The next few years were spent in confirmation class, usually taken by the rabbi. With bar mitzvah behind them, some boys dropped out. But most remained. Again, there was little interest in class. Students misbehaved in front of the rabbi. Continually he raised his voice, telling us we would never be good Jews if we knew nothing about the tradition. On one occasion, he screamed at one of the girls whose rubber band hit him on the nose. He called her a "scheming little bitch." The class froze. He went white and apologized profusely. Several months later his contract ended, and a new rabbi was hired. We always wondered if this was the result of his outburst. The girl whom he shouted at was the daughter of the Temple president.

These disspiriting experiences in religion school, however, did not dampen my interest in the Jewish faith. Unlike most of my high school friends, I found Judaism fascinating. I liked Temple services. I enjoyed the classes in Sunday school despite the raucous behaviour of the other students. At the age of thirteen, I had decided that I wanted to serve the Jewish people. My father was an orthopedic surgeon, but I wanted to be a congregational rabbi. Yet my experience of Judaism was limited. Throughout my childhood I had only encountered Reform Jews. I knew practically nothing about the other branches of the Jewish faith. Only rarely did I come across Hasidic Jews. I had never been to an Orthodox worship service.

When I went East to be a freshman at Williams College in Williamstown, Massachusetts, my exposure to the Jewish heritage was even more narrow. Nestled in the Berkshire mountains, Williams in the 1960s was an elite all-men's college. Although there were some Jewish students, they expressed little if any interest in Judaism. There was no Jewish chaplain. No rabbi ever visited the college. On Sunday some of the students attended Thompson Memorial Chapel, but I was not one of them. However, during my third year of college I was a Junior Year Abroad student in Athens, Greece. There I learned about ancient Greek civilization. During one of the holidays I went to Israel. The Jewish state had been in existence for less than twenty years. Jerusalem was divided by barbed wire into Arab and Jewish sectors. Alone I walked the city streets in bitter December weather. I was enthralled.

After graduation from Williams, I spent the summer taking an intensive Hebrew course at the Hebrew Union College in Cincinnati, Ohio—the main rabbinical school for Reform rabbis. Most of the students were from Reform homes, but a few had a traditional Jewish upbringing. The first evening I assembled with my classmates for an introductory session. The director of the summer school explained that we would be working very hard. In the past, rabbinic students were locked in the building, he continued. Only on the weekends were they released. We were fortunate because the regime had become more liberal. We were now free to go outside!

Such an nightmarish account caused considerable alarm. None of us had expected to work that hard. After the director's talk, the president of the college welcomed us. I knew what he looked like since I had seen his picture on the cover of *Time* magazine. He stood before us and took out a handkerchief. With tears in his eyes, he emphasized the importance of the rabbinate. "I don't have to tell you," he said, "that being a rabbi is a wonderful vocation. You will become leaders of our people." He then recounted his adventures in the Negev, where he had worked as an archaeologist. Throughout he wept. It was certainly moving. Later I discovered that the president always cried whenever he spoke, and it had a powerful effect on his hearers. Rich women, in particular, were so overwhelmed at fundraising gatherings that they unhesitatingly wrote large checks for the college.

The next three months were torture. Every week we suffered the ordeals of a Hebrew test. In bed I frequently fell asleep conjugating verbs. But at last the initiation program ended and normal classes began. During the first year, we were forced to translate texts. The Bible was reduced to syntax. Jewish liturgy and rabbinic sources were studied for their grammatical structure rather than religious content. At the end of the year we took what was called a "Readiness Exam." For three days we sat a battery of tests which determined whether we would be permitted to continue. Feverishly we struggled with tortuous translations.

Following this ordeal, all the first-year students were required to have an interview with a psychiatrist. Previously we had all completed an enormous multiple-choice questionnaire. It was not clear, however, what the psychiatrist was looking for. Arriving at the psychiatrist's office, I took a seat. When he entered, I stood up and shook hands. First he asked why I wanted to be a rabbi. He puffed on his pipe. The conversation quickly took a new course. He asked me a series of questions about my sex life. I stumbled through various exploits. Eventually, he asked about my mother. After making copious notes, he stood up, shook my hand, grimaced, and closed the door.

I had passed. But I was not certain why. During the five years I spent in rabbinical seminary, I was sent out to various congregations as a student rabbi. Invariably these small Jewish communities were composed largely of Reform Jews with a small sprinkling of traditionalists. I was there to conduct the service and encourage their observance of Jewish holidays. Yet, to my surprise, congregants did not appear to be interested in the tradition.

One congregation was so desperate to raise funds that they sponsored a gala bingo evening. On the night of the event the parking lot was full an hour before the doors opened, and a crowd of people gathered outside. At eight the doors opened, and masses of people flooded into the Temple. Members of the Temple dressed in outfits suitable for a casino directed them to the hall where long tables had been assembled. In the middle was a machine with bouncing, numbered ping-pong balls. Eventually it was time for the high point of the evening: bingo for the grand prize. Reluctantly I approached the ping-pong machine. The balls bounced against the glass sides of a large container. I reached into a suction cup and called out the numbers of the balls that emerged. A record number of bingo cards had been sold for the jackpot, and I watched as the players stared at them and clicked the plastic tabs. Tension increased as one number was called after another. Never before had I experienced such excitement in the Temple.

Once I was ordained, I served as a student rabbi in Melbourne, Australia. There I saw a similar disinterest in Jewish religious life. The same pattern was repeated in the other congregations that I briefly served in London, England, and Johannesburg, South Africa. Many of the Reform congregants were ignorant of Jewish law and lore and had no interest in following Jewish practice. On one occasion, for example, I sat on the Temple Board of a large congregation in Johannesburg, South Africa. Prior to the High Holiday services, we discussed a proposal to censure members of the congregation if they opened their stores on *Yom Kippur*. Listening to the debate, I was struck by the fact that those who proposed this motion kept their shops open on Saturdays. I pointed out that it would be inconsistent if we said nothing about such a violation of the law. The president of the Temple Board, who owned a large chain of stores that were open on Saturday was outraged. "I resent this," he sputtered. "I keep my shop open like everyone else," he said, "because that's the busiest day of the week. And quite frankly," he continued, "I don't think it's any of your business telling us how to run our businesses."

As a young rabbi in Johannesburg and elsewhere, I discovered the intractable nature of modern Jewish life. From Orthodoxy on the right to Reconstructionist and Reform Judaism on the left, Jews today seek to re-interpret the tradition in the light of their own religious assumptions and needs. No longer is the Jewish community bound by an inflexible code of law supervised by a strictly observant leadership. Instead Jewry is divided into sub-groups, each with its own ideology and interpretation of Judaism. Hence in the modern Jewish world, the vast majority of Jews draw from their heritage those elements that they find spiritually significant and reject the rest. As a consequence, Judaism has ceased to be a unified religion with a set framework for belief and practice.

Discouraged by my early experiences in the rabbinate, I studied for a Ph.D. at Cambridge University in England and applied for a job at the University of Kent, Canterbury, where I became a lecturer in 1975. Teaching at a university was a delight—in contrast to pupils in religion schools, undergraduates were actually interested in the subject and wrote down every word I said. How different this all was from my experience as a rabbi, when I had struggled to attract anyone to adult study groups. Sprinkled among the students was a handful of friars who were simultaneously studying at the Franciscan Study Center located next to the university camps. Occasionally, they came to my Judaism class dressed in their habits.

On one occasion I was explaining passages about *tefillin*. These, I said, are small leather boxes which contain passages from the Torah. They are worn by Orthodox male Jews on their arms and heads in fulfillment of a biblical commandment. Their purpose, I went on, is to remind the wearer to keep God's law. Listening to my explanation, one of the Franciscans held up his rosary. "We have something similar," he said. "The rosary is sup-

posed to aid concentration in prayer." I had never made the connection. I couldn't help but wonder what the rabbis with whom I
had worked or the congregants I had served would make of this
scene. I was lecturing to Christians bout Judaism, and they were
teaching me about their own faith in relation to mine.

As the years passed, I became increasingly interested in this
interconnection. Later I published a book dealing with Jewish-
Christian dialogue: *On Earth as It Is in Heaven: Jews, Christians
and Liberation Theology*. In this study I sought to illustrate some
of the areas in which Jews can unite with Christian liberation
theologians to bring about God's kingdom. In pursuit of the
common goal of freedom from oppression, committed Jews
and Christians, I argued, can become a saving remnant of the
modern world, embodying the liberation message of Scripture.
Like Abraham, they can hope against hope in laboring to build
a more just and humane world.

During this time I also taught an adult education class with
the Dean of Canterbury Cathedral. Our course attracted a sizable
number of students. For convenience's sake, we decided to meet
at the Deanery. Once a week a group of elderly ladies, the Dean,
and I sat around the dining room table, and we took turns leading
the class. Beginning with biblical origins, we traced the development of Jewish and Christian ritual to the present. As the course
was nearing its end, we arranged an outing to a nearby convent of
Anglican Benedictine nuns. The purpose of the trip was to give
our class an insight into the contemplative life. These experiences
increased my interest in Christian theology, and several years later
I wrote a *Dictionary of Judaism and Christianity* in which I compared theological ideas and observances in both traditions.

Living in Canterbury at the center of the Anglican world
stimulated my interest in Jewish-Christian dialogue, but as the
years passed I sought to place Judaism in the context of the universe of faiths. Although the field of interfaith theology has been
a prominent area of investigation in Christian circles, very little
has been written on this topic by Jewish scholars. In contrast to
attempts among Christian theologians to formulate a Christian

theology of the world's religions, contemporary Jewish thinkers have paid scant attention to the issue of religious pluralism. In my view, however, it is vital that the Jewish community understands Judaism in a universal context, and I published the first book dealing with Judaism and the world's religions: *Judaism and Other Faiths.*

In this study I first surveyed Jewish attitudes to other faiths over the centuries. From this overview I sought to demonstrate that Jewish writers through the ages have in different ways affirmed that monotheistic traditions should be regarded as religiously acceptable. Even though Jewish theologians perceive Judaism as the true faith, they view other religions—especially Christianity and Islam—as playing an important role in the unfolding of God's eschatological plan. Yet, I argued that in the contemporary world the Jewish community needs to adopt an even more open stance toward the world's faiths. What is required today is a shift from inclusivism to pluralism, in which the Divine—rather than Judaism—is placed at the center of the world's religions. Such pluralism would enable Jews to affirm the uniqueness of Judaism while acknowledging the validity of other religions. The theology underpinning this shift in perspective is based on the distinction between Ultimate Reality as it is in itself, and Reality as perceived. From this vantage point, the truth-claims of all religions should be regarded as human constructions rather than universally valid doctrines.

This conception of religious truth serves as the framework for this study of the Jewish tradition. In the past the Jewish people were united by a common religious inheritance which they believed to be the one true path to God. According to Scripture, God created the universe, chose the Jewish people from among all nations, delivered them from exile, revealed himself to Moses on Mount Sinai, and exercised providential care over his children throughout their history. For centuries, Jews were sustained by such a conviction through persecution, suffering, and death. In the post-Enlightenment period, however, such a theological framework has disintegrated for a variety of reasons: no longer

are most Jews able to accept such a depiction of God's nature
and activity. Thus, among the varying religious sub-groups
within the Jewish community there has been a loss of faith in
the theological framework of the past.

As a result of this disintegration of the tradition, I believe that
a new vision of Judaism that can provide a basis for religious
belief and practice is required. As I will explain, what is now
needed is a theological structure consonant with a contemporary
understanding of Divine Reality as conceived by the world's
faiths. Arguably such a revised theology of Judaism should be
based on the distinction between Divine Reality as it is in itself
and Divine Reality as conceived in human thought and experience. Such a contrast is a central feature of many of the world's
faiths. In Judaism God the transcendental Infinite is conceived
as *Ayn Sof* as distinct from the *Shekhinah* (God's Presence) which
is manifest in the terrestrial plane. In Hindu philosophy the
nirguna Brahman, the Ultimate in itself, beyond all human categories, is sometimes distinguished from the *saguna Brahman,*
the Ultimate as known to finite consciousness as a personal
deity, *Ishvara.* In Taoist thought it is said "the *Tao* that can be
expressed is not the eternal *Tao.*" In Mahayana Buddhism there
is a distinction between the unmanifest Buddha Realm and individual, manifest Buddha.

Given the diversity of images of the Real among the various religious systems that have emerged throughout history, it
is not surprising that there are innumerable conflicts between
the teachings of the world's faiths. In all cases, believers have
maintained that the doctrines of their respective traditions are
true and superior to competing claims. Thus Jews contend that
they are God's chosen people and partners in a special covenant—their mission is to be a light to the nations. In this sense
the Jewish people stand in a unique relationship with God. This
does not lead to the quest to convert others to Judaism, but it
does give rise to a sense of pride in having been born into the
Jewish fold.

Yet, within this new theological framework, absolute claims

about God within the Jewish tradition might be understood as human conceptions stemming from the religious experience of the ancient Israelites as well as later generations of Jewish sages: Jewish monotheism—embracing a myriad of formulations from biblical through medieval to modern times—is rooted in the life of the people. In all cases, pious believers and thinkers have expressed their understanding of God's activity on the basis of their own personal as well as communal encounter with the Divine. However, given that the Divine as it is in itself is beyond human comprehension, this Jewish understanding of God cannot be viewed as definitive and final. Rather, it must be seen as only one among many ways in which human beings have attempted to make sense of Ultimate Reality. In this light, it makes no sense for Jews to believe that they possess unique truth about God and his action in the world. On the contrary, universalistic truth-claims about Divine Reality must give way to a recognition of the inevitable subjectivity of beliefs about the Real.

The same conclusion applies to the Jewish belief about God's revelation. Instead of affirming that God uniquely disclosed his word to the Jewish people in Scripture and through the teachings of the sages, Jews might acknowledge that their Holy Writ is only one among many records of divine communication. Both the written and the oral Torah have special significance for the Jewish people, but this does not imply that these writings contain a uniquely true and superior divine communication. Instead the *Tanakh* and rabbinic literature should be perceived as a record of the spiritual life of the people and a testimony of their religious quest. As such, they should be viewed in much the same light as the New Testament, the *Qur'an,* the *Bagahavad Gita,* the *Vedas,* and so forth. For the Jewish people, the Torah has particular meaning—but it need not be regarded as possessing ultimate truth.

Likewise the doctrine of the chosen people must be revised. Although Jews have derived great strength from the conviction that God has had a special relationship with Israel, such a belief is based on a misapprehension of Judaism in the context of the world's religions. Given that the Divine as it is in itself transcends human understanding, the conviction that God selected a particular people as his agent is nothing more than an expression of the Jewish people's sense of superiority and impulse to spread its religious message. In fact, there is simply no way of knowing whether any people stand in a special relationship with the Divine.

Again this approach challenges the traditional conviction that God has a providential plan for the Jewish people and for all humankind. The belief that God's guiding hand is manifest in all things is ultimately a human response to the universe. It is not, as Jews have believed through the ages, certain knowledge. This is illustrated by the fact that other traditions have postulated a similar view of providence, yet maintain that God's action in history has taken an entirely different form. In other cases, non-theistic religions have formulated conceptions of human destiny divorced from the activity of God or the gods. Such differences of interpretation highlight the subjectivity of these beliefs.

The Jewish doctrine of the Messiah could also be seen in a similar light. Within a pluralistic theology of the world's religions, the longing for messianic deliverance should be perceived as a pious hope based on personal and communal expectation. Although this belief has served as a bedrock of the Jewish faith through the centuries, it is invariably shaped by human conceptualization. Like other doctrines in the Jewish tradition, it has been grounded in the experience of the Jewish people and has undergone a range of changes in the history of the nation. Because Divine Reality as it is in itself is beyond comprehension, there is simply no way of ascertaining whether the doctrine of a personal Messiah is true.

Finally, this new interpretation of Jewish theology demands a similar stance regarding the doctrine of the afterlife. Although the belief in the eschatological unfolding of history has been a central feature of the Jewish faith from rabbinic times to the present, it is, in my opinion, simply impossible to ascertain whether these events will occur in the future. In our finite world—limited by space and time—certain knowledge about life after death is unobtainable. Belief in the hereafter in which the righteous of Israel will receive their just reward has sustained the nation through suffering and tragedy, yet from a pluralistic outlook these doctrines are no more certain than any other features of the Jewish religious heritage.

The implications of this shift from the absolutism of the Jewish past to a new vision of Jewish theology are radical and far-reaching. Traditional Judaism, like all other religions, has advanced absolute, universal truth-claims about the nature of God. But given the separation between our finite understanding of the Divine and the Divine as it is in itself, there is no way of attaining complete certitude about the veracity of these beliefs. Divine Reality transcends human comprehension, and hence it must be admitted that Jewish religious convictions are no different in principle from those found in other religious traditions. All are lenses through which Divine Reality is conceptualized.

Unlike Orthodox, Conservative, Reform, Reconstructionist and Humanistic Judaism—all of which advocate varying systems of belief and practice, this new interpretation of Judaism advances a truly liberal ideology of personal choice. In short, in the contemporary Jewish world there is a conscious acceptance of the principle of personal autonomy, even if in some quarters it is only grudgingly accepted. This new vision of Judaism would thus be in accord with the spirit of its age—its endorsement of personal decision-making would be consonant with the nature of Jewish life in Israel and the Diaspora.

PART II

WRESTLING WITH THE MESSAGE

Chapter 2.

DIVINE UNITY

Throughout the history of the Jewish people, the belief in one God has served as the cardinal principle of the faith. From biblical times to the present, Jews daily recite the *Shema* prayer: "Hear O Israel, the Lord our God, the Lord is One." Yet, given the various notions of Divine Reality in the world's faiths, it should now be recognized that Jewish monotheism is simply one among many ways of conceptualizing Ultimate Reality.

Learning about God

In religion school, we were constantly reminded of Reform Judaism's emphasis on Jewish monotheism combined with prophetical religious ideals. Citing the story of the patriarch

Abraham in the Book of Genesis, our teachers emphasized that Abraham was born into a polytheistic society. Living in the Sumerian city of Ur in Mesopotamia, he was aware of the polytheistic practices of his countrymen. For the Sumerians life was under the control of the gods. To obtain happiness, it was essential to keep them in good humour through worship and sacrifice. Yet, the gods were unpredictable, and this gave rise to the practice of reading omens. In the birth of monstrosities, in the movements of animals, and in the shapes of cracks in the wall or of oil poured into a cup of water, these ancient peoples saw the fingers of the gods pointing to the future.

Rejecting such practices, Abraham believed he was called by the one true God to depart from Ur and travel to Canaan. Genesis records God's command: "Go from your country and your kindred and your father's house to the land I will show you. And I will make of you a great nation" (Genesis 12:1–2). Together with his father Terah, his wife Sarai, and his nephew Lot, he travelled first to Haran, a trading center in northern Syria. Later, during a famine in Canaan, he went to Egypt and proceeded to the Negeb, finally settling in the plain near Hebron. Here he experienced a revelation which confirmed that his deliverance from Ur was an act of providence. God declared: "I am the Lord who brought you from Ur of the Chaldeans, to give you this land to possess" (Gen. 15:7).

The Temple worship I attended as a child carried on this theme. God, we were told, created the universe and providentially watches over his people. Each week the rabbi began the Sabbath service with prayers of praise, emphasizing God's power:

> Lord of all worlds, not in reliance upon our own merit do we lay our supplications before Thee, but trusting in Thine infinite mercy alone. For what are we, what is our life, what our goodness, what our power? What can we say in Thy presence? Are not all the mighty men as naught before Thee and those of great renown as though they had never been; the wisest as if without knowledge, and men of understanding as if without discernment.[1]

This was followed by a series of prayers, culminating in the *Shema* :

> Hear, O Israel: The Lord our God, the Lord is One. Praised
> be His name whose glorious kingdom is forever and ever.

The congregation then recited a paragraph from Scripture stressing the importance of loving God and keeping his commandments:

> Thou shalt love the Lord, thy God, with all thy heart, with all
> thy soul, and with all thy might. And this word, which I com-
> mand you this day, shall be upon thy heart. Thou shalt teach
> them diligently unto thy children, and shalt speak of them
> when thou sittest in thy house, when thou walkest by the way,
> when thou liest down, and when thou risest up. Thou shalt bind
> them for a sign upon thy hand and they shall be for frontlets
> between thine eyes. Thou shalt write them upon the doorposts
> of thy house and upon thy gates: That ye may remember and do
> all My commandments and be holy unto your God.[2]

At the end of the Sabbath service we prayed for a time when all human beings will acknowledge the existence of the one God who is the Lord of all:

> May the time not be distant, O God, when Thy name shall be
> worshipped in all the earth, when unbelief shall disappear and
> error be no more. We fervently pray that the day may come
> when all men shall invoke Thy name, when corruption and
> evil shall give way to purity and goodness, when superstition
> shall no longer enslave the mind, nor idolatry blind the eye,
> when all who dwell on earth shall know that to Thee alone ev-
> ery knee must bend and every tongue give homage. O may all,
> created in Thine image, recognize that they are brethren, so
> that, one in spirit and one in fellowship, they may be forever
> united before Thee. Then shall Thy kingdom be established

on earth and the word of Thine ancient seer be fulfilled: The
Lord will reign forever and ever.

The choir then concluded this section of the service with the
traditional prayer: "On that day the Lord shall be One and His name
shall be One."[3]

Jewish Monotheism

Throughout the *Union Prayerbook,* Jewish monotheism was
continually affirmed. Like the other branches of the faith, the
Reform movement upheld the centrality of this belief, viewing dedication to one God as the basis of faith. Surveying the
history of Jewish theology from biblical times to the present, it
is apparent that such a conviction has always been paramount.
In the Hebrew Bible, the Israelites experienced God as Lord.
Deuteronomy 6:4 serves as the basis of the *Shema* prayer: "Hear
O Israel, the Lord our God, the Lord is One." The Bible proclaims
that the universe owes its existence to one God who is creator of
heaven and earth. Since human beings are created in his image, all
men and women are brothers and sisters. Thus the belief in one
God implies that there is one humanity and one world.

According to Scripture, God alone is to be worshipped. The
Ten Commandments proclaim:

> I am the Lord your God, who brought you out of the land of
> Egypt, out of the house of bondage. You shall have no other
> gods before me. You shall not make for yourself a graven image,
> or any likeness of anything that is in heaven above, or that is in
> the earth beneath, or that is in the water under the earth; you
> shall not bow down to them or serve them; for I the Lord your
> God am a jealous God, visiting the iniquity of the fathers upon
> the children to the third and the fourth generation of those who
> hate me, but showing steadfast love to thousands of those who
> love me and keep my commandments. (Exodus 20: 2–6)

Again, in the prophetic books God is perceived as Lord of all. As the prophet Isaiah declared:

> I am the Lord, and there is no other,
> besides me there is no God....
> I form light and create darkness,
> I make weal and create woe, *
> I am the Lord, who do all these things. (Isa. 45: 5, 7)

Continuing this tradition, the sages of the early rabbinic period stressed that any form of polytheistic belief is abhorrent. In all likelihood, Persian dualism had an influence on Jewish thought in the development of the idea of Satan. Yet, the rabbis were anxious to reject any form of dualistic belief which they referred to as "two powers." Hence the *Sifre* (*midrash* on Deuteronomy) declares in relation to Deuteronomy 32:39 ("See now that I, even I, am He, and there is no god with me"): "If anyone says that there are two powers in heaven the retort is given to him: 'There is no god with me.'"[4] The belief in two powers in heaven is based on the fact that when God proclaimed: "I am the Lord thy God" (Exod. 20:2) no one objected.[5] Continuing this theme, the Mishnah states that if a person says in his prayers: "We acknowledge Thee, we acknowledge Thee," he is to be silenced. According to the *Gemara* (the talmudic commentary on the Mishnah), the reason for an action is because such a person would appear to acknowledge the existence of two powers.[6] Despite such objections to dualistic tendencies, the doctrine of Satan and Metatron as well as the *Sitra Ahra* (Other Side) in kabbalistic sources suggests that the belief in two powers continued to influence Jewish theology. Yet it was continually stressed that evil powers in the universe do not have a divine status. Repeatedly Jewish sages emphasized that there is one God who created all things.

As Christianity gained in influence, a number of Jewish thinkers were troubled by the Christian doctrine of the Incarnation. In their view, such a belief is inherently dualistic. In the Middle

Ages, the Christian doctrine of the Trinity was frequently attacked since it appeared to undermine pure monotheism. According to these Jewish writers, God as Father and Jesus as Son should be understood as a form of dualism, implying the acceptance of the doctrine of two powers in heaven. In this regard R. Abahu of Caesarea stated: "God is not a man that He should lie, neither the son of man, that He should repent: When He hath said, will He not do it? Or when He hath spoken, will He not make it good?" (Num. 23:19) On the basis of this observation, he concluded: "If a man says to you, 'I am a god,' he is lying; 'I am the Son of Man,' he will end by being sorry for it; 'I am going up to heaven,' he will not fulfill what he has said."[7] Again, commenting on the verse, "I am the first, and I am the last, and beside Me there is no God" (Is. 44:6), R. Abahu declared: "'I am the first,' for I have no father; 'and I am the last,' for I have no brother; 'and beside Me there is no God,' for I have no son."[8]

Later in the Middle Ages, the doctrine of the Trinity was attacked by Jewish scholars. It was common for Christian exegetes to interpret the *Shema* with three references to God as implying the doctrine of the Trinity. Yet, Jewish scholars were anxious to illustrate that the *Shema* implies there is only one God rather than Three Persons of the Godhead. In response, however, Christian scholars insisted that Jewish criticisms of the doctrine of the Trinity are based on an inadequate understanding of Trinitarianism. Despite such Christian objections, Jewish thinkers were determined to illustrate that the unity of God is fundamental to monotheism, thereby rejecting any form of Trinitarianism. According to the twelfth century Jewish philosopher Ibn Daud, for example, God's absolute unity is derived from his necessary existence. For ibn Daud the belief in the unity of God precludes the possibility of ascribing positive attributes to Deity. Again, in the *Guide for the Perplexed*, the twelfth century Jewish philosopher Moses Maimonides argued that no positive attributes can be predicated of God since the Divine is an absolute unity. Thus when God is described positively in the Bible, such ascriptions must refer to his activity. The only true attributes, Maimonides maintained, are negative ones. They lead to a knowledge of God because in negation no plurality is involved. Each negative attribute excludes from God's essence some imperfection. Such negation, Maimonides believed, brings one nearer to the knowledge of the Godhead.

During this period the kabbalistic belief in divine unity was also a central doctrine. In Provence and Spain early kabbalists referred to God as the *Ayn Sof* (Infinite), the absolute perfection in which there is no distinction or plurality. The *Ayn Sof,* they argued, is beyond all thought. According to the *Zohar,* the *Ayn Sof* is the cause of all, yet it has no name because it transcends creation:

> Master of the worlds, you are the cause of causes, the first cause who waters the three with a spring; this spring is like the soul to the body, since it is like the life of the body. In you there is no image, nor likeness of what is within, nor of what is without....

> There is none that knows anything of you, and besides you there is no singleness or unity in the upper or the lower worlds. You are acknowledged as Lord over all. As for all the *sefirot* [divine emanations], each one has a known name and you are the perfect completion of them all. When you remove yourself from them, all the names are left like a body without a soul.[9]

Again, the *Zohar* declares that the *Ayn Sof* is beyond all human knowledge:

> Rabbi Eleazar asked Rabbi Simeon, "We know that the whole-offering is connected to the Holy of Holies so that it may be illumined. To what heights does the attachment of the will of the priests, the Levites and Israel extend?" He said, "We have already taught that it extends to *Ayn Sof* since all attachment, unification, and completion is to be secreted in that secret which is not perceived or known, and which contains the will of all wills. *Ayn Sof* cannot be known, it does

not produce end or beginning like the primal *ayin* (nothing), which does bring forth and end…there are no end, no wills, no lights, no luminaries in *Ayn Sof*."[10]

In kabbalistic sources creation is bound up with the emanation of God. According to the *Zohar*, the *sefirot* (divine emanations) come successively from above to below in a hierarchical structure. The common order of the *sefirot* and the names most frequently used are: *Keter Elyon* (Supreme Crown), *Hokhmah* (Wisdom), *Binah (Intelligence)*, *Gedullah* (Greatness), *Gevurah* (Power), *Tiferet* (Beauty), *Netzah* (Endurance), *Hod* (Majesty), *Yesod* (Foundation), Malkhut (Kingdom). These *sefirot* together illustrate how an infinite, unknowable, and undivided God can be the source of all modes of existence.

In their totality, the ten *sefirot* are represented as a cosmic tree that grows from its roots and spreads downward in the direction of the lower worlds to the *sefirot* which constitute its trunk and main branches. Another depiction of the ten *sefirot* is in the form a man: the first *sefirah* represents the head; the next three *sefirot* the cavities of the brain; the fourth and fifth *sefirot* the arms; the sixth the torso; the seventh and eighth the legs; the ninth the sexual organ; and the tenth the all-embracing totality of this image. Kabbalistic sources also describe this heavenly man as divided into two parts: the left column is made up of the female *sefirot* and the right column the male. Another arrangement presents the *sefirot* as ten concentric circles in descending order.

According to kabbalistic sources, the *sefirot* are dynamically structured; the divine energy flows from its source and separates into individual channels, reuniting in the lowest *sefirah*, *Malkhut*. These *sefirot* were also conceived as divine substances as well as containers of the divine essence. Despite their individuality, they are united with the *Ayn Sof* in the moment of creation. According to the *Zohar*, all existences are emanations of God. He is revealed in all things because He is immanent in them:

He brings everything from potentiality into actuality; He varies his deeds but there is no variety in him. It is He that puts the *sefirot* in order; there are among the *sefirot* great, intermediate and small. Each has its place in the order, yet there is no order in him. He created everything with *Binah*, but there is none that created him. He is a designer, designing everything with *Tiferet*, but he has no design or designer. He formed everything with *Malkhut*, but there is none that formed him. Since he is within these ten *sefirot*, he created, designed and formed everything with them. There he places his unity, so that they might recognize him there.[11]

To reconcile this process of emanation with the doctrine of creation *ex nihilo,* some kabbalists contended that the *Ayn Sof* should be understood as *ayin* (nothingness). Thus the manifestation of the divine through the *sefirot* is a self-creation out of divine nothingness. Other kabbalists maintained that creation does not occur within the Godhead. It takes place at a lower level where created beings are formed independent of God's essence.

The elaboration of these mystical ideas occurred in the sixteenth century through the teachings of the Issac Luria. Living in Safed, Luria reinterpreted the act of creation as a negative event. In his view, the *Ayn Sof* had to bring into being an empty space in which creation could take place since divine light was everywhere, leaving no room for creation. This was accomplished by the process of *tzimtzum*—the contraction of the Godhead into itself. This first act was not positive, but rather one that demanded withdrawal. God had to go into exile from the empty space so that the process of creation could be initiated. *Tzimtzum* (divine contraction) therefore postulates exile as the first step of creation.

The Lurianic concept of *tzimtzum* was subsequently embraced by *Habad* Hasidism, founded by Schneur Zalman in the eighteenth century. In his view, the doctrine of God's unity implies that there is only one God. In other words, God is all. From this point of view, there are no creatures, only God himself. The multiplicity of objects we observe as well as ourselves are thus the result of the screening of divine light. This *tzimtzum* does not in fact actually take place; rather, divine light is progressively concealed so that creatures experience existence from their standpoint rather than the divine perspective. On this monistic scheme the multiplicity of things is included in God's unity. It is God alone who embraces all and is in all. Here the doctrine of God's unity is taken to its utmost limit. Even though such mystical notions have not been adopted by the mainstream branches of Jewry, the doctrine of God's unity is today accepted within Orthodoxy as well as the other major branches of the Jewish faith as fundamental to Judaism. Modern Jewish monotheism is as central to Judaism as it was in ancient times.

Judaism and Other Religions

For thousands of years, Jews have proclaimed their belief and trust in the one God who created the universe and rules over creation. Such a claim is unconditional and absolute. In biblical times this conviction led to the renunciation of foreign deities and the proscriptions against idolatry. According to the biblical writers, the gods of other nations are non-entities. The religion of the Jews is depicted as the true faith. Yet, it should be noted that there was no harsh condemnation of pagan idolatry. In addition, the prophets foretold that at the end of days, all people will recognize that the God of Israel is the Lord of history. Thus there is hope even for non-Jews in the unfolding of God's scheme of salvation. Rabbinic teaching about gentiles continued this tradition of acceptance: those who follow the Noahide Laws (given originally to Adam and Noah) are viewed as worthy of eternal life. Even those who engage in seemingly polytheistic practices are admissable as long as the gods they worship are conceived as symbolically pointing to the one true God.

In the writings of medieval Jewish thinkers such as Rabbenu Tam, this earlier rabbinic conception of symbolic intermediacy was applied to Christian believers. In the view of these scholars, Christianity is not idolatry. Some writers such as Judah Halevi formulated an even more tolerant form of Jewish inclusivism. In their opinion, Christians as well as Muslims have a positive role in God's plan for humanity: as monotheistic faiths they can spread the message of monotheism to the nations and encourage them to adhere to the Noahide covenant. Here then is a form of Jewish exclusivism combined with an acceptance of religious practices in other traditions. Yet for the biblical writers and the rabbis, monotheistic belief is fundamental. Members of other faiths are acceptable only if they worship one God. Any form of dualism, polytheism or alternative conceptions of the Godhead is regarded with abhorrence.

It is understandable that in previous centuries when Jews had little contact with faiths other than Christianity and Islam, such religious absolutism was the predominant attitude. In the modern world, however, Jewry arguably needs to adopt a more religiously tolerant stance. Today it has become increasingly apparent that adherents of other faiths have conceptualized Divine Reality in various and conflicting ways. In Hinduism, for example, the vast majority of believers believe in many gods. Brahman is the supreme spirit, beyond all human understanding, time and space. He is the origin of all creation—pure intelligence and being. In addition, Vishnu has millions of followers: he is conceived as visiting the earth as an *avatar*. Vishnu's most popular *avatar* was Krishna, whom many Hindus worship as a god in his own right. Rama is another well-known *avatar*. The third of the *trimurti* is Shiva whose son Ganesha is the elephant-god.

Unlike Hinduism, both Theravada and Mahayana Buddhism deny the existence of a supernatural deity. Instead, the Four Noble Truths serve as the foundation for Buddhist practice. All life, Buddhists contend, involves suffering; its cause is a craving for life, pleasure and money. By eliminating such desire, suffering can be overcome. For Buddhists, the Middle Way—between asceticism and hedonism—serves as the only means to eliminate this craving. In addition to this scheme, the Eightfold Path provides a formula for right conduct including: the correct understanding of the Four Noble Truths; right thoughts leading to love of all things; right speech which must be well-intentioned; right action involving moral behaviour, right livelihood entailing the avoidance of living from anything that involves violence; right effort to banish evil thoughts; right mindfulness involving an awareness of the needs of others; and right concentration using meditation.

The followers of Taoism pursue a spiritual path, the Tao, which is conceived as the source of everything that exists in the world. The Tao is the primal force in the universe which is present in all things. It is at the heart of everything in heaven and earth, eternal and unchanging. As in Confucianism, two natural forces, *yin* and *yang* create the energy of life through their interaction. There cannot be darkness without light, nor movement without stillness. This dynamic tension which exists between the *yin* and the *yang* creates heaven and earth as well as humanity. Heaven and earth are the spiritual and physical realms, while humanity maintains the balance between them. This harmony can be disturbed by human iniquity, and Taoists seek forgiveness for this through prayer and offerings. All life is made possible by the *Ch'i*, the life energy of the universe. This breath is in everything, and Taoists seek to preserve their *Ch'i* in the quest for immortality. Within the Taoist system, the Three Pure Ones serve as the central deities: T'ai-Shang Tao-chun who is often identified as Lao-Tzu; T'ai-lao Tao-Chun, and Yu-Huang.

In Zoroastrianism, all of creation is caught up in the constant battle between the gods of good and evil. Basing their faith on the teachings of Zarathustra, Zoroastrians believe that Ahura Mazda created the world and is completely good in his dealings with humanity. His twin, Angra Mainyu, on the other hand, is the god of darkness and destruction, the creator of non-life who produces storms, plagues and monsters. The eternal fate of all individuals is determined by the choice they make between Ahura Mazda and Angra Mainyu. The good enjoy happiness in this life and eventually enter heaven, whereas the evil are punished everlastingly. In opposition to such dualism, the other major monothesitic faiths, including Christianity, Islam, and

Sikhism have in different ways formulated distinct theological systems. For Christians, Jesus is Christ and Lord, who has come to redeem the world. Muslims, however, insist that Muhammad is the greatest prophet to whom God has revealed his word in the *Qur'an*. For Sikhs the ultimate goal of human life is the restoration of the soul to unity with God. In the *Guru Granth Sahib*, God is presented as unknowable and without form but present in the world, particularly in the depths of the human soul.

How is one to make sense of these myriad notions of the Divine? In attempting to represent Ultimate Reality, the different religions have in my opinion conceptualized the Real in two distinct modes: the Divine personalized and the Divine as absolute. In the Christian faith God is understood as Father; in Judaism as Lord; in Islam as Allah; in the Indian traditions as Vishnu or Shiva. In each case these personal deities are conceived as acting within the history of the various faith communities. The concept of the Absolute is alternatively schematized to form a range of divine conceptualizations in the world's religions such as Brahman and the Tao. Unlike personal deities which are concrete and often visualized, the divine as absolute constitutes a variety of concepts (such as the Tao). These non-personal representations of the Divine inform modes of consciousness ranging from the experience of becoming one with the Infinite to finding total reality in a concrete historical moment of existence.

Given the diversity of images of the Real among the various religious systems that have emerged throughout history, it is not surprising that there are innumerable conflicts between the teachings of the world's faiths. In all cases, believers have maintained that the doctrines of these respective traditions are true and superior to competing claims. Thus, as we have seen, Jews contend that they are God's chosen people and partners in a special covenant—their mission is to be a light to the nations. In this sense the Jewish people stand in a unique relationship with God. This has not led to the quest to convert others to Judaism, but it does give rise to a sense of pride in having been born into the Jewish fold.

Within Islam, Muslims are convinced that Muhammad was the seal of the prophets and that, through the *Qur'an,* God revealed himself decisively to the world. Similarly, Christians affirm the unique superiority of the Christian faith since Jesus Christ was God himself, the second person of the Trinity in human form. On the basis of this central dogma, they view themselves as the heirs of the one and only true religion. Hindus, on the other hand, believe that it is possible to have access to eternal truth as incarnated in human language in the Vedas. Although they are tolerant of other faiths, it is assumed that in this life or in the life to come all will accept the fullness of Vedic understanding. Likewise, in the Buddhist tradition it is assumed that the true understanding of the human condition is presented in the teachings of the Buddha. The *Dharma,* Buddhists stress, contains the full and saving truth for all humanity.

Each of these religious traditions, then, affirms its own superiority—all rival claims are regarded as misapprehensions of Ultimate Reality. Yet, there is no way to ascertain which, if any, of these spiritual paths accurately reflects the nature of the Real as it is in itself. In the end, the varied truth-claims of the world's faiths must be in my opinion regarded as human images which are constructed from within particular social and cultural contexts. Thus, Jews lack any justification for believing that their tradition embodies the uniquely true and superior conception of the Divine. A new vision of Judaism calls for a complete reorientation of religious apprehension. What is now required is for the Jewish community to acknowledge that its conceptual system, forms of worship, life styles and Scripture are ultimately nothing more than lenses through which the Jewish people have perceived and Divine Reality. But the Divine as it is in itself is beyond human understanding.

Chapter 3.

OMNIPOTENCE
AND OMNISCIENCE

Although there are no terms for omnipotence and omniscience in the Bible, God is presented in Scripture as almighty and all-knowing. According to the Book of Genesis, he
created the universe, chose the Jews as his special people, and
exercises providential care over the Hebrew nation. The Psalms
declare that He knows all human intentions. Yet, there are numerous philosophical and theological perplexities connected
with these divine attributes.

A God of Power and Knowledge

In religion school, those who taught us about the Bible emphasized God's almighty nature. He was, they explained, the creator of all things. In six days he formed heaven and earth, resting on the seventh day after all his labours. After destroying all living things in the flood, He chose the Jews, liberated them from Egyptian bondage, and brought them into the Promised Land. Subsequently, He sent the prophets to warn the nation of impending doom and urge them to repent of their evil deeds. Following the exile, God comforted them in their distress, and through the centuries, He has continued to watch over his people.

In one of my classes, the teacher—a Holocaust survivor—was anxious to convey the religious message of the Book of Job. After telling us about the Nazi onslaught against the Jews, he explained how God's speech to Job helped him to survive the horrors of the Holocaust. At the end of the book, God rebuked Job for questioning his justice. In a series of rhetorical questions, God asked Job where he was when He created the universe. God's power and knowledge, our teacher stressed, are unfathomable:

> Where were you when I laid the foundations of the earth?
> Tell me, if you have understanding.
> Who determined its measurements—
> surely you know!
> Or who stretched the line upon it?
> On what were its bases sunk,
> or who laid its cornerstone,
> when the morning stars sang together,
> and all the sons of God shouted for joy? (Job 38:4–7)

In the Reform liturgy the theme of God's omnipotence and omniscience were continuously reinforced. Every *Shabbat* that I attended religion school, the rabbi began the morning service with the traditional prayer extolling God's glory:

Every living soul shall praise Thee; the spirit of all flesh shall glorify Thy name. Thou art God from everlasting to everlasting and besides Thee there is no redeemer nor savior. Thou art the first and the last, the Lord of all generations. Thou rulest the world in kindness and all Thy creatures in mercy. Thou art our guardian who sleepest not and slumberest not. To Thee alone we give thanks. Yet though our lips overflow with song, and our tongues with joyous praise, we should still be unable to thank Thee even for a thousandth part of the bounties which Thou hast bestowed upon our fathers and upon us. Thou hast been our protector and our savior in every trial and peril. Thy mercy has watched over us, and Thy lovingkindness has never failed us.[1]

Such affirmations of God's power were repeated in further readings which emphasized his interventions in Jewish history. Together the Congregation and Reader recalled his glorious deeds:

Praised be Thy holy name. Thou hast made Thine eternal law our portion, and hast given us a goodly heritage. Open our eyes to the beauty of Thy truth and help us so to exemplify it in our lives that we may win all men for Thy law of righteousness. Gather all Thy children around the banner of Thy truth that Thy name may be hallowed through us in all the world and the entire human family be blessed with truth and peace.[2]

Following the *Shema*, the rabbi began the recitation of a version of the traditional Eighteen Benedictions which emphasize God's eternal power:

Eternal is thy power, O Lord, Thou art mighty to save. In lovingkindness Thou sustainest the living; in the multitude of Thy mercies Thou preservest all. Thou upholdest the falling and healest the sick; freest the captives and keepest faith with Thy children in death as in life. Who is like unto Thee,

Almighty God, Author of life and death, Source of salvation. Praised be Thou, O Lord, who hast implanted within us eternal life.[3]

This message of divine power and knowledge has served as the framework for Reform Judaism's insistence that the God of the Jews acts in history. Even though the movement has viewed biblical miracles as mythological in character, Reform thinkers accepted the basic theological presuppositions of the faith: God is personal. God is almighty. God is merciful. Thus, week after week we heard the rabbi declare that God is Creator, Redeemer and Saviour. Joining in congregational recitations, we recited prayers which emphasized his continuing concern over our lives. We thanked him for his tender mercies. We praised him for his glorious deeds. We acknowledged his abiding love. We asked him to preserve us and heal those who were sick. There were no limits to his power and knowledge, we asserted. The God of Israel is creator and Lord of all.

All-Mighty and All-Knowing

From biblical times, the belief in God's all-mighty power has been a central feature of the faith. In the Book of Genesis, for example, God told Abraham that his wife Sarah, aged ninety, was pregnant. Expressing astonishment, Sarah laughed and was criticized: "The Lord said to Abraham, 'Why did Sarah laugh, and say, "Shall I indeed bear a child now that I am old?" Is anything too hard for the Lord?" (Gen. 18:13-14). Again, in the Book of Jeremiah when the prophet purchased a field while Jerusalem was being threatened by the Babylonians, He declared in similar terms: "Behold, I am the Lord, the God of all flesh: is anything too hard for me? Therefore, thus says the Lord: Behold, I am giving this city into the hands of the Chaldeans and into the hand of Nebuchadrezzar king of Babylon." (Jer. 32:27) These passages suggest that there is nothing God cannot do: even what appears impossible is within his power.

For the biblical writers as well as later Jewish sages, such a conviction was of fundamental importance. Yet, under the impact of Greek thought, Jewish writers—along with Islamic and Christian theologians—began to explore the concept of divine omnipotence. Prominent among their concerns was the question whether God can do anything. According to the tenth century Jewish theologian, Saadiah Gaon, the soul will not praise God for being able to cause five to be more than ten without adding the requisite number; nor for being able to put the world through the hollow of a signet ring, nor for being able to change the past. All of these actions would be absurd. Thus Saadiah wrote:

> Of course, certain heretics often ask us about such matters, and we do indeed answer them that God is not anything because it is absurd, and the absurd is nothing. It is, therefore, as though they were to ask: "Is God capable of doing what is nothing?" which is, of course, a real question.[4]

Subsequently, the fifteenth-century Jewish philosopher Joseph Albo discussed the same issue. In his opinion, there are two kinds of impossibility: some things are intrinsically impossible so that even God cannot bring them about. We cannot imagine, for example, that God can make a part equal to the whole, a diagonal of a square equal to one of its sides, or the angle of a triangle equal to more than two right angles. Moreover, it is not possible for God to make two contradictory propositions true simultaenously, or the affirmative and negative true at the same time. Likewise, it is impossible to believe that God could create another being like himself. In these cases, the human mind cannot conceive such a state of affairs. The other type of impossibility is that which contradicts the law of nature. In these instances, it is possible to imagine such an occurrence. Therefore, Albo asserted, God can bring about such events since they are not inherently impossible.

Arguing along similar lines in his *Guide for the Perplexed*, the twelfth-century Jewish philosopher Moses Maimonides explored the nature of God's omnipotence. In his view, even though God is all-powerful, there are certain actions He cannot perform because they are logically impossible:

> That which is impossible has a permanent and constant property, which is not the result of some agent, and cannot in any way change, and consequently we do not ascribe to God the power of doing what is impossible...it is impossible to produce a square with a diagonal equal to one of its sides, or a solid angle that includes four right angles, or similar things.... We have thus shown that according to each one of the different theories there are things which are impossible whose existence cannot be admitted.[5]

In the next century the biblical commentator Ezra ben Solomon made a similar point in his discussion of the Song of Songs:

> The fact that God is unable to bring about what is logically absurd, e.g., creating a square the diagonal of which is equal in length to one of its sides, or asserting and denying the same proportion, does not indicate any deficiency in God's power. Just as this does not indicate any deficiency in his power, so the fact that God cannot cause an emanation of something from nothing does not indicate that God is deficient in any way. This, also, would be logically absurd.[6]

Such theological observations were paralleled in the Christian world. In in the same century Thomas Aquinas warned against assuming that God can do everything:

> When you say that God has the power for everything, you are most correctly interpreted as meaning this: that since power is relative to what is possible, divine power can do everything that is possible, and on this account is God called omnipotent.... Now it is incompatible with the meaning of absolute possibility that anything involving the contradiction of simul-

tanteously being and not being should be conceived as divine omnipotence....Whatever does not involve a contradiction is in that realm of the possible with respect to which God is called omnipotent. Whatever involves a contradiction is not held by omnipotence, for it just cannot possibly make sense of being possible.[7]

It was not the intention of these thinkers to impose restrictions on God's power; rather, they were anxious to determine those acts that are logically inconceivable. Since certain actions are inherently absurd, they argued that it makes no sense to believe that God could perform them.

In modern times Jewish writers have not been preoccupied by such theological dilemmas. Instead, a number of Jewish thinkers have advanced the doctrine of a limited or finite God. Influenced by such Christian philosophers of religion as Charles Hartshorne, Jewish theologians such as Levi Olan conceived of God as limited by his own nature. This view has been propounded to account for the existence of evil: if God is limited in power, He should not be held responsible for human suffering. God does not desire that such a state of affairs exists—He would eradicate moral and physical evil if He could. But it is not in his power to do so. In this view, God should be conceived as a partner with human beings in the quest to create a better world. Within Judaism, this notion of a limited God has not gained many adherents. Instead, most religious believers have continued to embrace the traditional doctrine of an all-powerful God who created the universe and continues to guide its destiny without any limitation.

Alongside the doctrine of God's omnipotence, Jews throughout the ages have testified to God's unlimited knowledge. As the Psalmist declared:

The Lord looks down from heaven,
He sees all the sons of men....
he who fashions the hearts of them all,
and observes all their deeds. (Ps 33:13, 15)

Again, Psalm 139 states:

> Thou knowest when I sit down and when I rise up;
> thou discernest my thoughts from afar.
> Thou searchest out my path and my lying down,
> and art acquainted with all my ways. (Ps. 139: 2–3)

In line with this view, rabbinic sages maintained that God's knowledge is not limited by space and time. Rather, nothing is hidden from God. Moreover, the rabbis declared that God's foreknowledge of events does not deprive human beings of their free will. As the second century scholar Akiva stated in the Mishnah: "All is foreseen, but freedom of choice is given."[8] Subsequently Maimonides argued in his *Mishneh Torah* that God knows everything before it occurs. Nonetheless, human beings are unable to comprehend the nature of God's knowledge since it is of a different order from that of human beings. On this account, it is similarly not possible to understand how divine foreknowledge is compatible with human freedom:

> You may ask: God knows all that will happen. Before someone becomes a good or a bad man God either knows that this will happen or He does not know it. If He knows that the person will be good is it impossible for that person to be bad? If you reply that while God knows that he will be good it is still possible for him to be bad, then God has no clear foreknowledge. You must know that the solution to this problem is larger than the earth and wider than the sea, many main principles of faith and lofty mountains of thought depend upon it.… God does not "know" with a knowledge that is apart from him, like human beings whose self and knowledge are distinct one from the other. God's knowledge and his self are one and the same though no human being is capable of clearly comprehending this matter.[9]

Other medieval thinkers, however, were not convinced by this explanation. In *The Wars of the Lord*, the fourteenth-century philosopher Gersonides contended that God knows things only in general. According to Geronsides, God eternally perceives the general laws of the universe, namely those laws that order the movements of heavenly bodies and, through them, sublunar beings. Thus God is aware of what awaits all persons as members of collectivities but, as an individual, each person is able to exercise freedom of the will. When such free choice is made, human beings are able to liberate themselves from the constraints of determinism. They cease to be subject to the universal laws known by God, and their acts are therefore totally undetermined and unknown to the Deity.

In presenting this explanation of divine knowledge and human freedom, Gersonides asserted that God's knowledge does not undergo any modification; it remains true regardless of individual choices since each agent is no longer included in the necessary and universal propositions which are thought by God. For Gersonides, God's knowledge embraces all events of this world with the exception of freely chosen actions that cannot be foreseen. By means of this theory he believed he was able to resolve the seeming contradiction between omniscience and freedom of the will. In the same century, the Jewish theologian Hasdai Crescas held a radically different position. For Crescas, all human beings only appear to be free, but in reality all their deeds are determined by virtue of God's foreknowledge. Rather than attempting to reconcile free will and omniscience, he asserted that God's knowledge is absolute and free will is an illusion. Hence, unlike other Jewish thinkers of the Middle Ages, Crescas believed that human beings only appear to be free, but in reality they are not, since all deeds are determined by God's foreknowledge.

In modern times, the devout have been less interested in such philosophical problems. Instead, there has been a universal reaffirmation of the traditional belief that God knows past, present and future and that human beings have freedom of choice. In his explanation of the Jewish faith, *The Jewish Religion,* the twentieth century Jewish writer, Michael Friedlander, stated with regard to divine foreknowledge:

> His knowledge is not limited, like the knowledge of mortal be-
> ings by space and time. The entire past and future lies unrolled
> before his eyes, and nothing is hidden from him. Although we
> may form a faint idea of the knowledge of God by considering
> that faculty of man that enables him within a limited space of
> time, to look backward and forward, and to unroll before him
> the past and the future, as if the events that have happened
> and those that will come to pass were going on in the pres-
> ent moment, yet the true nature of God's knowledge no man
> can conceive. "God considereth all the deeds of man," without
> depriving him of his free will; he may in this respect be com-
> pared to a person who observes and notices the actions and the
> conduct of his fellow-men, without interfering with them. It is
> the will of God that man should have free will and should be
> responsible for his actions; and his foresight does not necessar-
> ily include predetermination. In some cases the fate of nations
> or of individual man is predetermined; we may even say that the
> development of mankind is part of the design of the Creation.
> But as the actual design in the Creation is concealed from man's
> searching eye, so is also the extent of the predetermination a
> mystery to him. To solve this problem is beyond the intellectual
> powers of short-sighted mortals; it is one of the "hidden things
> that belong to the Lord our God."[10]

Theological Perplexities

As we have seen, the doctrines of omnipotence and omniscience have given risen to a range of theological dilemmas.
From the earliest rabbinic period, Jewish thinkers have sought
to make sense of these notions. Regarding the belief that God is
all-powerful, Jewish theologians have discussed the idea of God
doing impossible things. Some writers, such as Maimonides, insisted that even though God is almighty, there are certain actions
He cannot perform. The range of examples of such impossible

actions include creating incoherent geometrical constructions (such as a round square), causing a small number to be larger than a greater number (making five more than ten), or bringing about an absurd state of affairs (such as putting the world through the hollow of a signet ring).

Other thinkers have extended this category to include acting evilly, annihilating himself, or creating a being equal to himself. In their view, the fact that God cannot do such things does not indicate any defect in his nature; nor do they seek to impose any restriction of the scope of his activities. Rather, they argued, God can only do what is possible. In that sense He is all-powerful. Yet, if God is limited in this way, is He truly omnipotent? Determined to defend the attribution of omnipotence, other theologians insisted that God can do anything, even if it involves doing what is logically absurd. In their opinion, a being lacking the power to do literally anything would not be God.

As we noted, other thinkers have sought to escape from this dilemma by formulating the concept of a limited God. In the nineteenth century the utilitarian philosopher John Stuart Mill maintained that the idea of God as the Designer of the universe implies that He is only able to create the universe out of the pre-existent material. Otherwise, why would He have had to design or plan the cosmos? The notion of a design, he stressed, implies that there are obstacles which must be overcome. Given that this is so, God is limited by the material out of which He created the universe. Further, the notion of a designing mind implies that chaos was pre-existent, calling for order to be imposed. More recently, process theologians contend that God is limited by his nature so that, although He is infinite in some respects, He is finite in others. Such views seek to provide a solution to the problem of evil. If God is not omnipotent, as these writers suggest, then He is unable to eradicate suffering.

On this account, God is not the cause of evil. Rather, because He is limited in power He is unable to prevent human misery. Recently a number of Holocaust theologians have propounded such a theory to account for the tragedies of the Nazi era. In

Rethinking Jewish Faith, for example, the Reform rabbi Steven Jacobs argued that Jewish theology must be reformulated in a radically new fashion. Today, he wrote, Jews must redefine God's nature:

> Such an understanding is…contingent upon accepting a notion of God as other than historically and traditionally presented by both Judaism and Christianity. A possible source of divine affirmation, to the degree to which such affirmation is either desired or acknowledged as desired, lies in the concept of a "limited Deity" who could neither choose nor reject action during the dark years of 1933 (39)-1945, who could not have responded to those humanly created and crafted processes of destruction even if he or she had wanted to do so. Notions of omniscience and omnipotence quickly fall by the wayside; the alternative possibilities are a Deity who was ignorant of the designs of his or her German children and their European cousins and impotent to act even when he or she learned of their plans, or a limited Deity whose own knowledge and limited power precluded foreknowledge and interference.[11]

This notion of a limited God is, however, subject to serious criticism. If God is not able to prevent evil, it is difficult to see why He created the universe in the first place. Arguably God would have known that his creation would be subject to physical catastrophes as well as gross immorality. If God is wholly good—as many of these thinkers affirm—it is unclear why He would have created the cosmos knowing that He would not be able to prevent such suffering. Further, even if there were more good than evil in the universe, this would not explain why God created a world full of sorrow. Finally, this theory logically implies severe limitations of God's power. If God is unable to eliminate those evils which plague humankind, He must be very feeble indeed.

The idea of divine omniscience is likewise beset with difficulties. The central issue regarding this belief is how to make sense of human free will given God's knowledge of future events. According to Scripture, human beings are at liberty to choose between good and evil. Thus God declares in Deut. 11:26–28:

> Behold, I set before you this day a blessing and a curse: the blessing, if ye shall hearken unto the commandments of the Lord your God, which I command you this day; and the curse, if ye shall not hearken unto the commandments of the Lord your God, but turn aside out of the way which I command you this day, to go after other gods, which ye have not known.

Again, in Deut. 30:15–18, we read:

> See, I have set before thee this day life and good, and death · and evil, in that I command thee this day to love the Lord thy God, to walk in his ways, and to keep his commandments and his statutes and his ordinances; then thou shalt live and multiply, and the Lord thy God shall bless thee in the land whither thou goest in to possess it. But if thy heart turn away, and worship other gods, and serve them; I declare unto you this day, that ye shall surely perish.

Yet given God's omniscience, how can such human choice exist? As we have seen, Jewish philosophers have advanced three alternative explanations. Some thinkers, like Maimonides, maintained that God has foreknowledge even though human beings are free. According to Maimonides, the knower, the thing known, and the process of knowing are all one since God does not acquire knowledge of something outside of himself of which He was ignorant. Even though it appears logically impossible for human foreknowledge of a person's actions to be compatible with that individual's freedom, divine knowledge is so radically different from human knowledge that there is not a real problem. Divine foreknowledge, Maimonides argued, is in fact compatible with human freedom, even though we are unable to understand how this can be so.

Although Maimonides did not offer any further explanation, other thinkers have appealed to the mystery of time and eternity. In their view, God exists in the "Eternal Now." As such, He is outside time. Explaining the nature of this notion, Bahya Ibn Asher stated in his *Commentary to the Pentateuch* : "All times, past and future, are in the present so far as God is concerned, for He was before time and is not encompassed by it."[12] In this view, in the "Eternal Now" God knows everything simultaneously, including the choices a person makes. For human beings these are real choices made in a temporal sequence, but for God they are known all at once.

For Gersonides, on the other hand, the fact that human beings have free will makes it impossible for God to have complete knowledge of the future. As we have seen, Gersonides maintained that God knows things in general, but not everything. Since human beings are free to choose, God knows only what these choices are. He does not know these decisions as certain outcomes. Thus, God is not omniscient in an absolute sense. He is unable to know beforehand what human beings will do.

Adopting a different approach, Hasdai Crescas argued that human beings only appear to be free. In reality, all their deeds are determined by virtue of divine foreknowledge. As a consequence, it would be misguided to reward or punish individuals because of their actions. A later thinker who embraced such a deterministic viewpoint was the nineteenth-century Hasidic master, R. Joseph Mordecai of Izbica, who remarked with regard to the Talmudic passage in Ber. 33b (Everything is in the hands of Heaven except the fear of Heaven) that even the fear of Heaven is predetermined. In this life, he stated, the illusion that human beings have free will is maintained as an incentive to worship the Creator. However, in the Messianic age the truth will be revealed that there is neither virtue nor sin since all is due solely to the will of God.

These various and conflicting theories concerning omnipotence and omniscience were propounded by Jewish scholars in the attempt to make sense of seemingly irreconcilable doctrines about the nature of God and his activity in the world. From rabbinic times to the present, Jewish thinkers have clashed with one another in this quest. Yet, arguably, no single theory provides a completely adequate solution, and an acknowledgement of the inevitable subjectivity of religious belief can liberate Jewish theology from such a struggle. The doctrines of omnipotence and omniscience generate religious perplexity precisely because Jews perceive God as all-powerful and all-knowing. However, if the Divine is beyond human comprehension and Jewish doctrines are consequently viewed as human attempts to make sense of the Infinite, then the puzzle of God's knowledge and power ceases to be an insoluble problem.

Chapter 4.

CREATION

For the Jewish people, the belief in creation is of central importance. God is the source of all things, and this doctrine is celebrated throughout the year in the liturgy. In rabbinic literature, the biblical narrative served as the basis of considerable speculation. This was particularly acute in mystical sources, where attempts were made to penetrate the meaning of creation. In the history of Jewish philosophy, speculation about the nature of creation also played a central role. Today, religious Jews continue to uphold this belief, yet the findings of modern science have challenged the biblical account of the origin of the universe.

The Origin of the Cosmos

In the first years of religion school, our teachers recited to us the biblical account of creation. For six days, we were told, God created Heaven and Earth. "In the beginning," they read, "God created the heavens and the earth. The earth was without form and void, and darkness was upon the face of the deep; and the Spirit of God was moving over the face of the waters." Then God created light. God saw that the light was good; He separated the light from the darkness. Then he called the light day, and the darkness night. This completed his creative work for the first day. On the second day He formed the firmament in the midst of the waters, thereby creating heaven. On the third day, the dry land and vegetation were made. God said: "Let the earth put form vegetation, plants yielding seed, and fruit trees bearing fruit in which is their seed, each according to its kind." On the fourth day God placed lights in the firmament of the heavens. He then proceeded to create birds and fish and He blessed them, saying: "Be fruitful and multiply and fill the waters in the seas, and let birds multiply on the earth."

Finally, on the sixth day, God bestowed life on animals and human beings. Quoting from the second chapter of Genesis, they explained that Adam was placed in the Garden of Eden where God commanded him to refrain from eating from the tree of the knowledge of good and evil: 'The Lord God took the man and put him in the garden of Eden to till it and keep it. And the Lord God commanded the man, saying, "You may freely eat of every tree of the garden; but of the tree of the knowledge of good and evil you shall not eat, for in the day that you eat of it you shall die." The Lord then created Eve as a helper for him, for as He said: "It is not good that the man should be alone." Eve, too, was told that she was free to eat from all the trees of the garden except for the tree that He had forbidden to Adam.

Although in ordinary school we had been taught scientific theories about the origin of the universe and the evolution of human beings, we did not question the biblical narrative. Instead we listened to the story of creation and accepted it as an essential part of the Jewish heritage. In the natural history museum I had seen prehistoric creatures. I knew that the universe was millions of years old. But I never puzzled over the biblical account. Admittedly, it seemed implausible that Adam and Eve could have been historical figures who were tricked by a wily serpent into eating forbidden fruit. But I did not challenge the claim that God was the creator of the universe. This seemed entirely believable.

Every Saturday morning, the rabbi repeated this belief in the worship service. God, we heard, had created all things, and we were encouraged to acknowledge his power over nature. At the beginning of the service, he quoted the traditional prayer of praise from the *Amidah:*

> Praised be Thou, O Lord our God, Ruler of the world, who in Thy mercy makest light to shine over the earth, and all its inhabitants, and renewest daily the work of creation. How manifold are Thy works, O Lord! In wisdom hast Thou made them all. The heavens declare Thy glory. The earth reveals Thy creative power. Thou formest light and darkness, ordainest good out of evil, bringest harmony into nature and peace to the heart of man.

> Thou didst lay the foundations of the earth and the heavens are Thy handiwork. They may perish but Thou shalt endure. The heavens shall have no end. O everliving God, Creator of heaven and earth, rule Thou over us forever. Praised be Thou, O Lord, Creator of light.[1]

God's creation of the universe was directly linked to Sabbath observance. Just as God had rested on the seventh day, so we too were told to remember the Sabbath. Lifting the wine cup, the rabbi recited the *Kiddush* prayer:

> Praised be Thou, O Lord our God, Ruler of the world, who

hast created the fruit of the vine. Praised be Thou, O Lord our God, King of the Universe, who hast sanctified us with Thy commandments. In love hast Thou given us, O Lord Our God, the holy Sabbath as a heritage, a remembrance of creation. For that day is the prologue to the Exodus from Egypt. For us did you choose and us did you sanctify from all the nations. And your holy Sabbath, with love and favour did you give us a heritage. Blessed are you, O Lord our God, who sanctifies the Sabbath.[2]

Thus within Reform Judaism—as in the other major modern Jewish movements—the belief in God's creation is of supreme importance. Despite the discoveries of modern science, Reform Jews join with their coreligionists in proclaiming with faith that God alone formed the universe, and rules over it in glory.

One Creator

From biblical times to the present, Jews have affirmed that God is the source of all things. In the Hebrew Bible, the term *bore* (Creator) is frequently used to describe God. In the traditional synagogue, a hymn recited before readings from the Psalms stresses that before God's creative act nothing existed: "Blessed be He who spake, and the world existed: Blessed be He; Blessed be He who was the Master of the world in the beginning."[3]

Another synagogue hymn emphasizes God's eternal nature: "Thou wast the same before the world was created; Thou hast been the same since the world hath been created."[4]

The *Ani Maamin* (I believe) prayer, formulated in the sixteenth century, echoes this theme: "I believe with perfect faith that the Creator, blessed be His name, is the Author and Guide of everything that has been created, and that He alone has made, does make, and will make all things."[5]

According to the twelfth-century Jewish philosopher, Maimonides, the belief in creation is one of the thirteen basic principles of Judaism. Unlike everything else, whose existence is contingent on God's creative action, He alone necessarily exists:

> The foundation of all foundations and the pillar of wisdom is
> to know that there is a First Being. He it is who brought all
> things into being and all beings in heaven and earth and in
> between only enjoy existence by virtue of His true being. If it
> could be imagined that He does not exist nothing else could
> have have existed. But if it could be imagined that no other
> beings, apart from Him, enjoyed existence, He alone would
> still exist and He could not cease because they have ceased.
> For all beings need Him but He, blessed be He, does not need
> them, not any of them. Consequently, His true nature is dif-
> ferent from the truth regarding any of them.[6]

In rabbinic literature, the sages speculated about the nature
of the creative process. Drawing on the Platonic concept of the
idea of the world in the mind of God, *Genesis Rabbah* (*midrash
on Genesis*), for example, asserts that God looked into the Torah
and created the cosmos.[7] Here the Torah is conceived as a primordial blueprint of creation. Regarding the order of creation, in
the first century C.E. the School of Shammai stated: "The heavens
were created first and then the earth" (following Genesis 1:1). The
School of Hillel, however, maintained that heaven and earth were
created at the same time.[8] In the same century, a philosopher said
to Rabban Gamaliel: "Your God is a great craftsman, but he found
good materials to help him in the work of creation, namely *tohu*
and *vohu*, darkness, spirit, water and the deep." In reply, Rabban
Gamaliel quoted other biblical verses to illustrate that these materials were themselves created by God.[9] In the third century, R.
Johanan stated that God took two coils, one of fire and the other
of snow, wove them into each other, and created the universe.[10]
According to another rabbinic source, all things were formed
simultaneously on the first day of creation, but appeared on the
other six days just as figs are gathered in one basket but each is
selected individually.[11] Again, in *Genesis Rabbah* the sages emphasize that God formed several worlds, but destroyed them before

creating this one.[12] The goal of creation is summed up in the rabbinic claim that whatever the Holy One, blessed be He, created in his world, He did this for his glory.[13]

In early mystical texts, Jewish sages propounded other theories concerning the nature of the creative process. In the *Sefer Yetsirah* (Book of Creation)—the earliest mystical cosmological tract—God is described as creating the universe by means of the letters of the Hebrew alphabet. According to this text, God hewed them, combined them, weighed them, interchanged them, and through them produced the whole creation and everything that is destined to come into being. These letters are of three types: mothers, doubles and singles. The mothers (*shin, mem, aleph*) symbolize the three primordial elements of all existing things; they represent in the microcosm (the human form), the head, the belly and the chest.

In addition to these three mother letters, there are seven double letters (*beth, gimel, daleth, caph, peh, resh, tau*) which signify the contraries in the universe. These letters were formed, designed, created and combined into the stars of the universe, the days of the week, and the orifices of perception in human beings. Finally, there are twelve simple letters (*he, vav, zayin, chet, tet, yod, lamed, nun, samek, ayin, tsade, and kof*) which correspond to the chief activities—sight, hearing, smell, speech, desire for food, the sexual appetite, movement, anger, mirth, thought, sleep, and work. These letters are also emblematic of the twelve signs of the zodiac in the heavenly sphere, the twelve months, and the chief limbs of the body. Thus, human beings, world, and time are linked to one another through the process of creation.

These recondite doctrines are supplemented in the *Sefer Yetsirah* by a theory of emanation. The first *sefirah* (divine emanation) is the spirit of the living God; air is the second of the *sefirot* and is derived from the first. On it are hewn the twenty-two Hebrew letters. The third *sefirah* is the water that comes from the air. The fourth of the *sefirot* is the fire which comes from water through which God made the heavenly wheels, the seraphim and the ministering angels. The remaining six *sefirot* are the six dimensions of space. These ten *sefirot* are the molds into which all created things were originally cast. They constitute form rather than matter. The twenty-two letters, on the other hand, are the prime cause of matter: everything that exists is due to their creative force, but they receive their form from the *sefirot*. According to this cosmological doctrine, God transcends the universe; nothing exists outside of him. The visible world is the result of the emanation of the divine. By combining emanation and creation in this manner, the *Sefer Yetsirah* attempts to harmonize the concept of divine immanence and transcendence. God is immanent in that the *sefirot* are an outpouring of his spirit, and he is transcendent in that the matter which was shaped into the forms is the product of his creative action.

In the Middle Ages, a number of Jewish theologians believed that God created the universe *ex nihilo*. The kabbalists (Jewish mystics), however, interpreted the doctrine of *ex nihilo* in a special sense. God, they argued, should be understood as the Divine Nothing because as He is in and of himself, nothing can be predicated. The Divine is beyond human understanding. As the *Zohar* (the thirteenth-century mystical text) explains, God as Infinite (*Ayn Sof*) is beyond human comprehension:

> Master of the worlds, you are the cause of causes, the first cause who waters the tree with a spring; this spring is like the soul to the body, since it is like the life of the body. In you there is no image, nor likeness of what is within, nor of what is without.... There is none that knows anything of you, and besides you there is no singleness or unity in the upper or the lower worlds. You are acknowledged as Lord over all. As for all the *sefirot*, each one has a known name and you are the perfect completion of them all. When you remove yourself from them, all the names are left like a body without a soul.[14]

Creation *ex nihilo*, therefore, refers to the creation of the universe out of God, the Divine Nothing. Embracing the theory of emanation in earlier sources such as the *Sefer Yetsirah*, kabbalists argued that this occurred through a series of divine emanations. In their view, the first verses of Genesis allude to the processes within the Godhead prior to the creation of the universe. Following the teaching of Isaac Luria in the sixteenth century, later Jewish mystics understood the notion of God creating and destroying worlds before the creation of this world as referring to spiritual worlds. Thus *tohu* (void) in Genesis denotes the stage of God's self-revelation known as *olam ha-tohu* (world of the void) which precedes *olam ha-tikkun* (world of perfection). Other kabbalists, such as the Hasidic scholar Kalonymous Kalman of Cracow, maintain that the void in Genesis is the primordial void remaining after God's withdrawal to make room for the universe (*tzimtzum*). On this reading, God's decree, "Let there be light" (Gen. 1:3), means that God caused his light to emanate into the void in order to provide sustaining power required for the worlds which were later to be formed.[15]

Regarding the question whether, in the process of creating the cosmos, God also created intelligent beings on other planets, the Bible offers no information. Even though rabbinic sources attest to the creation of other worlds, they similarly contain no reference to the existence of other sentient creatures. In the nineteenth century, however, Phineas Elijah ben Meir Hurwitz of Vilna discussed this issue. On the basis of Isaiah 45:18 ("For thus says the Lord who created the heavens {He is God!}, who formed the earth and made it, He established it; He did not create it a chaos, He formed it to be inhabited: 'I am the Lord; and there is no other'"), he maintains that there are creatures on other planets than the earth. In this connection he refers to a passage in the Talmud in which *Meroz* (Judg. 5:23) is a star. Since it is cursed, Hurwitz concludes that it is inhabited. He alleges that creatures on other planets may have intelligence, yet he does not think they would have free will since only human beings have such capacity. Therefore, he writes, there is only room for Torah and worship in this world; they would have no place where free will is absent.[16]

In a modern discussion of this issue, the Reform rabbi Gunther Plaut asks:

> Will the possibility that there are intelligent creatures on other planets impose any strain on our religious beliefs?... The modern Jew will answer this question with a firm "No." An earlier generation, rooted in beliefs in an earth-centred universe, might have had some theological difficulties, but we have them no longer.... Just as a father may love many children with equal love, so surely may our Father on high spread his pinions over the vastness of creation.[17]

An alternative Jewish view has been advanced by the Orthodox rabbi Norman Lamm. There are, he believes, three major challenges confronting Judaism. The existence of extraterrestrial beings underlines the conviction that human beings are the ultimate purpose of God's creation. The second challenge relates to the generation of life. If life is generated by natural processes on other planets, how is one to understand the doctrine of God as Creator? The final challenge concerns the temptation to view God in non-personal terms given this new vision of the universe. Lamm believes that Judaism is able to resolve these difficulties. He concludes: "We may yet learn that, as rational, sentient, and self-conscious creatures, 'we are not alone.' But then again we never felt before nor need we feel today or in the future that we are alone, 'For Thou art with me.'"[18]

The Jewish scholar Louis Jacobs points out that the challenges Lamm mentions are not the crucial ones. The most serious difficulty is the question of the uniqueness of the Torah:

> Lamm's arguments center around what the Torah means in the light of the new possible situation. But if this possibility is real, the far more difficult and radical question to be faced is that there are whole worlds for which the Torah, given to humans, can have no meaning. In asking what Judaism has to say about extraterrestrial life, Lamm begs the question whether Judaism has any relevance in this context.[19]

Leaving aside this debate about the existence of extra-terrestrial life, there is no doubt that the belief that God is the source of all continues to animate Jewish religious sensibilities. Maimonides' formulation of this principle in the beginning of his *Code* expresses what has remained the central feature of the Jewish religious system:

> The foundation of all foundations and the pillar of wisdom is to know that there is a First Being. He it is who brought all things into being and all the beings in heaven and earth and in between only enjoy existence by virtue of his true being.[20]

Science and Creation

The biblical account in the Book of Genesis was written in a pre-scientific age. Hence, it is not surprising that the depiction of the creation of the universe conflicts in numerous respects with the findings of modern science. According to Scripture, God created the world in six days and rested on the seventh. The verb *bara* used in Gensis 1:1 does not imply *creatio ex niilo*, but denotes a process whereby God utilized various primordial elements in creating the cosmos. The opening sentence begins with the temporal clause: "When God began to create the heaven and the earth," and continues with a reference to darkness and void. The first creative act was the formation of light: "And God said, 'Let there be light,' and there was light." (Gen. 1:2).

The six days of creation are divided into a symmetrical pattern of three days each, in which the creation of light and of day and night occurred on the first day, the sky on the second, and dry land, seas and vegetation on the third. Then follows the creation of luminaries on the fourth day, living creatures of the sea and sky on the fifth, and land animals and human beings on the sixth. Throughout it is stressed that "God saw that it was good, and there was evening and there was morning"—this is followed by the completion of each day's labour. The final act of the creation of Adam is preceded by a declaration of God's purpose announced in the heavenly council: "Let us make man in our image, after our likeness." (Gen 1:26) Adam is then blessed by God and told to be fertile, increase the earth, and master it. He is entrusted with sovereignty over the fish of the sea, the birds of the sky, and all living things that creep on earth. (Genesis 1:28) In the second account of creation in chapter 2, a much more anthropocentric version is given of God's dealings with Adam and Eve.

What are we to make of the biblical narrative? For centuries, Jews have viewed this account of creation as literally true. As the source of all things, God formed the heavens and earth in six days, but rested on the seventh. For this reason, the Jewish people are commanded to rest on the Sabbath day from all their labours. Yet, modern science provides a totally different picture of the development of the cosmos and the origin of life. Today there is widespread agreement amongst scientists that the cosmos was formed through a big bang. Scientists explain that, as the world emerged, the spatial order was formed; then space boiled in the rapid expansion of the inflationary era, blowing the universe apart with rapidity. The perfect symmetry of the original structure was later broken as the cooling brought about by expansion crystallized out the forces of nature. For some time the universe was a hot soup of quarks and gluons and leptons, but by the time it was one ten-thousandeth of a second old, this age of transformations ceased and matter took the form of protons, neutrons and electrons.

At this point, the entire cosmos was hot enough to be the arena of nuclear reactions which continued for three minutes. The gross nuclear structure was then left at a quarter helium and three-quarters hydrogen. It was then far too hot for atoms to form around these nuclei—this would not occur for half a million years. By then the universe had become cool enough for matter and radiation to separate. The world then suddenly became transparent and a sea of radiation was left to continue cooling. Gravity was the dominant force in the next area of cosmic history. This continued its battle against the original expansive tendency of the big bang, stopping the universe from being too dilute, but failing to bring about an implosive collapse. Even though the universe was nearly uniform at that stage, small fluctuations were present, producing sites at which there was excess matter. The effect of gravity enhanced these irregularities until, after about a billion years, the universe began to become lumpy and the galaxies and their stars began to form.

Within the stars, nuclear reactions began and the contractive force of gravity heated up the stellar cores beyond their ignition temperature. Hydrogen was burned to become helium, and eventually a delicate chain of nuclear reactions started which generated further energy and the heavier elements up to iron. After a life of ten billion years, stars began to die. Some were so constituted that they did this in supernova explosions. This resulted in the dissemination of the elements into the wider environment; at the same time, the heavier elements beyond iron were produced in reactions with the high energy neutrinos blowing off the outer envelope of exploding stars.

As more stars and planets condensed, the conditions of chemical composition, temperature, and radiation led to the next new development in cosmic history. A billion years after conditions on earth became favourable, long chain molecules formed with the power of replicating themselves. They rapidly used the chemical food in the shallow waters of early earth, and the three billion years of the history of life commenced. A genetic code was established, and primitive unicellular entities transformed the atmosphere of earth from one containing carbon dioxide to one containing oxygen. The process of photosynthesis evolved, and eventually life began to become more complex. About seven hundred million years ago, jellyfish and worms were the most advanced life forms. About three hundred and fifty million years ago, life moved from the sea onto dry land, and seventy million years ago, dinosaurs disappeared. Three and a half million years ago, Australopithecines began to walk erect; homosapiens appeared three hundred thousand years ago.

The clash between these two rival views of the origin of the cosmos illustrates the archaic nature of biblical speculation about the beginning of all things. For the writers of Scripture, God is at the center of this process: He is the source of all that exists. Modern scientists, on the other hand, are concerned to explain in physical terms the sequence of events that took place when the universe was formed. Basing their conclusions on physical, chemical, and biological evidence, they have provided a coherent picture of the process by which the cosmos came into being. Despite efforts made by contemporary theologians to reconcile the biblical narrative with modern scientific theory, it is obvious that the authors of Genesis had a limited understanding of the true nature of the origins of the cosmos. The Bible's presentation of events is wholly inaccurate. This is true as well of the kabbalistic understanding of divine emanation and the formation of the cosmos by means of letter combination and divine emanation. These theories are nothing more than mystical speculation based on unfounded religious presuppositions.

A new vision of Judaism calls for a reevaluation of the Biblical story. It could now be recognized that the cosmological mythology of the ancient Israelites emerged out of a particular social and cultural context. Influenced by Babylonian legends, the authors of Genesis reformulated these ancient Near Eastern epics to suit their own religious purposes. For these writers, it was the God of the Israelites—not the numerous deities of Babylonian mythology—who had fashioned the universe out of primordial elements. During the six days of creation, they believed, God did all his work and rested on the seventh day. As modern Jews, however, we might wish to set aside such unsophisticated notions, replacing them with a scientific understanding of the origins of the universe. In the quest to explain the true nature of reality, we can adopt modern methods of investigation and experimentation—such a Copernican shift in orientation is a precondition for the formulation of my vision of a reconstructed Judasim for the twenty-first century.

Chapter 5.

DIVINE PROVIDENCE

According to the Jewish tradition, God is not detached from the universe that He created; rather, He sustains his creation and is actively involved in human history. The Bible affirms that God chose the Jewish people from all nations, and will guide their destiny to its ultimate fulfilment. Such providential care is an overarching theme of rabbinic literature as well as later Jewish thought. Hence, from ancient times to the present, Jews have been comforted by the belief that God exercises providential care for his people and will redeem them in the final days. Yet, arguably, such a conception of God needs to be modified given its conceptual difficulties and in the light of modern Jewish history.

God's Intervention

In Sunday school we were taught that God created and sustains the universe. The stories we read in the Hebrew Bible continually emphasize this theme: God is an active agent in the universe, determined to accomplish his purposes. In the *Union Prayerbook*, such providential care is repeatedly stressed. The evening service for the Sabbath, for example, begins with a recitation of God's involvement in nature:

> Praised be Thou, O Lord our God, ruler of the world, by whose law the shadows of evening fall and the gates of morn are opened. In wisdom Thou hast established the changes of times and seasons and ordered the ways of the stars in their heavenly courses.[1]

In the same part of the service, God's love for Israel is extolled:

> Infinite as is thy power, even so is Thy love. Thou didst manifest it through Israel, Thy people. By laws and commandments, by statutes and ordinances hast Thou led us in the way of righteousness and brought us to the light of truth.[2]

In responsive readings, the congregation acknowledges God's power and involvement in Jewish life:

> And through thy power alone has Israel been redeemed. Great deeds hast Thou wrought on our behalf and wonders without number. Thou has kept us in life; Thou hast not let our footsteps falter. Thy love has watched over us in the night of oppression; Thy mercy has sustained us in the hour of trial. And now that we live in a land of freedom, may we continue to be faithful to Thee and Thy word. May Thy law rule the life of all thy children and Thy truth unite their hearts in fellowship. O God, our refuge and our hope, we glorify thy name now as did our fathers in ancient days:

Who is like unto Thee, O Lord, among the mighty? Who is like unto Thee, glorious in holiness, awe-inspiring, working wonders?[3]

In the Silent Prayer, worshippers are to turn to God for support and comfort:

O God, keep my tongue from evil and my lips from speaking guile. Be my support when grief silences my voice, and my comfort when woe bends my spirit. Implant humility in my soul, and strengthen my heart with perfect faith in thee. Help me to be strong in temptation and trial and to be patient and forgiving when others wrong me. Guide me by the light of Thy counsel, that I may ever find strength in Thee, my rock and redeemer.[4]

Similarly at the Passover service, God's involvement in the history of the Jewish people is the dominant theme. The *Haggadah* relates that, under Egyptian bondage, the Jewish people suffered persecution and oppression. Quoting from the Book of Exodus, the *Haggadah* narrates the travail of Jews under a new pharaoh:

Now there arose up a new king over Egypt, which knew not Joseph. And he said unto his people, Behold, the people of Israel are more and mightier than we...And Pharaoh charged all his people, saying, Every son that is born you shall cast into the river. (Exodus 1: 8–22)

Yet Moses, as God's servant, thwarted Pharoah's evil plans. Speaking to Moses, God instructed him to free the Jewish nation: "Come now therefore, and I will send thee unto Pharaoh, that thou mayest bring forth my people the children of Israel out of Egypt." (Exodus 2:11) By sending a series of plagues, God persuaded Pharaoh to release the Jews, and the dramatic account of their escape is recounted at length during the Passover *seder*. God's glorious actions on behalf of the Jewish people is recited in the *dayanu* (it were enough) recitation—here God's providential care is celebrated:

> Had He brought us out of Egypt, and not divided the sea for us, Dayanu!
>
> Had He divided the sea, and not permitted us to cross on dry land, Dayanu!
>
> Had He permitted us to cross the sea on dry land, and not sustained us for forty years in the desert, Dayanu!
>
> Had He sustained us for forty years in the desert, and not fed us with mana, Dayanu!
>
> Had He fed us with mana, and not ordained the Sabbath, Dayanu!
>
> Had He ordained the Sabbath, and not brought us to Mount Sinai, Dayanu!
>
> Had He brought us to Mount Sinai, and not given us the Torah, Dayanu!
>
> Had He given us the Torah, and not led us into the land of Israel, Dayanu!
>
> Had He led us into the land of Israel, and not built for us the Temple, Dayanu!
>
> Had He built for us the Temple, and not sent us prophets of truth, Dayanu!
>
> Had He sent us prophets of truth, and not made us a holy people, Dayanu![5]

Providential Care

As we have seen, in Scripture the notion that God controls and guides the universe is a central theme. The Hebrew term for such divine action is *hashgaha*, a term derived from the thirty-third Psalm: "From where he sits enthroned He looks forth (*hishgiah)* on all the inhabitants of the earth." (Psalm 33:14) This view implies that the dispensation of a wise and benevolent providence is manifest everywhere—all events are ultimately foreordained by God. According to Scripture, God's provision for the world is of two types: (1) general providence, namely God's concern for the world in general; and (2) special providence—God's provision for each person. In the Hebrew Bible, God's general providence is illustrated by his freeing the ancient Israelites from bondage in Egypt, guiding them in the desert, and leading them to the Promised Land. The belief in the fulfillment of a divine plan for salvation is a further manifestation of God's providential care for his creatures. Linked to this concern for all is God's preoccupation with the fate of each individual. As the prophet Jeremiah declared: "I know, O Lord, that the way of man is not in himself, that it is not in man who walks to direct his steps." (Jer. 10:23)

Later, the doctrine of divine providence was developed in rabbinic sources. The Mishnah states: "Everything is foreseen."[6] In the Talmud, we read: "No man suffers as much as the injury of a finger when it has been decreed in heaven."[7] Such a belief became a central element of the Rosh Hashanah (New Year) service. According to the New Year liturgy, God, the judge of the world, provides for the fortunes of individuals as well as nations on the basis of their actions.

In the Middle Ages, Jewish theologians were preoccupied with this belief. Maimonides defended both special and general providence. In his view, special providence extends only to human beings and is in proportion to a person's intellectual and moral character. In this regard, Maimonides argued that the ideal of human perfection involves reason and ethical action. To illustrate his view, Maimonides used a parable about a king's palace. Those who are outside its walls have no doctrinal belief; those within the city but with their backs to the palace hold incorrect positions; others wishing to enter the palace not knowing how to do so are traditionalists who lack philosophical sophistication. But those who have entered the palace have speculated about the fundamental principles of religion. Only the person who has achieved the highest level of intellectual attainment can be near the throne of God.

Such philosophical attainment, however, is not in itself sufficient; to become perfect a person must go beyond communion with God to a higher state. Quoting Jeremiah 9:23–24, Maimonides proclaimed:

> Let not the wise man glory in his wisdom, let not the mighty man glory in his might, let not the rich man glory in his riches; but let him who glories glory in this, that he understands and knows me.[8]

This view implies that God is concerned about the human species, but not with every individual. Only human beings come under divine care as they rise in intellectual and moral stature.

Arguing along similar lines, the twelfth-century Jewish philosopher Abraham Ibn Daud discussed the highest degree of prophecy:

> Divine providence on behalf of his creatures is already evident to all those who meditate, but since these are few in number, the perfect goodness of God makes it still more evident by making it repose on those men who are of perfect conduct and irreproachable morals, so that, as it were, they become intermediaries between God and his creatures. He elevates them to such a point that they have a power comparable to that of the eminent substances which incline towards them in prophecy.... Only perfect and pure souls can attain such a level. This perfection and this purity are sometimes in a man from the beginning of his formation, and also moral perfection, but study is of great utility, as is the society of virtuous men....[9]

In the fifteenth century, however, Hasdai Crescas maintained that God created human beings out of his love for them—thus his providential care is not related to their personal characteristics. All persons enjoy God's special providence. Intellectual perfection, he insisted, is not the criterion of divine providence, nor the basis for divine reward and punishment.

The kabbalists were also concerned with this topic. In his

Shomer Emunim, for example, the eighteenth-century scholar Joseph Ergas explained that there are various types of providence:

> Nothing occurs by accident, without intention and divine providence, as it is written: "Then will I also walk with you in chance." You see that even the state of "chance" is attributed to God, for all proceeds from him by reason of special providence.

Nevertheless, Ergas limited special providence to human beings:

> However, the guardian angel has no power to provide for the special providence of non-human species; for example, whether this ox will live or die, whether this ant will be trodden on or saved, whether this spider will catch this fly and so forth. There is no special providence of this kind for animals, to say nothing of plants and minerals, since the purpose for which they were created is attained by means of the species alone, and there is no need for providence to be extended to individuals of the species. Consequently, all events which happen to individuals of these species are by pure chance and not by divine decree, except...where it is relevant for the divine providence regarding mankind.'[10]

These views caused offense to various Hasidic teachers. Divine providence, they insisted, is exercised over all things. Thus in the eighteenth century Phineas of Koretz stated in his *Peer La-Yesharim* : "A man should believe that even a piece of straw that lies on the ground does so at the decree of God. He decrees that it should lie there with one end facing this way and the other end the other way."[11] Again, Hayim of Sanz in his *Divre Hayim* to *Mikketz* contended: "It is impossible for any creature to enjoy existence without the Creator of all worlds sustaining it and keeping it in being, and it is all through divine providence. Although Maimonides has a different opinion in this matter, the truth is that not even a bird is snared without providence from above."[12]

In the Middle Ages, Jewish theologians also wrestled with dilemmas concerning God's foreknowledge as it relates to human freedom. If God knows everything that will happen in the future, how can human beings be free to choose their actions? As we have seen, in the *Guide,* Maimonides mentioned that human beings are free despite God's knowledge of future events. This is possible, he argued, because God's knowledge is not our knowledge.

Other scholars disagreed. In the twelfth century, for example, Abraham Ibn Daud argued that God's foreknowledge is not determinative nor causative. Thus human beings are able to act freely. His knowledge, he argued, is not in the nature of a compelling decree, but can be compared to the knowledge of the astrologers who know, by virtue of some other power, how a certain person will act.

Some later scholars, such as the seventeenth-century thinker Yom Tobh Lippman Heller, quoting *Midrash Shemuel* of Samuel b. Isaac of Uceda, appealed to the concept of the Eternal Now to resolve this problem:

> When a man sees someone else doing something the fact that he sees it exercises no compulsion on the thing that is done. In exactly the same way the fact that God sees man doing the act exercises no compulsion over him to do it. For before God there is no early and late since he is not governed by time.[13]

In modern society such theological issues have ceased to preoccupy Jewish theologians. Rather, the rise of science has challenged the traditional understanding of God's providential care. In place of the religious interpretation of the universe as controlled by the Deity, scientific explanation has revealed that nature is governed by complex physical laws. Thus it is no longer credible for most Jews to accept the biblical and rabbinic notion of divine activity. As a consequence, many Jews have simply abandoned the belief in providence.

Others, however, envisage God as working through natural causes. As a creator of all, He established the laws that regulate the natural order. Concerning special providence, many Jews believe that God is concerned with each person even though he does not miraculously intervene in the course of human history. Divine providential concern should thus be understood as a mode of interaction in which God affects the consciousness of the individual without curtailing his free will. Knowing the innermost secrets of every human heart, He introduces into the conscious awareness of individuals aims consonant with his will. Viewed in this light, special providence involves a dynamic relationship between the human and the divine.

Such a view was propounded by Arthur A. Cohen in his theological investigation of the religious implications of the Holocaust. According to Cohen, it is a mistake to blame God for inaction during the Nazi era. God, he stated, does not intervene magically in the course of human affairs. If there were such a God, the created order would be an extension of God's will rather than an independent domain brought about by God's creative love. "God," he wrote:

> is neither a function nor a cause of the historical nor wholly other and indifferent to the historical. I understand divine life to be rather a filament within the historical, but never the filament that we can identify and ignite according to our requirements, for in this and all other respects God remains God. As filament, the divine element of the historical is a precarious conductor always intimately linked to the historical....[14]

Similarly, the Jewish theologian Edward Feld, emphasized that God must be conceived as a fragile light of the spirit rather than an omnipotent Deity. As such, He inspires human beings: He is a small voice calling to us out of the depths:

> We believe not in a God of strength but in a fragile light of the spirit that is always threatened by the power of night and

that must always be fought for. A place can be made to let that spirit in, human beings can act in a way that affirms another world than that of the Nazis; it is for us to choose that world we want to enter. We believe not in an omnipotent God who will transform the reality closing in around us, which is the given of our lives, but in a God who in a delicate voice calls us from within that reality to break through its hardness and create a resting place for the Divine Presence.[15]

This reinterpretation of the traditional doctrine of providence has enabled many contemporary Jews to affirm the ancient formulation of the *Ani Maamin* prayer: "I believe with perfect faith that the Creator, blessed be his name, is the author and guide of everything that has been created, and that He alone has made, does make, and will make all things."

Divine Action

For the Jewish people, the belief in God's intervention in the world is of cardinal importance. As we have seen, within the Bible and rabbinic literature the belief that God providentially guides human history is a central motif. Yet, there are serious conceptual difficulties with this doctrine. First, the belief in God's intervention is problematic in that it presupposes his active involvement in human affairs, particularly at times of crisis. Yet, it is arguable that the universe is better organized without such supernatural involvement.

Let us imagine what the world would be like if God were constantly to prevent all human suffering. In a universe where all possibility of suffering was eliminated there would be no causal regularities. A chair, for example, would have to be firm enough to sit on, but soft and yielding if we stumbled against it. A fire would have to provide warmth and heat, but not when we came into contact with it. Water would have to be liquid enough to drink, but not to drown us. God would have to control our driving and braking a car so that we never caused an accident.

Hence, if a child ran across our path, our car would have to halt instantly by divine fiat so that we would suffer no effects of deceleration. In such an environment, everyone would be friends or lovers; no two people would ever fall in love with the same person at the same time. Crops would grow even if they were not planted; wheat would change into bread and be delivered even if farming and processing food halted. Houses, furniture, and clothes would come into being even if no one made them.

The negative impact of such a state of affairs is that no human activity would fulfill any purpose—if we failed to do something, God would always put things right. Only in this way could human suffering be prevented. There would be nothing to avoid, and nothing to seek. No occasion for co-operation or mutual help would arise. There would be no stimulus for civilization or culture. Humans would lack any positive character without the dignity of responsibility or potential for achievement. Not only would there be nothing to do, moral activity would be impossible. If God constantly intervened to prevent harmful consequences, there could be no right or wrong. In such altered conditions, there could be no courage or honesty. There would be no real love. There would be no stable environment for human growth and development. Moreover, evolution would not have taken place in such a world since it would lack a stable structure in which species that failed to adapt would die out. Arguably, the world as it is—devoid of divine intervention—is far preferable. A stable, material universe in which suffering is a possibility is the only environment in which the virtues of love, sympathy, devotion, courage, mutual cooperation and understanding can develop.

Added to these problems, it has become increasingly difficult for many Jews to embrace the traditional notion of a God who acts in history. In the light of the Holocaust, a number of Jewish theologians have argued that the traditional concept of God must be modified. Preeminent among Holocaust theologians, Richard Rubenstein called for a reevaluation of the the the doctrine of God. This conclusion was triggered by an encounter with a distinguished German clergyman, Heinrich Grüber, Dean of

the Evangelical Church in East and West Berlin. At an interview in his home in the West Berlin suburb of Dahlem, Grüber
affirmed that God was active in history and was responsible
for the Holocaust. Quoting Psalm 44:22 (For Thy sake are we
slaughtered every day), Grüber explained that it was part of
God's plan that the Jews died.

Shocked by Grüber's words, Rubenstein became convinced
that he could not avoid the issue of God's relation to the
Holocaust. Though Grüber's view of God as involved in human history was in harmony with Scripture, Rubenstein could
not believe in such a divine being. It seemed amazing to him that
Jewish theologians still subscribed to the belief in an omnipotent, beneficent God after the death camps. Traditional Jewish
theology maintains that God is the ultimate actor in history—it
interprets every tragedy as God's punishment for Israel's sinfulness. But Rubenstein was unable to see how this position could be
maintained without viewing Hitler as an instrument of God's will:
"The agony of European Jewry cannot be likened to the testing of
Job. To see any purpose in the death camps, the traditional Jewish
believer is forced to regard the most demonic, anti-human explo-
sion of all history as a meaningful expression of God's purposes.
The idea is simply too obscene for me to accept."[16]

According to Rubenstein, a void now exists where once the
Jewish people experienced God's presence. This demythologiz-
ing of the Jewish tradition is, he stated, acknowledged in contemporary Jewish life even if it is not made explicit in Jewish
theology. In the Diaspora and in Israel the myth of an omnipotent God of history is effectively repudiated in the lives of most
Jewish people. After the Nazi period, life is lived and enjoyed
on its own terms without any superordinant values or special
theological relationship. What is now required is a reorientation
of belief. In Rubenstein's words, modern Jewry must recognize
that we live in a universe devoid of supernatural action: "We
stand in a cold, silent, unfeeling cosmos, unaided by any power
beyond our own resources. After Auschwitz, what else can a Jew
say about God."[17]

While most Jews are unfamiliar with Rubenstein's writings, there is widespread disbelief in a God who intervenes in the course of human affairs. Despite the words of the traditional Jewish liturgy, most Jews today find it inconceivable that the natural course of everyday affairs could be interrupted by a divine agent. In contemporary society, the vast majority of Jews conduct their lives without recourse to supernatural agency. As a result a new theology of Judaism is called for—one that provides a framework for life in a post-Holocaust age.

Chapter 6.

REVELATION AND INSPIRATION

The Jewish faith is a revealed religion. Its basis is the Bible. According to tradition, the Five Books of Moses were revealed by God to Moses on Mount Sinai. In addition, the Oral Torah—consisting of the interpretation of the Written Torah—was also given to Moses. The prophetic books and the remaining books of the Hebrew Bible are viewed as divinely inspired. In modern times, however, biblical scholars have highlighted the improbability of this traditional view of Scripture. Today many Jews have distanced themselves from the binding authority of biblical law and have sought spiritual guidance from other sources.

Torah

From its origins in the nineteenth century, Reform Judaism emphasized the centrality of Scripture. In 1885 Reform leaders who gathered in Pittsburgh, Pennsylvania to formulate a theological statement for the movement emphasized their dedication to the biblical tradition. In their view, Scripture was to serve as a framework for Jewish life, even though these reformers sought to apply modern standards of relevance to its teachings:

> We recognize in the Bible the record of the consecration of the Jewish people to its mission as priest of the One God, and value it as the most potent instrument of religious and moral instruction.... We recognize in the Mosaic legislation a system of training the Jewish people for its mission during its national life in Palestine, and today we accept as binding only the moral laws and maintain only such ceremonies as elevate and sanctify our lives.[1]

Fifty years after the Pittsburgh meeting, the Reform movement issued a reinterpretation of Reform Judaism's mission in the Columbus Platform. Yet these Reformers continued to express their allegiance to Scripture:

> God reveals himself not only in the majesty, beauty and orderliness of nature, but also in the vision and moral striving of the human spirit. Revelation is a continuous process, confined to no one group and to no one age. Yet the people of Israel, through its prophets and sages achieved unique insight in the realm of religious truth. The Torah, both written and oral, enshrines Israel's ever-growing consciousness of God and of the moral law. It preserves the historical precedents, sanctions and norms of Jewish life, and seeks to mould it in the patterns of goodness and holiness.[2]

Such sentiments served as the background to the theological views expressed in the *Union Prayer Book,* published first in 1940, which was used at the weekly services I attended as a child. Repeatedly we were told that the Jewish people had received a goodly inheritance. Prior to the reading of the Torah on the Sabbath, the congregation stood when the scroll was taken from the ark and said:

> Let us declare the greatness of our God and render honor unto the Torah.

The Choir then sang:

> Praised be He who in his holiness has given the Torah unto Israel.

Before reading from the Torah, the rabbi recited the traditional blessing:

> Praised be Thou, O Lord Our God, Ruler of the world, who hast given us the law of truth and hast implanted within us everlasting life. Praised be Thou, O Lord, Giver of the Law.

Before the reading of the *Haftarah,* the rabbi recited the traditional *Haftarah* blessing:

> Praised be the Lord our God, for the law of truth and righteousness which He has revealed unto Israel, for the words of the prophets filled with His spirit and for the teachings of the sages whom He raised up aforetime and in these days.

Following the *Haftarah,* another blessing was recited thanking God for his revealed word:

> For the Torah, for the privilege of worship, for the prophets, and for this Sabbath day, given us for sanctification and rest, for honor and for glory, let us thank and bless the Lord our God.

When the Torah was returned to the ark, the congregation again stood and the rabbi stressed the significance of biblical law:

> The law of the Lord is perfect, restoring the soul; the testimony of the Lord is sure, making wise the simple. The precepts of the Lord are right, rejoicing the heart; the judgements of the Lord are true; they are righteous altogether. Behold, a good doctrine has been given unto you; forsake it not.

Finally the Choir declared:

> It is a tree of life to them who hold fast to it, and its supporters are happy. Its ways are ways of pleasantness and all its paths are peace.

Such sentiments were reinforced by the Torah and *Haftarah* portions recounted to us each week. The centrality of these Scriptural readings in the worship service illustrated that the words of Scripture were to resonate in our lives. Repeatedly the rabbi emphasized that the stories we heard about the patriarchs, Moses, and the prophets continue to have contemporary relevance. We were to be inspired by these ancient tales and the values they championed. In this way, as modern Jews, we could link ourselves to the Jewish past.

Divine Revelation

According to tradition, the entire Hebrew Bible was communicated by God to the Jewish people. As Maimonides stated in his formulation of the thirteen principles of the Jewish faith:

> The Torah was revealed from heaven. This implies our belief that the whole of the Torah found in our hands this day is the Torah that was handed down by Moses, and it is all of divine origin. By this I mean that the whole of the Torah came unto him from before God in a manner which is metaphorically

called "speaking"; but the real nature of that communication is unknown to everybody except to Moses (peace to him!) to whom it came.[3]

In rabbinic sources a distinction is made between the revelation of the Torah (Five Books of Moses) and the prophetic writings. This is expressed by saying that the Torah was given directly by God, whereas the prophetic books were given by means of prophecy. The remaining books of the Bible (referred to as the Hagiographa) were conveyed by means of the holy spirit rather than through prophetic inspiration. Nonetheless, all these books constitute the canon of Scripture. The Hebrew term for the Hebrew Bible is *Tanakh*—this word is made up of the first letters of the three divisions of Scripture: Torah (Pentateuch), *Neviim* (Prophets); and *Ketuvim* (Writings).

In the rabbis' view, the expositions and elaborations of the Law contained in the Torah were also revealed by God to Moses on Mount Sinai. This is referred to as the Oral Torah. Subsequently they were passed from generation to generation, and through this process additional legislation was incorporated. This process is referred to as the *Torah She-Be-Al Peh* (Torah by word of mouth). Thus, traditional Judaism affirms that God's revelation to the Jewish nation is two-fold and authoritative. Committed to this belief, Jews pray in the synagogue that God will guide them to do his will as recorded in their sacred literature:

> O our Father, merciful Father, ever compassionate, have mercy upon us: O put it into our hearts to understand and to discern, to mark, learn and teach, to heed, to do and to fulfil in love all the words of instruction of thy Torah. Enlighten our eyes in thy Torah, and let our hearts cling to thy commandments, and make us single-hearted to love and fear thy name, so that we be never put to shame.[4]

In the early rabbinic period the doctrine of *Torah MiSinai* (Torah from Sinai) was a constant theme. Thus, R. Levi b.

Hama said in the name of R. Simeon b. Lakish: The verse:

> "And I will give thee the tables of stone, and the law and
> the commandment, which I have written thou mayest teach
> them" (Exod. 24:12) means as follows: "The tables of stone"
> are the Ten Commandments, "the law" is the Pentateuch; "the
> commandment" is the *Mishnah*, "which I have written" are the
> Prophets and the Hagiographa, "that thou mayest teach them"
> is the *Gemara* (*Talmud*). This teaches that all these things were
> given on Sinai.[5]

In the medieval period this doctrine was continually affirmed.
Like Maimonides, the thirteenth-century Jewish theologian
Nahmanides in his *Commentary on the Pentateuch* wrote that
Moses composed the Five Books of Moses at God's dictation.
It is likely, he observed, that Moses wrote Genesis and part of
Exodus when he descended from Mount Sinai. At the end of
forty years in the wilderness, he completed the rest of the Torah.
Nahmanides pointed out that this interpretation follows the
rabbinic tradition that the Torah was given scroll by scroll. For
Nahmanides, Moses was like a scribe who copied an older work.
Underlying this conception is the mystical idea of a primordial
Torah that contains the words describing events before the creation of the world. Further, Nahmanides maintained that the
secrets of the Torah were revealed to Moses and are referred to
in the Torah by the use of special letters, the numerical values of
words and letters, and the adornment of Hebrew characters.

Paralleling Nahmanides' understanding of the Torah, the thirteenth-century mystical work, the *Zohar*, asserts that the Torah
contains mysteries beyond human comprehension:

> Said R. Simeon: "Alas for the man who regards the Torah as a
> book of mere tales and everyday matters! If that were so, even
> we could compose a Torah dealing with everyday affairs, and
> of even greater excellence. Nay, even the princes of the world
> possess books of greater worth which we could use as a model

for composing such a Torah. The Torah, however, contains in all its words supernal truths and sublime mysteries…. Thus had the Torah not clothed herself in garments of this world, the world could not endure it. The stories of the Torah are thus only her outer garments, and whoever looks upon that garment as being the Torah itself, woe to that man—such a one has no portion in the next world."[6]

In the sixteenth century the Jewish scholar Moses b. Joseph di Trani similarly maintained that the Torah is the blueprint of all worlds. After stating that all the words in the Torah—from the first word of Genesis to the last word of Deuteronomy—are from the Almighty, he questioned why the Torah is not recorded in the first person. Why, he asked, does the text not say: "In the beginning I created with My name *Elohim* the heavens and the earth…And I said with My name *Elohim:* 'Let there be light'…And I called the firmament heaven and I divided the light from the darkness." The answer is that, since the Torah is a preexistent plan for all worlds, it does not speak directly about God's involvement in creating this world. If it did so, it would suggest that God was only concerned with the formation of our universe.[7]

Despite the centrality of this doctrine, in the modern period it has become increasingly difficult to sustain the belief in *Torah MiSinai.* As early as the sixteenth century, scholars noted that the Five Books of Moses appear to be composed of different sources. In 1520, A. B. Carlstad argued that both the style and diction were the same in the Torah passage dealing with Moses' death and in the preceding passages. In a commentary to Joshua published in 1574 the Catholic A. Masius maintained that the Torah was compiled by Ezra from ancient documents. In 1670 Baruch Spinoza noted that some of the stories in the Torah are repeated more than once with various differences. At the same time Richard Simon, a Catholic priest, put forward the view that the Torah is a compilation of various documents of different dates.

In the middle of the nineteenth century sustained investigation by two German scholars, Karl Heinrich Graf and Julius Wellhausen, concluded that the Five Books of Moses are composed of four main documents that once existed separately but later were combined by a series of editors or redactors. The first document, "J," dating from the ninth century B.C.E. attributes the most anthropomorphic character to God, referred to by the four Hebrew letters YHWH. The second source, "E," stemming from the eighth century B.C.E., is less anthropomorphic and utilizes the divine name *Elohim*. In the seventh century B.C.E. the "D" source was written, concentrating on religious purity and the priesthood. Finally the "P" source from the fifth century B.C.E., has a more transcendental conception of God, emphasizing the importance of the sacrificial cult.

Graf and Wellhausen argued that this framework makes it possible to account for the manifold problems and discrepancies in the biblical text. The Graf-Wellhausen hypothesis was later modified by other scholars. Some preferred not to speak of separate sources, but of circles of tradition. On this view, J, E, P and D represent oral traditions rather than written documents. Further, these scholars emphasized that the separate traditions themselves contain early material; thus, it is a mistake to think they originated in their entirety at particular periods. Other scholars have rejected the theory of separate sources altogether. They argued that oral traditions were modified throughout the history of ancient Israel and eventually were compiled into a single narrative. Yet despite these different theories there is a general recognition among both non-Jewish and Jewish scholars that the Torah was not written by Moses. Rather, it is seen as a collection of traditions originating at different times in ancient Israel.

In addition to biblical criticism, textual studies of ancient manuscripts highlight the improbability of the traditional view of Scripture. According to rabbinic Judaism, the Hebrew text of the Torah used in synagogues today (the Masoretic text) is the same as that given to Moses. Yet it is widely accepted that the script of contemporary Torah scrolls is not the same as that which was current in ancient Israel from the time of the monarchy until the sixth century B.C.E. It was only later, possibly under Aramaic influence, that the square script was adopted as the standard for Hebrew writing. Further, the fact that the ancient translations of the Hebrew Bible into languages such as Syriac and Greek contain variant readings from the Masoretic text suggests that the Hebrew text of the Five Books of Moses now in use is not entirely free from error.

A final aspect of modern studies that bears on the issue of Mosaic authorship concerns the influence of the ancient Near East on the Hebrew Bible. According to Orthodoxy, the Torah was essentially created out of nothing. Yet there are strong parallels in the Bible to laws, stories, and myths throughout the ancient Near East. It is unlikely that this was simply a coincidence: the similarities offer compelling evidence that the Torah emerged in a specific social and cultural context. The authors of the biblical period shared much the same world view as their neighbors and no doubt transformed this framework to fit their own religious ideas. In this light, most contemporary biblical scholars would find it impossible to reconcile the traditional conception of Mosaic authorship with the findings of modern biblical scholarship and archeological discovery.

For the Orthodox, such investigations are irrelevant. Orthodox Judaism remains committed to the view that the Written and the Oral Torah were imparted by God to Moses on Mount Sinai. This act of revelation serves as the basis for the entire legal system as well as doctrinal beliefs about God. Despite such an adherence to tradition, many Orthodox Jews pay only lip-service to such a conviction. The gap between traditional belief and contemporary views of the Torah is even greater in the non-Orthodox branches of Judaism despite their alleged dedication to the Jewish past. Here there is a general acceptance of the findings of biblical scholarship. The Five Books of Moses are perceived as divinely inspired but at the same time the product of human thought.

Thus the Pentateuch is viewed as a unified text—combining centuries of tradition—in which a variety of individual sources

were woven together by a number of editors. Such a non-fun-
damentalistic approach, which takes account of scholarly developments in the field of biblical studies, rules out the traditional
belief in the infallibility of Scripture and thereby provides a
rationale for changing Jewish law. The same applies to the Oral
tradition. Non-Orthodox Jews similarly regard the chain of rabbinic teaching as the product of human reflection rather than the
unfolding of the divine will. This shift in orientation has brought
about considerable uncertainty within the ranks of Conservative,
Reconstructionist, Reform, and Humanistic Judaism. If the law
needs to be altered, what criteria should be implemented in de-
ciding which laws should be retained, discarded or changed? By
what criteria is one to decide which elements of the Torah were
revealed to Moses? The lack of satisfactory answers to these
questions points to the religious confusion that exists in the
various branches of non-Orthodox Judaism.

Authority and Personal Freedom

As we have seen, the conviction that God revealed the Written
Torah (*Torah Miktav*) and Oral Torah (*Torah She-Be-Al-Peh*) to
Moses on Mount Sinai has been of central importance in the
life of the Jewish people. This bedrock of divine disclosure has
provided a basis for Jewish observance through the ages. Yet in
modern times, the rise of biblical scholarship and a critical understanding of the development of Judaism have challenged this
doctrine. Today, within the Jewish world it is widely accepted that
the Pentateuch evolved over centuries and that the Oral Law underwent continual development. Hence, the authority of Scripture
and of the rabbinic tradition has been called into question. No
longer does Jewry feel compelled to follow biblical and rabbinic
law, nor accept the account of God presented in Scripture.

Such a new situation calls for a reevaluation of the traditional commitment to both belief and practice based on divine
revelation. In the past the doctrines of the faith were regarded
as binding upon all Jews. In his formulation of the principles

of Judaism, for example, Maimonides stressed that those who ceased to subscribe to these divinely revealed tenets were to be deemed heretics. In his view, such individuals had departed from the body of Israel and should be despised by all true believers—religious belief was here conceived as determinative of Jewishness. Similarly, through the centuries rabbinic authorities insisted that it is obligatory for all Jews to adhere to the Code of Jewish Law since it is based on the Written and Oral Torah revealed at Sinai. Anyone who deliberately violated the *mitzvot* was guilty of transgressing against God's sacred word. Judaism as a monolithic religious system was thus grounded in the inviolate communication of divine truth.

However, if the Jewish faith is a human construct growing out of the experiences of the nation for nearly four millennia, it must be susceptible to reinterpretation and change. Many Jews may now feel free to draw from the tradition those elements that he or she finds spiritually meaningful. The authoritarianism of the past, based on divine disclosure, could give way to personal autonomy in which all individuals are at liberty to construct for themselves a personal system of religious observance relevant to their own needs.

The central feature of this new understanding of Judaism is, the principle of personal liberty. Such a new vision of Judaism would allow all individuals the right to select those features from the tradition which they find of importance. This approach is not an innovation—it has always been a tenet of Reform Judaism, for example, that members of the community are at liberty to practice those observances that they regard as meaningful. However, the principle of autonomy has not always been carried to its logical conclusion. Instead, throughout the history of the Reform movement, reformers sought to impose their religious views on others. This is evident in the way the Reform liturgy emphasizes the centrality of Scripture. But this new approach to the tradition would actively encourage individuals to make up their own minds about religious belief and practice. In my opinion, no one—no rabbi or rabbinical body—should be allowed to decide which observances are acceptable for the community as a whole.

This new conception of Judaism would foster personal liberty and freedom. Rabbis who subscribe to such a stance would have the duty to instruct their congregations about the Jewish way of life, yet such teaching would be descriptive rather than prescriptive. Any return to centralized rules or regulations laid down by a small self-appointed body of rabbis would, in reality, be nothing more than Orthodoxy in disguise.

It might be objected that such extreme liberalism would simply result in chaos, leading to the dissolution of the faith. Such criticism, however, fails to acknowledge the state of religious diversity within contemporary Jewish society. In all the branches of Judaism there has been a gradual erosion of centralized authority. Although many rabbis have attempted to establish standards for the members of their communities, there is a universal recognition, that in the end, all Jews will define for themselves what aspects of the Jewish heritage are personally relevant. Modern Jews are ultimately guided by their own consciences, not by the traditional understanding of God's revelation. As a radical alternative to the more structured models of the Jewish faith presented by the major branches of Judaism, this reinterpretation of the faith provides a non-dogmatic foundation for integrating Jewish belief and practice into modern life. Rather than following the dictates of the Written and Oral Torah, Jews would be encouraged to chart their own paths through the tradition.

Chapter 7.

TORAH AND COMMANDMENTS

A ccording to tradition, Moses received the law contained in the Five Books of Moses; in addition, the Oral Law, consisting of the interpretations of the Written Law, was revealed on Mount Sinai. This corpus of legislation constitutes the authoriative framework of Jewish observance. Through the centuries, Jews have faithfully observed these commandments. In modern times, however, serious doubts have been raised about the doctrine of *Torah MiSinai*. As a consequence, most Jews have set aside the bulk of presecriptions contained in the Torah and rabbinic sources, and such neglect has resulted in the erosion of the legal heritage.

Reform Judaism and the *Mitzvot*

When I was a child, my family followed various religious practices. On Friday night my mother lit the Sabbath candles and my father recited the traditional *Kiddush* prayer (Sabbath blessing) over wine. At Passover my parents, grandmother, and cousins gathered together for the *seder*. My great uncle led the recitation of the Reform *Haggadah* which commemorates the exodus from Egypt. Every Rosh Hashanah I went with my parents to Temple for the New Year Service; this was followed ten days later by the Day of Atonement. In addition, we celebrated Hanukkah, Purim, and various other festivals. Yet, I was aware that our religious observance was far less rigorous than that of my Orthodox and Conservative friends.

In religion school we were taught about the principles of Reform Judaism. In one of my classes, the teacher recounted the history of the movement. Reformers in the nineteenth century, she explained, were anxious to distance themselves from the Judaism of the ghetto. Judaism, they believed, had always undergone change and development. As a result, Reform rabbis sought to modernize the Jewish faith to make it relevant for contemporary society. This process, she went on, resulted in the abandonment of a wide range of Jewish practices, such as *kashrut* (dietary laws), wearing *kippot* (skullcaps) and *tallit* (prayer shawls), and celebrating Jewish festivals for two days. Instead of observing these outmoded precepts, Reform Judaism emphasized the moral commandments.

Despite this orientation, the Reform prayer book frequently stresses the importance of God's commandments, and I recall reciting prayers in Sabbath services that extolled this feature of the tradition. At the beginning of the evening service, for example, the congregation and reader declared:

> Infinite as is Thy power, even so is Thy love. Thou didst manifest it through Israel, Thy people. By laws and commandments, by statutes and ordinances hast Thou led us in the way

of righteousness and brought us to the light of truth. Therefore at our lying down and our rising up, we will meditate on Thy teachings and find in Thy laws true life and length of days. O that Thy love may never depart from our hearts. Praised be Thou, O Lord, who hast revealed Thy love through Israel.[1]

Later in the service, such sentiments were reiterated in a prayer concerning Sabbath observance:

Our God and God of our fathers, grant that our worship on this Sabbath be acceptable to Thee. Sanctify us through Thy commandments that we may share in the blessings of Thy word. · Teach us to be satisfied with the gifts of Thy goodness and gratefully to rejoice in all Thy mercies. Purify our hearts that we may serve Thee in truth. O help us to preserve the Sabbath as Israel's heritage from generation to generation, that it may bring rest and joy, peace and comfort to the dwellings of our brethren, and through it Thy name be hallowed in all the earth. Praised be Thou, O Lord, who sanctifies the Sabbath.[2]

Responsive readings similarly stressed the significance of the *mitzvot*:

For He is our God and we are His people, consecrated to His service. Remember all the commandments of the Lord, and do them; that ye go not about after your own heart and your own eyes. It is He who redeemed us from the hand of oppressors, and revived our spirits when our own strength failed us. His works and wonders surpass our understanding, His gifts and blessings are without number. We rejoice in His sovereign power; we praise and give thanks unto His name.[3]

In the Torah service the significance of God's law was highlighted. Quoting from Isaiah 2:1-4, the rabbi proclaimed that in the end of days the law will go forth from Zion:

It shall come to pass, in the end of days, that the mountain of the Lord's house shall be exalted above the hills, and all nations shall flow unto it. And many peoples shall go and say: Come ye, and let us go up to the mountain of the Lord, to the house of the God of Jacob; that He may teach us of His ways, and we will wlk in His paths. For out of Zion shall go forth the law, and the word of the Lord from Jerusalem.[4]

The rabbi continued by stating that it is God's covenant, enshrined in the law, that binds Israel to God:

This is the covenant which dedicates Israel to the One and Eternal God. This is the Torah, the pillar of right and of truth. This is the Law, that proclaims the Fatherhood of God and the Brotherhood of man.[5]

Thus, Reform Judaism emphasizes the centrality of God's commandments. We were to live in accordance with the Law. The commandments are a tree of life to those who hold fast to them. They are to enlighten our eyes and direct us to follow the path of truth. Such traditional sentiments were continually expressed in worship. Yet, it was clear that most Reform Jews had rejected the multitude of prescriptions that had regulated Jewish life in previous ages. We were to be faithful to a sacred inheritance, but for our parents and for us Jewish law had lost its significance. I was conscious of the incongruity of the liturgy and the realities of Reform Jewish life. Yet, I assumed that such seeming inconsistency was of little consequence—that those who had compiled the *Union Prayer Book* had been able to resolve such apparent discrepancies.

Divine Commandments

As we have seen, through the centuries Jews have subscribed to a belief in *Torah MiSinai*. According to this doctrine, God revealed all 613 commandments contained in the Torah to Moses on Mount Sinai. These prescriptions, which are to be observed as part of the divine covenant, are of two types: (1) statutes concerned with ritual performances characterized as obligations between human beings and God; and (2) judgments consisting of ritual laws that would have been adopted by society even if they had not been decreed by God. These 613 commandments are further categorized in terms of negative laws (365 commandments), and duties to be performed (248 prescriptions).

Traditional Judaism maintains that, in addition to the Written Law, Moses received the Oral Torah. This was passed down from generation to generation and was the subject of rabbinic debate. As the Mishnah records: "Moses received the Torah on Sinai, and handed it down to Joshua; Joshua to the elders; the elders to the prophets; and the prophets handed it down to the Men of the Great Assembly."[6]

The first authoritative collection of Jewish law is the Mishnah composed by Judah Ha-Nasi, the head of the Sanhedrin, in the second century C.E. This work is the most important legal code after Scripture; its purpose was to supply teachers and judges with a guide to the evolving Jewish legal tradition. In later centuries, scholars continued to discuss the nature of Jewish law—their deliberations are recorded in the Palestinian and Babylonian Talmuds.

The Palestinian Talmud developed in Israel and was redacted in a formal collection in the middle of the fifth century C.E. This *Gemara* and the Mishnah are also known as the *Talmud Yerushalmi*. The second *Gemara* developed in Babylonia and was compiled by Ashi and Ravina whose work was completed by the middle of the sixth century C.E. However, a great deal of later editorial work was done on this text over the next 250 years; hence the final version was not completed until around 800 C.E. The *Gemara* is never printed by itself; it is always printed along with the Mishnah. The Babylonian *Gemara* and the Mishnah printed together are also called the *Talmud Bavli*.

The Babylonian Talmud is much more complete than the Jerusalem Talmud. Nonetheless the *Gemara* only exists for 37 out of the 63 tractates of the Mishnah. In the usual printed editions the Babylonian Talmud comprises the full Mishnah, the 37 *Gemaras,* and the extra-canonical minor tractates. As the major source of Jewish observance, this multi-volume work forms the framework for Jewish living, and is regarded by the Orthodox as an authoritative legal code.

After the completion of the Talmuds in the sixth century C.E., outstanding rabbinic sages continued the development of Jewish law by issuing answers to specific questions. These responses—known as *responsa*—touched on all aspects of Jewish law and insured a standardization of observance. In time, various sages felt the need to produce collections of Jewish law so that all members of the community would have access to the legal tradition. In the eleventh century, Isaac Alfasi produced a code that became a standard legal text for Sephardic Jewry; two centuries later, Asher ben Jehiel wrote a code written that served as a legal guide for Ashkenazi Jews. In the twelfth century Moses Maimonides wrote the *Mishneh Torah,* which had a wide influence, as did the code by Jacob ben Asher in the fourteenth century. In the sixteenth century, Joseph Caro published the *Shulkhan Arukh* which, together with glosses by Moses Isserles, has served as the standard code of Jewish law for Orthodox Jews to the present day.

In kabbalistic thought, observance of the *mitzvot* has cosmic implications. For the mystic, *tikkun* (deeds of cosmic repair) sustain the world, activate nature, and bring about the coupling of the tenth and sixth *sefirot* (divine emanations). Such repair is accomplished by keeping the *mitzvot,* which were conceived as vessels for establishing contact with God. Such a religious life provided Jewish mystics with a means of integrating themselves into the divine hierarchy; in this way the *kabbalah* was able to guide the soul back to its ultimate source.

The highest rank attainable by the soul at the end of its sojourn on earth is the mystical cleaving to God. The early kabbalists of Provence defined such cleaving as the ultimate spiritual goal. According to the thirteenth-century Jewish kabbalist,

Isaac the Blind, the principal task of the mystic and of those who contemplate the divine name is "And you shall cleave unto him" (Deut. 13:4). This is the central principle of the Torah, blessings and prayer. The aim is to harmonize one's thought above, to conjoin God in his letters, and to link the ten *sefirot* to him. For Nahmanides in the thirteenth century, such cleaving is a state of mind in which one constantly remembers God and his love to the point that when one person speaks with another person, his or her heart is not with that person at all, but is still before God. Whoever cleaves in this way to his Creator, he continues, becomes eligible to receive the Holy Spirit. According to Nahmanides, the pious are able to attain such a spiritual state. Mystical cleaving does not completely eliminate the distance between God and human beings; rather it denotes a state of beatitude and intimate union between the soul and its source.

Within the Lurianic kabbalistic system, these notions were elaborated. According to the sixteenth-century Jewish mystic Isaac Luria, when the vessels were shattered, the cosmos was divided into two parts. The kingdom of evil in the lower part was separated from divine light in the upper realm. For Luria, evil is opposed to existence; therefore, it was not able to exist by its own power. Instead it had to derive spiritual sustenance from the divine light. This was accomplished by keeping the sparks of the divine light that fell captive when the vessels were broken. Divine attempts to bring unity to all things now had to focus on the struggle to overcome the evil forces.

At first this was accomplished by a continuing process of divine emanation which first created the *sefirot*, the sky, the earth, the Garden of Eden, and human beings. Humans were intended to serve as the battleground for this conflict. In this regard Adam reflected the dualism in the cosmos: he possessed a sacred soul while his body represented the evil forces. God's intention was that Adam conquer the evil within himself and thereby bring about Satan's downfall. However when Adam failed, a catastrophe occurred parallel to the breaking of the vessels. Instead of divine sparks being saved and uplifted, new divine lights fell and evil became more powerful.

Rather than relying on the action of one person, God then chose the people of Israel to triumph over evil and raise up the captive sparks. The Torah was given to symbolize the Jewish people's acceptance of this allotted task. When the ancient Israelites undertook to keep the law, redemption seemed imminent. Yet the people of Israel then created the golden calf—this was a sin parallel to Adam's disobedience. Again, when divine sparks fell, the forces of evil were renewed. According to Luria, history is a record of attempts by the powers of good to rescue the divine sparks and unite the earthly and heavenly spheres. Luria and his disciples believed they were living in the final stages of this last attempt to overcome evil, in which the coming of the Messiah would end the struggle.

Related to the contraction of God, the breaking of the vessels, and the exiled sparks was Luria's belief in *tikkun*. For Lurianic mystics, this concept refers to the mending of what was shattered at creation. After the catastrophe in the divine realm, the process of restoration commenced and every disaster was perceived as a setback. In this conflict, keeping God's commandments was understood as contributing to repair: the divine sparks that fell can be redeemed by ethical and religious deeds. According to Luria, these sparks are attached to all prayers and moral acts. If the Jew keeps the ethical and religious law, these sparks are redeemed and lifted up. When the process is complete, evil will disappear. But every time a Jew sins, a spark is captured and plunges into the satanic abyss. Every deed thus has cosmic significance in the Lurianic kabbalistic system.

In the modern world, such traditional mystical beliefs have lost their force except among the Hasidim. Today Orthodox Judaism has possibly the greatest number of adherents; nonetheless, the majority of those who profess allegiance to Orthodox Judaism do not follow the *Code of Jewish Law*. Instead each individual Jew feels free to determine his own path through the tradition. This is also so within the other branches of Judaism. The legal tradition has lost its hold on Jewish consciousness—the bulk of rituals and observances appear anachronistic and irrelevant. In previous centuries this was not the case; despite the divisions within the Jewish community, all Jews accepted the authority of Scripture as binding. Hence, food regulations, stipulations concerning ritual purity, the moral code, as well as other *mitzvot* served as the framework for an authentic Jewish way of life.

Throughout Jewish history the validity of the Written Torah was never questioned. In modern society, however, most Jews of all religious positions have ceased to view the legal heritage in this light. Instead individual Jews—including those of the Orthodox persuasion—feel at liberty to choose which *mitzvot* have personal spiritual significance. Such an anarchic approach to the legal tradition highlights the fact that Jewish law no longer serves as a cohesive force for contemporary Jewry. In short, many modern Jews no longer believe in the doctrine of *Torah MiSinai*, which previously served as a cardinal principle of the tradition. Instead, they subscribe to a limited number of legal precepts that for one reason or another, they find meaningful. Such a lack of uniformity of Jewish observance means that there is a vast gulf between the requirements of legal observances and the actual lifestyle of the majority of Jews, both in Israel and the Diaspora.

Jewish Practice in a New Age

In modern times the major branches of non-Orthodox Judaism do not accept biblical and rabbinic law as binding. In their different ways, these movements have redefined the scope of Jewish law. Yet despite such liberalism, Conservative, Reform, Reconstructionist and Humanistic Judaism are prescriptive in their view of the legal tradition.

The lack of biblical and rabbinic authority, however, raises serious questions about such a legalistic approach to contemporary Jewish life. A new conception of *halakhah* (Jewish law) is urgently needed in the light of this orientation. Arguably, what is now required is a reorientation of Jewish existence in which all Jews are encouraged to determine for themselves which practices are religiously significant. Here, personal autonomy is of paramount importance. The more traditionally-minded supporters of this new approach might wish to follow the Orthodox pattern of Jewish observance, including daily worship, attendance at Sabbath and Festival services, and a strict adherence to ritual law. In terms of outward appearances, their Jewish lifestyle would resemble that of pious Orthodox or Conservative Jews. Indeed such individuals might feel most comfortable within the Orthodox community. Yet, as followers of this new approach to Judaism, they would acknowledge that their personal religious choices are no more valid than those of the less observant.

Jews less conservative in approach, on the other hand, might wish to abandon or modify various features of Jewish law. Such individuals, for example, might distance themselves from the vast number of prescriptions surrounding Jewish worship, home observance, and personal piety—instead they would seek to formulate a Jewish lifestyle more in keeping with the demands of modern life. This has been the policy of Reform Judaism from its inception: for these less observant Jews, Reform Judaism would in all likelihood offer the most acceptable religious attitude. Nonetheless, even if they were members of a Reform congregation, they would recognize that their individual decisions should in no way set a standard for others. Rather, they should respect the choices of all Jews, no matter how observant or loose.

This new vision of Judaism would also accept as valid the resolve of Jews who wish to express only a minimal acknowledgement of their Jewishness. Such persons, for example, might choose to ignore Jewish law altogether in their everyday lives and only attend synagogue on the High Holy Days, or for the *yartzeit* (anniversary of a death) of a parent. Alternatively, they might simply wish to be married or buried under Jewish auspices without belonging to a synagogue. A new, more flexible conception of Judaism for the modern age—as an all-embracing, fluid system extolling personal autonomy—would accept the legitimacy of even such a nominal form of Jewish identification.

This new vision of Judaism would not set out to establish itself as another organized movement within the ranks of Jewry. Unlike the various branches of religious Jewish life with their own seminaries, rabbis, congregational structures, and educational facilities, it should be understood as an ideology, a new idea of Judaism based on a revised conception of divine Reality. Liberal in orientation, it would offer all Jews—no matter what their particular religious affiliation—a remodelled conceptualization of Jewish life more in accord with the realities of Jewish existence. As an overarching framework for Jewish observance, it would respect the manifold religious choices made by contemporary Jews.

Such a view of Judaism would encourage a spirit of tolerance concerning each Jew's choice of Jewish observance. In addition, it would be opposed in principle to the traditional *Code of Jewish Law* as an authoritative legal structure for all Jews or to the foundation of a contemporary system of Jewish law. As a radical alternative to the more structured models of the faith, such an approach would provide a non-dogmatic foundation for integrating Jewish practice into modern life. Respecting liberty and freedom, this new vision of the Jewish faith would afford the adherents of all the branches of Judaism a new perspective on religious faith in an everchanging world.

Chapter 8.

SIN, REPENTANCE, AND FORGIVENESS

According to Orthodox Judaism, all Jews are under the yoke of the Law. Within this context, sin is understood as a violation of the covenant. Nonetheless, sinners are forgiven for their transgressions as long as they truly seek pardon and, if possible, make restitution to those whom they have offended. Daily prayer as well as the Day of Atonement provide a framework for such repentance to take place. In contemporary society, however, many Jews have ceased to view the *Code of Jewish Law* as binding and therefore do not consider themselves to have sinned if they violate the legal precepts. Such a shift in perception calls for a reinterpretation of the traditional notion of transgression in terms of moral responsibility rather than obedience to a legal code.

Sin and Atonement

During Sabbath services in the Temple where I was a student, reference was made to personal responsibility and obligation. Repeatedly we were reminded of our ethical responsibilities. A typical reading from the Sabbath morning service emphasizes the importance of moral responsibility:

> Help us, O Father, to keep alive this sense of our high lineage amid the labors and duties of our common life. When selfishness and greed prompt us to wrongdoing, may the sense of Thy nearness restrain our desires and save us from degradation. May the inspiration of this hour open our hearts that we may receive the helpless and despondent with sympathy and love.[1]

This emphasis on moral responsibility was highlighted in the High Holiday services. On Rosh Hashanah, we were reminded of our failings during the previous year:

> Unto Thee, O Lord my God, do I open my heart at this time of the turn of the year. As I review my conduct during the months that are passed, I am deeply conscious of my shortcomings. Often righteousness called to me in vain and I yielded to selfishness, anger and pride. I acknowledge my failings and I repent of them. I pray for Thy forgiveness and for the forgiveness of those whom I have wronged and hurt. Whatever life has brought me during the year now ended, grant that it may become unto me a source of strength and wisdom. O that the year now begun may be for me a new year indeed; new in consecration of purpose and in renewal of earnestness and sincerity; steadfast in rejecting all that is unworthy of me and of my heritage. Grant me strength of will to live as Thou wouldst have me live. Incline Thine ear unto

me; be gracious unto me, O Lord. Lead me and guide me for my times are in Thy hand. Amen.[2]

On the Day of Atonement, similar sentiments were expressed, emphasizing the sinfulness of the congregation of Israel. In the evening service, the reader and congregation asked for forgiveness for their transgressions:

> For the sin which we have sinned against Thee under stress or through choice;
> For the sin which we have sinned against Thee openly or in secret;
> For the sin which we have sinned against Thee in stubbornness or in error;
> For the sin which we have sinned against Thee in the evil meditations of the heart;
> For the sin which we have sinned against Thee by word of mouth;
> For the sin which we have sinned against Thee by abuse of power;
> For the sin which we have sinned against Thee by the profanation of Thy name;
> For the sin which we have sinned against Thee by disrespect for parents and teachers;
> For the sin which we have sinned against Thee by exploiting and dealing treacherously with our neighbor,
> For all these sins, O God of forgiveness, bear with us! pardon us! forgive us![3]

At the end of the Yom Kippur service, the congregation committed itself to turning aside from evil. As the responsive reading records:

> O God whose deeds are mighty, grant pardon for our sins, as the closing hour draws nigh.
> O Lord, we stand in awe before Thy deeds. We who are

few in number, lift our eyes in worship, and trembling we approach Thee as the closing hour draws nigh.

O Lord, we stand in awe before Thy deeds.

We pour out our hearts before Thee; blot out our transgressions, grant our sins forgiveness as the closing hour draws nigh.

O Lord, we stand in awe before Thy deeds.

Give us Thy protection; deliver us from danger; grant us joy and honor as the closing hour draws nigh.

O Lord, we stand in awe before Thy deeds.

All their sins forgiving, show favor to Thy chosen as the closing hour draws nigh.

O Lord, we stand in awe before Thy deeds.

O God whose deeds are mighty, grant pardon for our sins as the closing hour draws nigh.

O Lord, we stand in awe before Thy deeds.[4]

Transgression and Forgiveness

In the Bible, sin is understood as a transgression of God's commandments. In biblical Hebrew the word *het* means "to miss" or "to fail"—in this context, sin is understood as a failing, a lack of perfection in carrying out one's duty. The term *peshah* means a "breach"; it indicates a broken relationship between man and God. The word *avon* expresses the idea of crookedness. Hence, according to biblical terminology sin is characterized by failure, waywardness, and illicit action. A sinner is one who has failed to fulfill his obligations to God.

Within the rabbinic tradition, sins can be classified according to their seriousness as indicated by their respective punishments: the more serious the punishment, the graver the offense. A distinction is also made in rabbinic sources between sins against other human beings (*bain adam la-havero*) and offenses against God alone (*bain adam la-Makom*). Atonement for sins against God can be made through repentance, prayer, and charity. In cases of wrongdoing against others, however, restitution and placation are required.

In rabbinic literature the *yetzer ha-ra* (evil inclination) is often identified with the sex drive (which embraces human physical appetites in general as well as aggressive impulses). Frequently it is depicted as the force which impels human beings to satisfy their longings. Even though it is portrayed as the evil inclination, it is essential to life itself. Thus the *midrash* remarks that, if it were not for the *yetzer ha-ra*, no one would build a house, marry, have children, or engage in trade. For this reason, Scripture states: "And God saw everything that He had made and behold, it was very good." (Gen 1:31)[5] Here "good" refers to the good inclination; "very good" to the evil inclination. In this light the Talmud relates that the men of the Great Synagogue (Ezra and his colleagues) sought to kill the *yetzer ha-ra*, but the evil inclination (who is here personified) warned them that this would result in the destruction of the world. As a consequence, he was imprisoned, and they subsequently put out his eyes so that he would not be able to entice men to incest.[6]

According to rabbinic Judaism, human beings are engaged in a continual battle with the *yetzer ha-ra*. In this struggle, the Torah serves as the fundamental defense. Hence the Talmud states that the Torah is the antidote to the poison of the *yetzer ha-ra*.[7] The implication of this passage is that, when human beings submit to the discipline offered by the Torah, they can be liberated from the influence of the evil inclination. The rabbis stated that this is like a king who struck his son and later urged him to keep a plaster on his wound. When the wound was protected in this way, the prince could eat and drink without coming to harm. But if he removed the plaster, the wound would grow worse as long the prince indulged his appetites. For the rabbis, the Torah is the plaster that safeguards the king's son.

Rabbinic literature also teaches that this conflict with the *yetzer ha-ra* is unending. No person can destroy it. All one can do is to subdue it through self-control. Arguably, such a view parallels the Christian concept of original sin; yet, unlike Christian exegetes, the rabbis interpreted Genesis chapters 2–3 as simply indicating how death became part of human destiny.

In the view of the rabbis, death was the direct result of Adam's disobedience. Even though they did not teach a doctrine of original sin on this basis, they did accept that "the wickedness of man was great in the earth, and that every imagination of the thoughts of his heart was only evil continually." (Gen. 6:5) They explain this by positing the existence of the evil inclination within every person.

In the Hebrew Bible the notion of repentance is of central importance. Throughout the prophetic books, sinners are told to give up their evil ways and return to God. Thus 2 Kings declares: "Yet the Lord warned Israel and Judah by the hand of every prophet, and of every seer, saying: 'Turn from your evil ways, and keep my commandments and my statutes in accordance with all the law which I commanded your fathers, and which I sent to you by my servants the prophets.'" (2 Kings 17:13) According to tradition, atonement can only be attained after a process of repentance involving the recognition of sin. It requires remorse, restitution, and a determination not to commit a similar offense. Both the Bible and rabbinic sources stress that God does not want the death of the sinner, but desires that he turn from his evil ways. Unlike the Christian faith, in Judaism God does not instigate this process through prevenient grace; instead, atonement depends on a sinner's sincere act of repentance. Only at this stage does God grant forgiveness and pardon.

With regard to unwitting offenses against ritual commandments, a sin offering was required in ancient times as a sacramental act that restored the relationship between God and the transgressor. However, following the destruction of the Second Temple in 70 C.E., prayer replaced sacrifice. In addition, fasting, kindly acts, and the giving of charity were also perceived as a means of atonement. In the Jewish yearly cycle, ten days (Ten Days of Penitence) are set aside to aid Jews to seek pardon for their sins. This period begins with Rosh Hashanah (New Year) and ends with Yom Kippur (Day of Atonement) which is devoted to prayer and fasting. An echo of the ancient scapegoat ritual is observed by some Orthodox Jews on the Day of Atonement, whereby an individual's sins are expiated by the death of a white fowl. The Day of Atonement, however, only brings forgiveness for sins committed against God; for offenses committed against others, atonement is granted only after the sinner has made final restitution and sought forgiveness from the offended party.

Maimonides summarized the rabbinic view in the *Mishneh Torah*. For Maimonides, when a person knowingly or unknowingly sins and repents for his wrongdoing, he is obliged to confess his sins to God. However, since the Temple is no longer standing, repentance itself atones for sins. True repentance occurs if the sinner has had the opportunity of sinning, but refrained from doing so because he has repented. The sinner must also confess verbally, and it is praiseworthy for him to do so in public: "Whoever is too proud to confess his sins to others," Maimonides stated, "but keeps them to himself, is not a true penitent."[8] This, however, does not apply to offenses against God where a declaration of sinfulness can be made to him alone. With regard to offenses against others, the sinner must make restitution and ask for forgiveness—in some cases this may entail repeated efforts:

> There is no forgiveness for offenses against one's neighbour such as assault or injury or theft and so forth until the wrong done is put right. Even after a man has paid the restitution due to a victim, he must beg his forgiveness. Even if all he did was to taunt his neighbour he must appease him and beg his forgiveness. If the victim does not wish to forgive him he should go to him in the company of three friends and they should beg him to grant his pardon. If their efforts were of no avail he should repeat the procedure with a second and a third group, but if the victim still persists in his attitude he should be left alone and the victim is then sinful in refusing his pardon.[9]

Here Maimonides maintained that repentance is effected by a resolve to give up the transgression by confession and restitution.

Mortification is to play no role in this process. Yet other medieval scholars differed regarding the necessity of ascetic actions. In his *Shaare Teshuvah*, for example, the thirteenth-century writer Jonah ben Abraham Gerondi listed twenty elements of sincere repentance, some of which involve mortification:

> (1) remorse; (2) relinquishing sin; (3) pain for the sin; (4) affliction of the body through fasting and weeping; (5) fear of the consequences of the sinful act and of repeating it; (6) shame; (7) submission to God; (8) gentleness in future actions; (9) overcoming physical lust through asceticism; (10) the use of the organ with which the sinner transgressed to do good; (11) self-observation; (12) reflection on the suitable appropriate punishment; (13) treating minor sins as major; (14) confession; (15) prayer; (16) compensating the victim; (17) almsgiving; (18) consciousness of sin; (19) refraining from repeating the transgression; (20) leading others away from sinfulness.[10]

In another medieval work, the eleventh-century legalist Isaac Alfasi outlined twenty-four things that act as a barrier to repentance:

> (1) slander and gossip; (2) anger; (3) evil thoughts; (4) association with evil people; (5) partaking of food so as to deprive the host of his share; (6) looking lustfully at women; (7) partaking of the spoils of robbery; (8) sinning with the intention to repent at a later stage; (9) attaining fame at others' expense; (10) separating oneself from the community; (11) holding parents in disgrace; (12) holding teachers in disgrace; (13) cursing the public; (14) preventing the public from performing good acts; (15) leading a neighbor astray; (16) using a pledge obtained from the poor; (17) taking bribes to pervert justice; (18) keeping a lost article that one has found; (19) refraining from preventing one's son from doing evil; (20) eating the food of widows and orphans; (21) disagreeing with sages; (22) suspecting the innocent; (23) hating rebuke; (24) mocking Jewish practices.[11]

In contemporary society, such speculation about the nature of repentance as well as obstacles toward true remorse has given way to the more simple view that human beings are responsible for their actions and should repent of their sins. For Jews of all religious persuasions, such action is fundamental to the faith. Although non-Orthodox Judaism does not accept the code of biblical and rabbinic law, it nevertheless affirms that all Jews are required to search their ways and make atonement for transgression. The Day of Atonement is designed to remind the Jewish people of this divinely sanctioned task, as the Conservative prayerbook makes clear:

> We have ignored Your commandments and statutes, and it has not profited us. You are just, we have stumbled. You have acted faithfully, we have been unrighteous. We have sinned, we have transgressed. Therefore we have not been saved. Endow us with the will to forsake evil; save us soon.... Our God and God of our fathers, forgive and pardon our sins on this *Yom Kippur.* Answer our prayers by removing transgressions from Your sight. Subdue our impulse to evil; submit us to Your service, that we may return to You. Renew our will to observe Your precepts. Soften our hardened hearts so that we may love and revere You.... You know our sins, whether deliberate or not, whether committed willingly or under compulsion, whether in public or in private.... You always forgive transgressions. Hear the cry of our prayer. Pass over the transgression of a people who turn away from transgression. Blot out our sins from Your sight.[12]

Responsibility in the Modern World

In previous centuries Jews held themselves under the obligation to follow all the 613 commandments in Scripture—any willful violation of these *mitzvot* was considered a sin. In ancient times the legal code stipulated a wide range of punishments for such infringements, and the rabbis formulated an elaborate eschatological system involving eternal punishment and reward based on the observance of these religious precepts. In modern times, however, most Jews have ceased to observe the vast corpus of law contained in the *Code of Jewish Law*. Instead, they have come to regard the Jewish legal system as antiquated and no longer regulative of Jewish life. As we have seen, the various branches of non-Orthodox Judaism have in different ways sought to justify their deviation from traditional Jewish practice.

Early in the history of the Reform movement, for example, reformers emphasized that, although biblical law had an important function in ancient Israel, it has lost its relevance for modern Jews. The Pittsburgh Platform formulated at the end of the nineteenth century, for example, emphasizes that change is now urgently needed to adapt Judaism to a changing world. Commenting on the place of law in the life of the ancient Israelites, the Pittsburgh Platform reformers stated that:

> We recognize in the Bible the record of the consecration of the Jewish people to its mission as priest of the One God, and value it as the most potent instrument of religious and moral instruction…. We recognize in the Mosaic legislation a system of training the Jewish people for its mission during its national life in Palestine, and today we accept as binding only the moral laws and maintain only such ceremonies as elevate and sanctify our lives, but reject all such as are not adapted to the views and habits of modern civilization. We hold that all such Mosaic and rabbinic laws as regulate diet, priestly purity and dress originated in ages and under the influence of ideas altogether foreign to our present mental and spiritual state. They fail to impress the modern Jew with a spirit of priestly holiness; their observance in our days is apt rather to obstruct than to further modern spiritual elevation.[13]

Fifty years after the Pittsburgh meeting of 1885, the world had undergone major changes. Yet the Columbus Platform of 1937 continued to emphasize that legal reform was vital. Although the

Columbus reformers stated that the "Torah, both written and oral, enshrines Israel's ever-growing consciousness of God and of the moral law," they stressed that much of the law is anachronistic. "Being products of historical processes," they concluded, "certain of its laws have lost their biding force with the passing of the conditions that called them forth."[14] A later Platform, the San Francisco Platform of 1976, continued to stress the necessity for legal reform. "For millennia," it stated, "the creation of Torah has not ceased and Jewish creativity in our time is adding to the chain of tradition."[15] The Pittsburgh Platform of 1999 repeated these assertions.

Within Conservative Judaism, a similar emphasis has been placed on the necessity of adapting the legal code to contemporary Jewish life. At the beginning of the twentieth century the Cambridge scholar Solomon Schechter, who later became the guiding figure of Conservative Judaism in the United States, emphasized the importance of placing traditional rituals, customs, and observances in an historical context. Only in this way, he believed, would Jews be able to understand the evolutionary character of Jewish life and be able to adapt Judaism to meet the needs of modern Jewry. From its beginnings, the founders of this new movement insisted that the Jewish past must serve the present; religious law, they stressed, should continue to be observed if it animates the spiritual life of adherents.

Paralleling this approach, Reconstructionist Judaism has sought to maintain Jewish observance as long as it continues to have religious significance. According to Mordecai Kaplan, the founder of the movement, the Jewish people should not be understood primarily as a religious denomination—rather the nation has produced a civilization. Within this context, Jewish religious practices constitute the symbols through which an individual is able to express identification with the community. For Kaplan, Jewish rituals should be perceived as *minhagim* (customs) rather than *mitzvot* (commandments). Such practices serve as the means through which a group is able to externalize the reality of its collective consciousness. Seen in this light, religious ceremonies should be understood as folkways rather than divine immutable laws. On this basis, Reconstructionist Jews seek to formulate a basis for determining which traditional laws should be retained in contemporary society.

For Humanistic Jews, Jewish law has lost its authoritative force altogether. Without a divine lawgiver, the *mitzvot* must be understood as human regulative precepts. Unlike Orthodox Judaism, which is based on the doctrine of *Torah MiSinai*, Humanistic Jews rely on reason as the most effective means of determining which Jewish practices continue to have religious significance. Both Scripture and rabbinic sources are perceived as human in origin: thus they must be submitted to critical evaluation. Jewish law is significant only if it is based on moral principles that continue to have relevance in the lives of modern Jews.

This survey of non-Orthodox approaches to Jewish law illustrates that, for the majority of modern Jews, the legal precepts of the past have lost their religious significance. Today, most Jews feel at liberty to select from the vast corpus of legal prescriptions those that animate their lives. The notion of sin has thereby undergone a major transformation. As we have seen, the traditional concept of sinfulness was directly related to legal transgression. The covenant was sacrosanct in the lives of Jewish believers, and any infringement of the legal code was regarded as offensive to God. Bound by the covenant, Jews were to live by God's dictates; if they willfully transgressed the law, they were punished by religious authorities and cautioned that God would exact punishment in the hereafter.

In contemporary society, however, such an understanding of transgression and punishment is no longer meaningful for the vast majority of Jews. With the exception of strictly observant Orthodox and Hasidic Jews, there is widespread neglect of the Jewish legal tradition. The laws in the Torah as well as the legal rulings of rabbinic sages are no longer regarded as authoritative. In most cases Jews do not feel any sense of remorse if they violate the Jewish legal code. Yet the notion of sinfulness has not disappeared from Jewish life. Across the religious spectrum—from the most Orthodox to the most liberal—Jews continue to express shame and sorrow for various transgressions. The focus today, however, is on ethical misconduct. As we have seen, moral wrongdoing is central to the Reform liturgy for the High Holidays, as it is for all the various branches of Judaism in the modern world.

Hence, a new vision of Judaism for the future requires in my opinion a recognition of this change of perception. No longer does Jewry feel bound by the legal dictates of previous centuries. Instead, many Jews today envisage religious duty largely in moral terms. Sinfulness, repentance, and forgiveness are all conceived in terms of ethical irresponsiblity rather than loyalty to a legal code. Such a shift in understanding is reflected in the Conservative movement's formulation of transgression and sin in the Yom Kippur liturgy. Here innumerable moral offenses are elaborated in detail, and this reorientation of religious responsibility has become universal throughout the Jewish community:

> We abuse, we betray, we are cruel.
> We destroy, we embitter, we falsify.
> We gossip, we hate, we insult.
> We jeer, we kill, we lie.
> We mock, we neglect, we oppress.
> We pervert, we quarrel, we oppress.
> We steal, we transgress, we are unkind.
> We are violent, we are wicked, we are xenophobic.
> We yield to evil, we are zealots for bad causes....
> We have sinned against you through sexual immorality.
> And we have sinned against you knowingly and deceitfully.
> We have sinned against you by wronging others.   ·
> And we have sinned against you by deriding parents and teachers.
> And we have sinned against you by using violence.
> We have sinned against you through foul speech.
> And we have sinned against you by not resisting the impulse to evil....

We have sinned against you by fraud and by falsehood.
And we have sinned against you by scoffing.
We have sinned against you by dishonesty in business.
And we have sinned against you by usurious interest.
We have sinned against you by idle chatter.
And we have sinned against you by haughtiness.
We have sinned against you by rejecting responsibility.
And we have sinned against you by plotting against others.
We have sinned against you by irreverence.
And we have sinned against you by rushing to do evil....
For all these sins, forgiving God, forgive us, pardon us, grant
us atonement.[16]

Chapter 9.

CHOSEN PEOPLE

The belief that the Jews are the chosen people is based on the covenant between God and Abraham; this covenantal relationship was renewed on Mount Sinai. Nonetheless, the election of Israel was made conditional on their observance of the Torah. The Jewish people is spoken of in Exodus as a kingdom of priests and a holy nation; the prophets taught that election is based on righteousness. In the Mishnah and the Talmud, the role of Israel as the teacher of all natons is emphasized. Today, however, this doctrine has been challenged by Jewish modernists.

God and Israel

Within the Reform movement, the belief that God chose the

Jews is treated with a degee of ambivalence. In religion school we were taught that God has a special relationship with the Jewish people. Yet the doctrine of chosenness was not explicitly stated. As Jews, we were to see ourselves as bound in a covenantal relationship with God, obligated to carry out his will. Nonetheless, there was a degree of reluctance to express such a notion in terms of divine election.

On some occasions the Hebrew prayers in the worship service retained the traditional language of chosenness, but it was noticeable that the English translations deliberately avoided mentioning that God chose the Jews from all peoples to be his own. Thus the *Kiddush,* which is recited on Friday night, retained the phrase *"ke vano vharta, votanu kidashta'"*(for you have chosen us and sanctified us), but the English renders the Hebrew differently:

> Thou hast ennobled us, O God, by the blessings of work, and in love hast sanctified us by Sabbath rest and worship as ordained in the Torah.[1]

Elsewhere, however, there were frequent references to God's call to his people, implying a divinely appointed mission. For example, in the section before the silent prayer during the Friday night service, the reader declared:

> Almighty and merciful God, Thou hast called Israel to Thy service and found him worthy to bear witness unto Thy truth among the peoples of the earth. Give us grace to fulfil this mission with zeal tempered by wisdom and guided by regard for other men's faiths.[2]

Some responsive readings were more explicit about the relationship between God and Israel:

> For He is our God, and we are His people, consecrated to His service. Remember all the commandments of the Lord, and do them; that ye go not about after your own heart and your own

eyes. It is He who redeemed us from the hand of oppressors, and revived our spirits when our own strength failed us.[3]

Special readings for the Holidays repeated such conviction. On the evening service for the Sabbath during *Pesach* (Passover), the liturgy recounts God's deliverance of the Jewish people from Egypt:

> On this festival of Passover, we are gathered in Thy house to recall Thy wonders of old. When we were slaves in Egypt and suffered under the lash of taskmasters, Thou didst send Thy servants, Moses and Aaron, to stand in the presence of Pharaoh and proclaim in Thy name: Let My people go that they may serve Me. The cruel heart of the tyrant and the might of his armies did not avail against Thy liberating word and Israel marched forth from Egypt with songs and rejoicing to find freedom in Thy service.[4]

Again, during the Sabbath morning service for *Sukkot*, the liturgy stresses God's providential care for his people during their wanderings in the desert:

> We recall today with grateful hearts Thy loving providence which guided our fathers in their wanderings through the barren desert and the trackless wilderness. Under Thy protection the weary pilgrims found shelter and security. In famine Thou didst sustain them and from the flinty rock Thou didst slake their thirst.[5]

The High Holiday services similarly referred to God's relationship with His people, implying the doctrine of chosenness. Thus, during the *shofar* service on the morning of the New Year, the rabbi proclaimed:

> The stirring sound of the *shofar* proclaimed the covenant at Mount Sinai which bound Israel to God as a kingdom of

priests and a holy people. Ever since that distant day, the voice
of the *shofar* has resounded through the habitations of Israel
awakening high allegiance to God and His commandments.[6]

Likewise, on the Day of Atonement the theme of election was
implied in the readings from Scripture. During the morning service, passages from the Book of Deuteronomy highlighted God's
relationship with the Jewish nation through the generations:

> Ye are standing this day all of you before the Lord your God:
> your heads, your tribes, your elders, and your officers, even all
> the men of Israel, your little ones, your wives, and the stranger
> that is in the midst of thy camp, from the hewer of the wood
> unto the drawer of the water; that thou shouldest enger into the
> covenant of the Lord thy God—and into His oath—which the
> Lord thy God maketh with thee this day; that He may establish
> thee this day unto Himself for a people, and that He may be
> unto thee a God, as He spoke unto thee, and as He swore unto
> thy fathers, to Abraham, to Isaac, and to Jacob. Neither with
> you only do I make this covenant and this oath; but with him
> that standeth here with us this day before the Lord our God,
> and also with him that is not here with us this day.[7]

We can see, therefore, that even though the Reform movement has in certain respects retained traditional notions associated with chosenness, the language of the liturgy was not
always clear. At times, there was a conscious avoidance of the
terminology of divine election, yet frequent references to God's
relationship with the Jewish people and the notion of covenantal
responsibility implied the acceptance of traditional ideas of
God's special relationship with Israel.

Jewish People

The notion of Israel as God's chosen people has been a constant feature of the Jewish faith from biblical times to the pres-

ent. In Scripture the Hebrew root "*bhr*" (to choose) denotes the belief that God selected the Jewish nation from all other peoples. As the Book of Deuteronomy relates, "For you are a people holy to the Lord your God; the Lord your God has chosen you to be a people for his own possession out of all the peoples that are on the face of the earth." (Deut. 7:6) According to the Hebrew Bible, this act was motivated by divine love: "It was not because you were more in number than any other people that the Lord set his love upon you and chose you for you were the fewest of all peoples; but it is because the Lord loves you." (Deut. 7:7–8) Such love for Israel was later echoed in the synagogue liturgy, especially in the *Kiddush* prayer for the Sabbath:

> Blessed art thou, O Lord our God, king of the universe, who has hallowed us by thy commandments and hast taken pleasure in us, and in love and favor has given us thy holy Sabbath as an inheritance, a memorial of the creation—that day being also the first of the holy convocations, in remembrance of the departure from Egypt. For thou hast chosen us and hallowed us above all nations, and in love and favour hast given us thy holy Sabbath as an inheritance. Blessed art thou, O Lord, who hallowest the Sabbath.[8]

Through its election, Jews have traditionally believed that Israel was given a historic mission to bear divine truth to humanity. Thus, before God proclaimed the Ten Commandments on Mount Sinai, He admonished the people to carry out this appointed task:

> You have seen what I did to the Egyptians, and how I bore you on eagles' wings, and brought you to myself. Now therefore, if you will obey my voice, and keep my covenant, you shall be my own possession among all peoples; for all the earth is mine, and you shall be to me a kingdom of priests and a holy nation. (Exod. 19:4–6)

God's choice of Israel therefore carries with it numerous responsibilities. As Genesis proclaims: "For I have chosen him, that he may charge his children and his household after him to keep the way of the Lord by doing righteousness and justice." (Gen. 18:19)

Divine choice demands reciprocal response. Israel is thus obligated to keep God's statutes and ordinances and observe his laws. In doing this the nation will be able to persuade other peoples that there is only one universal God. Israel is to be a prophet to the nations, bringing them to salvation. Yet, despite this obligation, the Bible asserts that God will not abandon his chosen people even if they violate the covenant. The wayward nation will be punished, but God will not reject them: "Yet for all that, when they are in the land of their enemies, I will not spurn them, neither will abhor them so as to destroy them utterly and break my covenant with them: for I am the Lord their God." (Lev. 26:44)

In rabbinic literature the biblical doctrine of the chosen people is a constant theme. While upholding the belief that God chose the Jews from all peoples, the rabbis argued that their election was due to an acceptance of the Torah. This conviction was based on Scripture: "If you will hearken to my voice, indeed, and keep my covenant, then you shall be my own treasure from among all peoples." (Exod. 19:5) According to the rabbis, the Torah was offered first to the other nations of the world, but they all rejected it because its precepts conflicted with their way of life. Only Israel acquiesced. According to one tradition, this occurred only because God suspended a mountain over the Jewish people, threatening to destroy the nation if they refused: "If you accept the Torah it will be well with you, but if not, here you will find your grave." The dominant view, however, was that the Israelites accepted God's law enthusiastically. For this reason Scripture states that the Jewish people declared: "All that the Lord has spoken we will do." (Exod. 24:7), showing a willingness to obey God's law without knowledge of its contents.

Rabbinic Judaism asserts that there is a special relationship between Israel and God based on love; this is the basis of the allegorical interpretations in rabbinic sources of the Song of Songs, and is also expressed in the Talmud by such sayings as: "How beloved is Israel before the Holy One, blessed be He; for wherever they were exiled the *Shekhinah* [divine presence] was with them." Rabbinic literature also emphasizes that God's election of the Jewish people is due to the character of the nation and of the patriarchs in particular. According to the Talmud, mercy and forgiveness are characteristic of Abraham and his descendents.

During the medieval period the Jewish claim to be God's chosen people was disputed by the Church, which viewed itself as the true Israel. In response, such thinkers as the tenth-century Jewish philosopher Saadiah Gaon maintained that God chose the Jews from all peoples and bestowed the law upon them:

> The first of his acts of kindness towards his creatures was the gift of existence, i.e., his act of calling them into existence after they had been non-existent, as he said to the men of distinction among them, "Everyone that is called by my name, and whom I have created for my glory." (Isa. 43:7) Thereafter he offered them a gift by means of which they are able to obtain complete happiness and perfect bliss, as is said, "Thou makest me to know the path of life; in thy presence is fulness of joy, in thy right hand bliss for evermore."(Psalm 16:11) This gift consists of the commandments and prohibitions which He gave them.[9]

In the next century the Jewish scholar Judah Halevi emphasized that the basis of the Jewish faith is the belief that God chose the Jews and guides his people through their history. In the *Kuzari*—a dialogue between a rabbi and representatives of other faiths—the rabbi declares:

> "I believe in the God of Abraham, Isaac and Israel who led the Israelites out of Egypt with songs and miracles; who fed them in the desert and gave them the Land, after having made them traverse the sea and the Jordan in a miraculous way; who sent Moses with his law, and subsequently thousands of prophets

who confirmed his law by promises to those who observed, and threats to the disobedient.... In the same strain Moses spoke to the Pharaoh, when he told him 'The God of the Hebrews sent me to thee'—viz. the God of Abraham, Isaac and Jacob. For the story of their life was well known to the nations, who also knew that the Divine power was in contact with the Patriarchs, caring for them and performing miracles for them."[10]

Like Halevi, other Jewish philosophers of the medieval period emphasized Israel's special role in God's plan of salvation. For Abraham ibn Daud, only Israel is privileged to receive prophecy. For Maimonides, the Jewish faith is the one true revelation which will never be superseded by another divine encounter. Among these Jewish thinkers, the doctrine of election was stressed largely as a reaction to oppression by the non-Jewish world. Forced to withdraw into the imposed confines of an enclosed world, Jews sought consolation from the belief that despite their sufferings they were God's special people whom he loved above all others.

The concept of Israel's chosenness is also a central theme of medieval kabbalistic thought. According to the *kabbalah*, the Jewish people on earth has its counterpart in the *Shekhinah* in the sefirotic realm. The *sefirah Malkhut* is known as the "community of Israel," which serves as the archetype of the Israelites on earth. For the kabbalists, Israel's exile mirrors the cosmic disharmony in which the *Shekhinah* is cast into exile. The drama of Israel's exile and its ultimate restoration reflects the dynamic of the upper worlds. In later *Habad* mysticism the Jew has two souls—the animal soul and the divine soul. This divine soul is possessed only by Jews; even the animal soul of Israel is derived from a source which is mixture of good and evil. The animal souls of Gentiles, on the other hand, derive from an unclean source. For this reason, no Gentile is capable of acting in a completely moral fashion.

During the Enlightenment, in Western Europe Jewry underwent a major transformation. No longer was the community confined to a ghetto existence. This change challenged the concept of Jewish uniqueness. At the end of the eighteenth century the Jewish philosopher Moses Mendelssohn argued that the intellectual content of Judaism is identical with the religion of reason. In response to the question, Why should one remain a Jew? he responded that Jewry was singled out by the revelation on Mount Sinai. For this reason, it was compelled to carry out a divinely appointed mission to the peoples of the earth.

Subsequently this conception has remained a central teaching of the various branches of the Jewish religious community. Within Reform Judaism, for example, the nation of Jewish mission was developed, stressing the special message of God which is to be passed on to all the nations. In a statement of principles for the Reform movement adopted at the 1999 Pittsburgh Convention of the Central Conference of American Rabbis, for example, the Reform movement expressed its commitment to Israel's mission: "We are Israel, a people aspiring to holiness, singled out through our ancient covenant and our unique history among the nations to be witnesses to God's presence."[11]

Nonetheless, within the non-Orthodox movements a number of writers have expressed considerable unease about the claim that the Jews constitute a divinely chosen people. The rejection of this traditional doctrine derives from universalistic and humanistic tendencies; unlike traditionalists, progressive Jews believe that Jews are inherently no different from the rest of humanity. Although the Jewish community has a unique history, they believe, this does not imply that God has chosen the nation as his very own. Rather, the God of Israel is also the Lord of history who loves all people and guides the destiny of humanity to its ultimate conclusion.

From Chosenness to Global Theology

As we have seen, until the time of the Enlightenment the Jewish people were unified by a common religious inheritance which they believed to be the one true path to God. According to Scripture, God created the universe, chose the Jews from among all nations, delivered them from exile, revealed himself to Moses on Mount Sinai, and exercised providential care over his children through their history. For centuries, Jews were sustained by such a conviction through persecution, suffering, and death.

Of central importance in this theological scheme was the belief in the special relationship between God and the Jews. Yet, given the shift in orientation from a Judeo-centric to a theo-centric conception of the world's religions, it is now possible to view Judaism in a new light. No longer need Jews regard their faith as the fullest expression of God's will. Rather, in the contemporary world the Jewish community could adopt a more open stance in which the Divine—rather than the Jewish faith—is placed at the center of the universe of faiths. Such a pluralistic outlook would enable Jews to affirm the uniqueness of their own heritage which acknowledging the validity of other religions.

Given such a transition from absolutism to religious pluralism—in which the Jewish tradition is perceived as simply one among many paths to the Divine—the way is open to interfaith encounter on the deepest level. In the past, Jewish theologians asserted that Judaism is the superior tradition because of the doctrine of divine election; even the most liberal thinkers maintained that, in the future, humanity will acknowledge the truth of Jewish monotheism. Today, however, in our religiously diverse world, it is no longer possible to sustain this position. What is now required is a redefinition of the theological task.

The new vision of Judaism advanced in this study provides a framework for such theological exploration. The pursuit of religious truth calls for a global, dialogical approach based on two preconditions. First, Jews must learn about religious traditions other than their own. Global theology undertaken from a divine-centred perspective requires religious thinkers to investigate what the world's faiths have experienced and affirmed about the nature of Ultimate Reality, the phenomenon of religious experience, the nature of the self, the problem of the human condition, and the value of the world.

Second, Jews should seek to enter into the thought-world as well as the religious experiences of other faiths. They must pass over to the experience and the mode of being in the world that nurtures the creeds, codes, and cults of other faiths. In this way they can imaginatively share in the faith of other religions. By entering into the subjectivity of other traditions, they should be able to bring the resulting insights to bear on their own understanding of religion: such reflection demands a multi-dimensional, cross-cultural, inter-religious consciousness.

Jewish thinkers who subscribe to this new vision of Judaism should place the spiritual quest in a trans-religious context. This enterprise requires an encounter in which Jews confront others who hold totally different truth-claims—such individuals can help Jewish thinkers to discover their own presuppositions and underlying principles. In this process, Jewish partners should be able to acknowledge the limitations of their own tradition, and as a result make a conscious effort to discover common ground with other faiths. Such interchange is vital to the formulation of a multi-dimensional theological outlook.

Given the possibility for this type of respectful and open-minded inter-religious exploration, there are a number of central issues that Jews and adherents of other faiths could fruitfully explore together:

1. Symbols: Jews and members of other traditions could profitably explore the nature of religious symbols.

2. Worship: In many of the religions of the world, worship is a response to the Divine, and acknowledgement of a reality independent of the worshipper. It would be helpful to discuss the ways in which various forms of worship provide some glimpse into the nature of Divine Reality.

3. Ritual: Like worship, ritual plays a major role in the world's religions, and there are areas worthy of joint investigation. First, an examination of formal and elaborate practices as well as simple actions could reveal the ways in which the believers see

their action as making contact or participating in the Divine. Second, a comparative study of ritualist practice could clarify the ways in which an outer activity mirrors an inner process. Third, it might be beneficial to examine the contemplative and mystical activities in different traditions that are seen as disclosing various aspects of the Divine.

4. Ethics: Traditional Jews believe that God chose the Jewish nation to be his people and gave them his law on Mount Sinai. The moral law is thus embodied in immutable, divine commandments. In other faiths, however, ethical values are perceived in a different light. An exploration of the moral frameworks of the different faiths and their underlying religious foundations could result in a deepening of ethical perception.

These subject areas by no means exhaust the possibilities for interfaith activity, but they do indicate the type of joint activity that could take place. In addition, those who embrace this new vision of Judaism—freed from the belief in the special relationship between God and the Jewish people—could also engage in interfaith encounter on a practical level. No longer should Jews feel constrained to stand aloof from the worship services of other faiths. Instead, a pluralist standpoint, in which all faiths are recognized as authentic paths to the Divine, would encourage adherents of all the world's faiths—including Jews—to participate in common religious activities. Through such personal engagement, Jewish believers could enrich their understanding of the spiritual life.

Chapter 10.

PROMISED LAND

According to Scripture, Abraham was the father of the Israelites. He left the country of his birth and travelled to Canaan at God's command: "Go from your country and your kindred and your father's house to the land that I will show you. And I will make of you a great nation." (Gen. 12:1–2) Centuries later, under Moses' leadership, the Jewish people fled from Egypt and wandered in the desert for forty years before entering the Promised Land. There they prospered until the Babylonian exile in 586 B.C.E. At the end of the century, they returned to Judah, where they remained until the first century C.E., when the Romans destroyed the Temple and drove the Jews from Jerusalem. For two millennia the Jewish nation longed for messianic deliverance and a return to the Holy Land. In modern times, the creation of a Jewish state has enabled the Jewish people to claim their own homeland, yet the conflict between Jews and non-Jews has led to continual instability in the Middle East.

The Holy Land

Throughout the nineteenth century, Reform Judaism officially opposed the creation of a Jewish homeland. According to early Reformers, it was unnecessary for Jews to create a state of their own; rather, they believed, Jews should seek to integrate into the societies in which they live. By this means, the Jewish people would be able to free themselves from previous disabilities. At the Pittsburgh gathering of American Reform leaders in 1885, the movement formulated its response to Zionist aspirations:

> We recognize in the modern era of universal culture of heart and intellect the approach of the realization of Israel's great messianic hope for the establishment of the kingdom of truth, justice and peace among all men. We consider ourselves no longer a nation but a religious community, and therefore expect neither a return to Palestine, nor a sacrificial worship under the administration of the sons of Aaron, nor the restoration of any of the laws concerning the Jewish state.[1]

In the same vein, the leader of American Reform Judaism, Isaac Mayer Wise proclaimed at the close of the First Zionist Congress: "We denounce the whole question of a Jewish state as foreign to the spirit of the modern Jew of this land, who looks upon America as his Palestine and whose interests are centered here."[2]

In time, however, Reform Judaism reversed its previous attitudes. Fifty years after the Pittsburgh meeting, the Jewish world had undergone major changes: America was the center of the Diaspora; Zionism had become a vital force in Jewish life; Hitler was in power. The Columbus Platform of the Reform movement of 1937 reflected a new approach to Jewish statehood. With regard to Israel, it stated:

In the rehabilitation of Palestine, the land hallowed by memories and hopes, we behold the promise of renewed life for many of our brethren. We affirm the obligation of all Jewry to aid in its upbuilding as a Jewish homeland by endeavoring to make it not only a haven of refuge for the oppressed but also a center of Jewish culture and spiritual life.[3]

Such an endorsement of Jewish statehood pervaded my religious education. Although as American Jews we viewed the United States as our home, we remained committed to the establishment of a strong and secure Jewish nation in Israel. In religion school, we were taught Jewish history as it evolved through the centuries, culminating in the heroic efforts of Jewish pioneers who settled in Palestine at the end of the nineteenth century. It was through their efforts, we believed, that Jewry would be able to protect itself from future persecution. The Holocaust had cast its shadow on Jewish life in the Diaspora, and we were determined to ensure that Israel would become a safe haven for all Jews.

The *Union Prayer Book* reflected such sentiments. Despite its endorsement of universalism, various prayers focused on the significance of Israel in the life of modern Jews. Typical of such recitations was the reading before the Silent Prayer during the Sabbath evening service. After asking God to extend his mercy to Jews wherever they live, the rabbi referred to Jewish pioneers in Israel, extolling their efforts:

Uphold also the hands of our brothers who toil to rebuild Zion. In their pilgrimage among the nations, Thy people have always turned in love to the land where Israel was born, where our prophets taught their imperishable message of justice and brotherhood and where our psalmists sang their deathless songs of love for Thee and of Thy love for us and all humanity. Ever enshrined in the hearts of Israel was the hope that Zion might be restored, not for their own pride or vainglory, but as a living witness to the truth of Thy word which shall lead the nations to the reign of peace. Grant strength that with Thy help we may bring a new light to shine upon Zion. Imbue us who live in the lands of freedom with a sense of Israel's spiritual unity that we may share joyously in the work of redemption so that from Zion shall go forth the law and the word of God from Jerusalem.[4]

Throughout my youth, Jews eagerly followed events taking place in the Middle East. As Reform Jews, we identified with those who were shaping the destiny of the Jewish nation. Although we did not share their hardships, their sufferings became our own. They were our brave brothers and sisters who labored for us all. Stained with their blood, the Holy Land became a symbol of hope in a post-Holocaust world.

Israel

Through the centuries the Jewish people have longed for a land of their own. God's call to Abraham was repeated to his grandson Jacob who, after wrestling with God's messenger, was renamed Israel (meaning "he who wrestles with God"). Later, after Jacob's son Joseph became vizier in Egypt, the Israelite clan settled in Egypt for several hundred years. Finally, Moses led the Jewish nation out of Egyptian bondage, and the people settled in the land that was promised to them. There they established a monarchy, but due to the corruption of the Israelites, God punished his chosen people: foreign powers devastated the northern kingdom in the eighth century B.C.E., and the southern kingdom two centuries later.

Even though the Temple lay in ruins and Jerusalem was destroyed, the Jews, who had been exiled to Babylonia, did not lose their faith in God. Sustained by the belief that God would eventually deliver them from exile, a number of Jews sought permission to return to their former home. In 538 B.C.E., King Cyrus of Persia allowed them to leave. The Book of Ezra records Cyrus' decree:

> Concerning the house of God at Jerusalem, let the house be
> rebuilt, the place where sacrifices are offered are brought...let
> the gold and silver vessels of the house of God which
> Nebuchadnezzar took out of the Temple that is in Jerusalem
> and brought to Babylon, be restored and brought back to the
> Temple which is in Jerusalem...let the governor of the Jews
> and the elders of the Jews rebuild this house of God on its site.
> (Ezra 6:3–7)

Under the leadership of Joshua and Zerubbabel, restoration of
the Temple began. After the destruction of the First Temple, the
Jews had strayed from the religious faith of their ancestors. To
combat such laxity, the prophet Nehemiah asserted that the community must purify itself; in this effort he was joined by the priest
Ezra. Although religious reforms were carried out, the people
continued to abandon the Torah, and the Temple was destroyed a
second time in the first century C.E. by the Romans.

Once the Temple had been devastated and the Jewish people
driven out of their homeland, the nation was bereft. In their despair the ancient Israelites longed for a kingly figure who would
deliver them from exile and rebuild their holy city. As we have
seen, rabbinic sages drew on messianic notions in Scripture, the
Apocrypha and the Pseudepigrapha in their description of the
Messianic Age. For nearly twenty centuries, the Jewish people
were persuaded that a divinely appointed Messiah would lead
the nation back to its ancient homeland in fulfilment of God's
promise to Abraham.

With the conversion of Shabbatai Tzevi, whom many had
regarded as the Messiah, to Islam in the seventeenth century,
however, such messianic aspirations diminished. Many Jews became disillusioned with centuries of messianic anticipation and
disappointment: the longing for the Messiah who would lead
the Jewish people to the Holy Land and bring about the end
of history seemed a distant hope. Yet, the aspiration to return
to Zion remained a fervent desire in the face of virulent anti-
Semitism. According to a number of early secular Zionists, no

reform of Judaism could eliminate Jew-hatred. In the view of the nineteenth century thinker, the German socialist Moses Hess, anti-Jewish sentiment is unavoidable. In his view, the only solution to the Jewish problem is the creation of a Jewish state which will enable world Jewry to undergo a renaissance and serve as a spiritual centre for all of humanity.

Similarly, another early Zionist, the Russian writer Leon Pinsker contended that Judaeophobia is inextricably part of Western society—the only remedy for anti-Semitism, he believed, is for Jews to reconstitute themselves as a separate people in their own land. Echoing such sentiments, the Viennese journalist Theodor Herzl espoused the creation of a Jewish homeland and undertook political steps to bring about its realization. Through Herzl's determination, the first Zionist Congress took place in August, 1897 in Basle. Subsequently Herzl engaged in extensive negotiations with political leaders through the world. By the time he died, Zionism had became an organized movement and Zionists continued to press for the creation of a Jewish homeland.

Eventually the British government approved of such a plan although Britain insisted that the rights of the non-jews be safeguarded. The Balfour Declaration, formulated in 1917, stated that Britain supported the creation of a national home for the Jewish people in Palestine:

> His Majesty's Government view with favour the establishment in Palestine of a national home for the Jewish people and will use their best endeavours to facilitate the achievement of this object, it being clearly understood that nothing shall be done which may prejudice the civil and religious rights of existing non-Jewish communities in Palestine, or the rights and political status enjoyed by Jews in any other country.[5]

After the First World War Herbert Samuel was appointed High Commissioner in Palestine to oversee this policy, but he met with considerable resistance from the Zionists who did not wish to appease the non-Jew populace. Although the British government initially allowed free immigration to Palestine, this policy was superseded by increased restrictions on the number of Jewish immigrants. In May 1939 an the British government limited the number of immigrants to 75,000 over the next five years, and none thereafter except with non-Jew permission.

This policy evoked widespread Jewish resistance, and the Jewish military forces engaged in conflict with the British. After a campaign of terror, Britain handed over the Palestinian problem to the United Nations, and a special committee was appointed to formulate a plan for the future of the country. On November 29, 1947 a recommendation that there be both a non-Jewish and a Jewish state was passed by the UN General Assembly. Immediately the non-Jews began to attack Jewish settlements and the Israelis were forced to defend their new state. On May 14, 1948 Prime Minister David Ben Gurion read out the Scroll of Independence in the Tel Aviv Museum:

> The Land of Israel was the birthplace of the Jewish people. Here their spiritual, religious and national identity was formed. Here they achieved independence and created a culture of national and universal significance. Here they wrote and gave their Bible to the world.
>
> Exiled from Palestine, the Jewish people remained faithful to it in all the countries of their dispersion, never ceasing to pray and hope for their return and the restoration of their national freedom.
>
> Impelled by this historic association, Jews strove throughout the centuries to go back to the land of their fathers and regain their Statehood. In recent decades they returned in their masses. They reclaimed the wilderness, revived their language, built cities and villages and established a vigorous and ever-growing community, with its own economic and cultural life. They sought peace yet were prepared to defend themselves. They brought the blessings of progress to all the inhabitants of the country. In the year 1897 the First Zionist Congress, inspired by Theodor Herzl's vision of the Jewish State, pro-

claimed the right of the Jewish people to national revival in their own country.

This right was acknowledged by the Balfour Declaration of November 2, 1917, and reaffirmed by the Mandate of the League of Nations, which gave explicit international recognition to the historic connection of the Jewish people with Palestine and their right to reconstitute their national home.

The Nazi holocaust, which engulfed millions of Jews in Europe, proved anew the urgency of the reestablishment of the Jewish State, which would solve the problem of Jewish homelessness by opening the gates to all Jews and lifting the Jewish people to equality in the family of nations...

On November 29, 1947 the General Assembly of the United Nations adopted a Resolution for the establishment of an independent Jewish State in Palestine, and called upon inhabitants of the country to take such steps as may be necessary on their part to put the plan into effect.

This recognition by the United Nations of the right of the Jewish people to establish their independent state may not be revoked. It is, moreover, the self-evident right of the Jewish people to be a nation, like all other nations, in its own soverign state...[6]

In subsequent years non-Jews and Jews have repeatedly engaged in battle. The Sinai War of 1946 was followed by the Six Day War in 1967 and the Yom Kippur War in 1973. In 1978 Egypt signed a peace agreement with Israel; however, other non-Jew neighbours refused to follow this precedent. In recent years Arab-Israeli conflict has intensified in the Occupied Territories.

The Jewish aspiration for a homeland reveals the utopian character of the yearning. Through four millennia, Jewry has often been guided by the belief that it is possible to create God's kingdom on earth. In ancient Israel the state was to be a theocracy. Continually the prophets reminded the nation of its divine obligations. With the destruction of Jerusalem and the Temple the desire for a Jewish home was transformed in to an eschatological vision of messianic redemption in Zion. The Jews were to return with the Messiah at their head. As time passed, however, this dream faded, yet the longing for a Jewish home did not die out. Increasingly, many Jews came to believe that its eternal quest could be realized only through the labours of the Zionists. The early pioneers were infused with home and enthusiasm. Their task was to create a Jewish society that would become a light to the nations.

The Jewish State

With the onset of Jewish emancipation in the late eighteenth and early nineteenth centuries Jewish assimilationists argued that human beings were progressing towards a one-world culture. In all countries economic and social developments led to the diminution of national characteristics. Hence, they believed, it was a mistake to return to Jewish nationalism. As we have seen, early Reform Judaism was deeply critical of Jewish nationalism for such reasons. Such a view led to the elimination of all references to a personal Messiah in the Reform liturgy; instead Reform Jews prayed for the realization of the messianic era in modern society.

Following the Second World War, however, such antipathy toward the creation of a Jewish state gave way to an endorsement of a Jewish homeland in the Middle East. Having endured the horrors of the Holocaust, world Jewry became more committed to Jewish survival: the rallying call of the Jewish people has now become: "Never Again!"

But how is the Jewish community to respond to the social responsibilities of political empowerment? In discussing this issue, a number of Jewish writers from across the religious and political spectrum have argued that pragmatic considerations must be paramount as the State of Israel struggles to survive. A policy of *realpolitik*, they maintain, will inevitably countenance the occasional use of immoral strategies to achieve desired ends. According to these pragmatists, if Judaism and the Jewish people are to continue into the twenty-first century, there must be constant vigilance about those forces that seek to undermine the existence of Jewry.

However, scripture speaks of positive action to prevent exploitation and oppression from becoming widespread. In the light of such teaching, a new vision of Judaism calls for an awareness of the suffering of others, particularly the Palestinian people. A number of early Zionists were acutely aware of the need of the Arab population in Palestine. Such writers as Ahad Ha-Am warned about the dangers of ignoring the Arabs' presence and trampling on their rights.

> One thing we certainly should have learned from our past and present history…and that is not to create anger among the local population against us…We have to treat the local population with love and respect, justly and rightly. And what do our brethren in the land of Israel do? Exactly the opposite.[5]

Again, the Jewish philosopher Martin Buber stressed that Jews must attempt to live in peace with their Arab neighbors and respect them as human beings. In an "Open Letter to Mahatma Gandhi," he stated:

> I belong to a group of people who from the time Britain conquered Palestine have not ceased to strive for the concluding of a genuine peace between Jew and Arab. By a genuine peace we inferred and still infer that both peoples should develop the land without the one imposing its will on the other.[6]

Despite such aspirations, the non-Jewish and Jewish communities have so far failed to reach such reconciliation.

Chapter 11.

MESSIAH

From ancient times to the present, the Jewish people longed for a redeemer who would deliver them from exile and inaugurate an era of peace and reconciliation. According to Scripture, such a figure would usher in a new age in which swords would be turned into ploughshares and war would be no more. Such eschatological predictions animated Jewish consciousness through the centuries and provided hope and consolation for persecution and suffering. However, in the modern world, most Jews have ceased to believe in the advent of the messianic age and instead insist on the necessity of human effort to bring about peace and harmony for all peoples.

The Messianic Age

From the earliest period, Reform Judaism disassociated itself from the traditional belief in the coming of the Messiah. In the Pittsburgh Platform of 1885, Reform rabbis and lay leaders officially declared that they no longer anticipated divine deliverance. Instead, they adopted a naturalistic interpretation of the messianic age: "We recognize in the modern era of universal culture of heart and intellect the approach of the realization of Israel's great messianic hope for the establishment of the kingdom of truth, justice and peace among all men."[1]

This aspiration to bring about an improvement of human life is a central feature of the *Union Prayerbook*. Eschewing any reference to the Messiah, it repeatedly emphasizes the importance of ameliorating society and building a better future. As children in religion school, we were exposed to these ideas in the Sabbath service. The morning service, for example, begins with a supplication to God for inspiration:

> Help us, O God, to banish from our hearts all vain-glory, pride of worldly possessions, and self-sufficient leaning upon our own reason. Fill us with the spirit of meekness and the grace of modesty that we may grow in wisdom and reverence. May we never forget that all we have and prize is but lent to us, a trust for which we must render account to Thee. O heavenly Father, put into our hearts the love and awe of Thee, that we may consecrate our lives to Thy service and glorify Thy name in the eyes of all men.[2]

Prayers for the improvement of society precede the *Barchu* prayer:

> We come into Thy house, O Lord, to voice the longings of our hearts in prayer. In the pressure of daily living, we often forget Thee, and stifle the nobler impulses of our nature. On the Sabbath Day, in this hour of worship, we regain the feel-

ing of our kinship with Thee. Help us, O Father, to keep alive this sense of our high lineage amid the labors and duties of our common life. When selfishness and greed prompt us to wrong-doing, may the sense of Thy nearness restrain our desires and save us from degradation. May the inspiration of this hour open our hearts that we may receive the helpless and despondent with sympathy and love. When summoned to give our strength to a noble cause, let the influence of our Sabbath worship fill us with eagerness and ardor that we may bring our offering with joy. May it be Thy will that our prayers be not barren of results; aid us to make them meaningful and fruitful.[3]

Such sentiments were repeated in the afternoon Sabbath service. Here the reader and congregation join together in praying for divine assistance to create a better world;

Heavenly Father, Thou art One, and Thy name is One; may Thy truth unite all mankind into one holy bond of brother-hood, and may our love for one another be our crown of glory and armor of strength. Bless us, O God, on this Sabbath, and grant that it be unto us a day of perfect rest and sanctification. May it strengthen us in all noble purposes and holy resolves; may it encourage us to seek truth from Thy fountain of truth, and inspire us to become holy as Thou art holy.[4]

On Passover, prayers were recited dealing with human free-dom and liberation:

O Lord, our God, on this closing eve of the feast of our free-dom, we gather to thank Thee for the blessings which it has bestowed and for the message it has brought. Delivered by Thy hand form the tyrant's might, Israel sang a song of praise unto Thee by the shore of the Red Sea. Many times since hast Thou saved us from the fury of men and from the floods of destruc-tion. In peril and in need hast Thou been our tower of strength. O continue to redeem us and all Thy children from danger and oppression. Wherever men groan under the yoke of servitude, hasten to deliver them. Cleanse the hearts of men and their rulers of the passions of hate and strife, of greed and lust for power, and fill them with good will and the love of justice.[5]

What is salient about these and other prayers is the absence of any reference to messianic deliverance. It is not God's appointed agent who will deliver humanity from oppression. Rather, it is our allotted task as Jews to bring the message of the ancient prophets to the modern age. Inspired by their words, we are to create a better world and, in this way, bring about God's kingdom on earth. The messianic age will dawn, but it will come about through human action rather than through a miraculous act of divine intervention.

Messianic Deliverance

In the Hebrew Bible, God declared to Abraham, Isaac, and Jacob that their descendants would inherit a land of their own. In later biblical history, Scripture tells of a future redemption which will be brought about through an anointed agent of the Lord. The early prophets maintained that the redeemer would be a descendant of David and his throne would be secure for all time. Eventually the view arose that the house of David would rule over the Northern and Southern Kingdoms as well as neighboring peoples. Later the eighth century B.C.E. prophets, such as Amos and Hosea, predicted the destruction of the nation because of its iniquity, yet in accordance with the divine promise they prophesied that there would be an ingathering of the exiles and the dominance of the Israelites over surrounding nations.

The destruction of Israel was to serve as means of moral reform: Israel was to endure devastation before redemption could take place. Then the Lord would have compassion upon his chosen people and return them to their former glory. This message of destruction and restoration continued in the ministries of the later pre-exilic prophets: for such figures as Isaiah,

Micah, Zephaniah and Jeremiah, God would in time deliver the Israelites—they would not be cut off forever. A new redemption, they proclaimed, would bring about a new spiritual life. In the post-exilic period, the message of hope and consolation was a predominant theme: again the prophets reassured the nation that God would be reunited with his people and Zion would enjoy future glory. The theme of a future redemption was echoed in the Psalms: there, too, the promise of a future king became a predominant theme. Finally, the Book of Daniel predicted the coming of a divinely appointed deliverer—the Son of Man was to be given dominion over all the earth.

Once the Temple had been destroyed and the Jewish people driven out of their homeland, the nation was bereft. In their despair, the ancient Israelites longed for a kingly figure who would deliver them from exile and rebuild the holy city. Drawing on messianic ideas found in Scripture, the Apocrypha, and Pseudepigrapha, they foresaw the coming of a future deliverance when all peoples would be converted to the worship of the one true God. Such conceptions animated rabbinic speculation about the eschatological unfolding of history, when God would intervene on behalf of Jewry. According to a number of early rabbinic sages such a process of redemption would be brought about through charity, repentance, and the observance of Jewish law.

Nevertheless, prior to the coming of such messianic deliverance, the world would be subject to serious tribulations defined as "the birth pangs of the Messiah." These would be followed by the arrival of Elijah, the forerunner of the Messiah. Subsequently a second figure—the Messiah ben Joseph—would engage in conflict with Gog and Magog, the enemies of the Israelites. Although he would be killed in battle, the King-Messiah (Messiah ben David) would eventually be victorious, and with his coming, the dispersion of Israel would cease. All exiles will be returned to Zion, and earthly life will be totally transformed. At the end of this messianic period, all human beings will undergo judgment and either be rewarded with heavenly bliss or punished everlastingly. This vision of a future hope was animated by the Jewish conviction that God would not abandon the Jews to exile. The promise of messianic redemption and return to Israel served as a basis for overcoming the nation's despondency at losing the Holy Land and the people's sacred institutions.

In the first century, a Jewish sect emerged which believed that Jesus would return to bring about the fulfillment of biblical prophecy. Although mainstream Jewry rejected such a claim, the Jewish community continued to long for divine deliverance, and in 132 B.C.E. a messianic revolt against Rome was led by the warrior Simeon bar Kochba. This rebellion was inspired by the conviction that God sought to overthrow Roman oppression. When this uprising was crushed, Jews put forward the year of messianic deliverance until the fifth century. In fulfillment of this prediction, a figure named Moses appeared in Crete, declaring that he would be able to lead Jews across the seas to Judaea.

After this plan failed, Jews continued to engage in messianic speculation, believing that they could determine the date of their deliverance on the basis of Scriptural texts. Their reflections are recorded in a number of midrashic sources. In the ninth century, the rabbinic scholar and philosopher Saadiah Gaon continued this tradition of messianic calculation. During these centuries of heightened messianic awareness, a series of pseudo-Messiahs such as Abu Isa al-Ispahani, Serene, and Yugdan appeared, and the traveller Eldad Ha-Dani brought reports of the ten lost tribes, an event that stimulated the Jewish desire to return to Zion.

At the time of the Crusades, Jewish aspirations for the advent of the Messiah intensified. As a consequence, when the massacres of this period occurred, the Jewish community envisaged this disaster as the birth pangs of the Messiah. In later years, the same desire for redemption and return to Zion was expressed by Jews who continued to suffer at the hands of Christians. In the following two centuries a number of Jewish scholars attempted to ascertain the date of divine deliverance.

Simultaneously several pseudo-Messiahs appeared in the Jewish world. Initially such figures came from Asia Minor, Babylonia, and Persia, but with the movement of Jewry to

Mediterranean countries, other would-be Messiahs emerged in Western Europe. The most important figure of this period was David Alroy who, even after his death, was viewed by his disciples as the Redeemer of Israel. In the following centuries, messianic calculators sought to determine the year of deliverance and return of the exiles to the Holy Land on the basis of scriptural texts. Often they relied on kabbalistic modes of exegesis in their computations. Mystical tracts of this era, such as the *Zohar*, also contain speculations about the messianic age. In the thirteenth century another messianic figure, Abraham Abulafia, appeared; although he attracted a wide following, he evoked considerable animosity from the scholarly community.

Despite the failure of the Messiah to appear, the Jewish community continued to await the advent of the messianic age. As a result, various messianic treatises were composed, and such writers as Simeon ben Duran and Isaac Abrabanel speculated about the year of his arrival. This tradition of messianic calculation was practised by other scholars such as Abraham Halevi, Mordecai ben Jacob Dato, Isaac Luria, Naphtali Herz ben Jacob Elhanan, Gedalia ibn Yahya and David ben Solomon ibn Abi Zimra. In addition, a number of false Messiahs including David Reuveni and Solomon Molko appeared in the early modern period, claiming to usher in the period of deliverance.

Undaunted by the failure of these false Messiahs to lead the Jewish people to the Promised Land and bring about redemption, other calculators persisted in their investigations. Pre-eminent among these messianic speculators was Hayyim Vital, the disciple of Issac Luria, who announced that he was the Messiah ben Joseph. Another major figure of this period was Manasseh ben Israel who maintained that the hour of redemption was at hand. Convinced that this momentous event was about to take place, he sought to persuade Oliver Cromwell to admit the Jews to England. Eventually, the Cossack Rebellion, which began in 1648 and devastated Polish Jewry, heightened the expectation that the coming of the Messiah was at hand.

By the beginning of the seventeenth century, Lurianic mysticism had made a major impact on Sephardic Jewry and messianic expectations had become a central feature of Jewish life. In this milieu the arrival of a self-proclaimed messianic king, Shabbatai Tzevi brought about a transformation of Jewish life and thought. In 1665 his messiahship was proclaimed. In time he travelled to Constantinople but, on the order of the grand vizier, he was arrested and placed in prison. Within a short time the prison quarters became a messianic court. Eventually Shabbatai was given the choice between conversion and death. In the face of this alternative he converted to Islam, an act which caused despair among most of his followers.

With the conversion of Shabbatai Tzevi in the seventeenth century, the Jewish preoccupation with messianic calculation diminished. Nonetheless, there emerged a number of religious Zionists who continued to subscribe to the belief in the advent of the messianic era. Prominent among such figures was Yehudai Alkalai, who maintained that Jewish settlers should establish Jewish colonies in Palestine in anticipation of the coming of the Messiah. A similar view was adopted by Zwi Hirsch Kalisher, who argued that the messianic era will not take place immediately; instead, the redemption of the Jewish people will occur gradually, through the ingathering of the Jewish nation to their ancient homeland. Later Abraham Isaac Kook sought to harmonize messianic aspirations with the efforts of modern, secular Zionists.

Opposed to this reinterpretation of messianic deliverance, Orthodox critics of Zionism united in their opposition to what they perceived as a betrayal of traditional Jewish values. In their view, it is impossible to accelerate divine redemption through human efforts. Distancing themselves from the traditional belief in messianic redemption, other Jews adopted a secular approach to Jewish nationalism. In the view of such figures as Moses Hess, Leon Pinsker, and Theodor Herzl, the creation of a Jewish homeland was required to solve the problem of anti-Semitism. Only by establishing their own nation would Jews be able to protect themselves from anti-Jewish hostility. Rejecting the Zionist cause, liberal Jews attacked both messianic and secular

Zionism for its utopian character. According to these reformers, what was required was for Jews to accomodate themselves to the cultures in which they lived and to achieve security through a policy of assimilation.

Despite the significance of the messianic idea for Jewish life in the past, many modern Jews have found it increasingly difficult to believe in a miraculous divine intervention which will change the course of human history. Further, doctrines connected with the coming of the Messiah—including the belief in the resurrection of the dead, the miraculous ingatheriing of the exiles, final judgment, and reward and punishment in the Hereafter—have seemed totally implausible. With the exception of strictly Orthodox Jews and the Hasidim, most Jews have ceased to adhere to these traditional convictions.

Traditional rabbinic eschatology, with the Messiah at its center has thus lost its force for a large number of Jews in the modern period, and in consequence there has been a gradually increasing this-worldly emphasis in Jewish thought. Significantly, this has been accompanied by a strong attachment to the State of Israel. For many Jews the founding of the Jewish State is the central focus of their religious and cultural identity. Jews throughout the world have deep admiration for the astonishing achievements of Israelis in reclaiming the desert and building a viable society, and great respect for the heroism of Israel's soldiers and leaders. As a result it is not uncommon for Jews to equate Jewishness with Zionism, and to see Judaism as fundamentally nationalistic in character—this is a far cry from the rabbinic view of history, which placed the advent of the Messiah at the center of Jewish life and thought.

Post-Messianic Judaism

As we have seen, from biblical times to the modern age the Jewish community anticipated the coming of the Messiah, who would redeem the nation from earthly travail and usher in a new era of peace. As we have seen, this doctrine underwent consider-

able development over time, yet despite the various interpretations
of messianic deliverance its central affirmation remained constant:
human history will find its ultimate fulfillment in a future age
when cosmic harmony will be restored. Despite the centrality of
messianic belief in the history of the nation,the modern period
has witnessed the disintegration of this doctrine. Increasingly
Jews have found it difficult, if not impossible, to believe in the
advent of messianic redemption. With the exception of the strictly
Orthodox as well as the Hasidim, most Jews have abandoned the
Jewish eschatological picture of divine redemption.

Two major factors have led to this change in attitude. In contemporary society it has become apparent that both biblical and
rabbinic conceptions of the universe were based on a pre-scientific
and mistaken understanding of nature. As a result of the expansion
of scientific knowledge, most modern Jews are unable to accept
the scriptural account and subsequent rabbinic view of the origin
of the universe as well as God's activity in the world. The climate
of thought in the twentieth century was one in which scientific
explanation has taken over the role of religious interpretation.

Although the sciences have not disproved the claims of
Judaism, they have provided a rational explanation of events that
were previously seen as the result of divine agency. In this light,
religious convictions have been perceived as subjective in origin,
to be ousted eventually from the central areas of human knowledge. In other words, the sciences have effectively established
the autonomy of the natural world. Nature is studied without
any reference to God, and the universe is investigated as though
the Deity does not exist. In essence, the contemporary period
has witnessed scientific advance on the one hand and the retreat
of traditional belief on the other.

A second factor which has brought about the eclipse of Jewish
theism is the fact of evil. For many Jews today, the existence of
human suffering makes the idea of an all-good and all-powerful
God utterly implausible: after the events of the Holocaust, the
traditional belief that God is a loving father who watches over
his chosen people has become impossible to sustain. In modern

society, faith in such a Deity has been overshadowed by an over-whelming sense that the universe is devoid of divine presence.

I wish to propose a new consciousness is therefore needed which is in tune with this shift in outlook. As we have seen, a growing number of contemporary thinkers have drawn attention to the inevitable subjectivity of religious belief; in their view, the world faiths should be understood as different human responses to the Divine. In the light of this interpretation, Jewish views of divine deliverance, final judgement, resurrection of the dead, and reward and punishment should be seen as rooted in the life of the nation rather than ultimate truths that have been revealed from on high.

Such a transformation of perspective calls for a revolutionary change in Jewish life and thought. In the past the community looked to God for release from their travail. In the biblical period, the prophets reassured the nation that God would not forsake his chosen people. Subsequently the nation awaited the arrival of a descendant of King David who would restore Israel to its former glory. In the exile that followed the destruction of the Temple, the Jewish people longed for the coming of a messianic redeemer who would lead them back from exile. Coupled with this belief was the conviction that the righteous will be rewarded in the World to Come.

Today, however, such longing for supernatural intervention might be understood as a pious hope nurtured through centuries of persecution and tragedy. Rather than wait for the Messiah to come to redeem the world, Jews today could rely on themselves to shape their own destiny. A new vision of Judaism calls for a radical reevaluation of the messianic hope: the messianic-centered conception of Judaism should now be replaced by a human-centered model of Jewish existence that acknowledges that the belief system of the Jewish faith is ultimately a human construction. Such a version of Judaism would also highlight the significance of human action in the world as opposed to the messianic belief in the coming of a divinely-appointed deliverer who will redeem all humankind.

Hence, despite the meaningfulness of the concept of the Messiah for Jewish existence in the past, the messianic idea of divine deliverance as presented in the Hebrew Bible, post-biblical writings, and rabbinic sources could be set aside. Rather than looking to a heavenly form of redemption, the Jewish community might now rely on itself for its own survival and the redemption of the world. Such a reorientation of the faith can be summarized by a new credo for the post-Messianic age:

A Suggestion for a Post-Messianic Credo

1. I believe that despite the significance of the process of messianic redemption in the life of the Jewish nation, it must be recognized that Jewish eschatological beliefs are human in origin. Paralleling the development of religious doctrines in other faiths, the messianic idea was elaborated by sages and scholars to provide an explanation for God's dealing with his chosen people.

2. I believe that the attempt of Jewish scholars to determine the date of the advent of the Messiah was a pious, though misguided quest.

3. I believe that the various Jewish messianic figures of the past were all pseudo-Messiahs; despite the sincerity of their followers, these messianic pretenders suffered from a delusion about their messianic role.

4. I believe that, given the subjective character of messianic belief, it makes more sense for Jews today to set aside the hope for final deliverance and redemption through a divine agent who will usher in a period of peace and harmony and bring about the end of history.

5. I believe that, with the demise of the messianic hope, the Jewish people must look to themselves for survival. It is only through the actions of the nation on its own behalf that a Jewish future can be secured.

6. I believe that the humanistic values of the Jewish heritage should serve as guiding principles for regulating national affairs within the Jewish state. Israel's political policies should not be

determined solely on the basis of pragmatic concerns; ethical ideals rooted in the tradition should be at the forefront of the nation's decision-making.

7. I believe that Jews in the Diaspora have the responsibility to engage in social action; the quest to create a better world through human endeavor is at the heart of the Jewish faith. Jews today must actively engage in this process rather than wait for a miraculous divine intervention to bring peace and harmony on earth.

8. I believe that, in the struggle to ameliorate social problems, Jews should look beyond their own faith community. Together with members of other faiths, they should strive to improve the lives of all human beings as well as the world they live in.

Here, then, is a new humanistic creed for post-Messianic Judaism. In place of the messianic vision of an unfolding providential scheme leading to divine reward and punishment, this Credo envisages Jewish existence as determined by the Jewish people themselves.

Chapter 12.

AFTERLIFE

In biblical times, the Jewish people did not look to reward in a future life as a conslation for human suffering. The biblical writers were preoccupied with earthly life. In their view, reward and punishment would take place in the here and now, depending on one's loyalty to the covenant. In time, however, rabbinic sages argued that, with the advent of the Messiah, the dead will be resurrected and eventually the virtuous will be rewarded in the World to Come. This belief in eternal life sustained the Jewish people through centuries of persecution—in the the modern world, however, many Jews have abandoned such notions, believing instead that the soul is immortal and will return to God. Yet, such a notion is itself beset with difficulties.

Immortality of the Soul

From its inception, Reform Judaism rejected the elaborate eschatological framework of Orthodoxy. In the view of early reformers, belief in messianic redemption, as well as reward in *Gan Eden* (Heaven) and punishment in *G'henna* (Hell) are outmoded concepts. Officially Reform Judaism subscribed to belief in the immortality of the soul. As the Pittsburgh Platform of 1885 states, Reform Jews:

> reassert the doctrine of Judaism that the soul is immortal, grounding this belief on the Divine nature of the human spirit, which forever finds bliss in righteousness and misery in wickedness. We reject as ideas not rooted in Judaism the belief in bodily resurrection and in *G'henna* and Eden as abodes for eternal punishment or reward.[1]

Such a conviction is reflected the Reform liturgy. The funeral service highlights the centrality of this conviction. Prior to the eulogy, the rabbi prays:

> Out of the depths we call unto Thee, O God, our heavenly Father. In Thy hands are the souls of all the living and the spirits of all flesh. Thy loving kindness is never withdrawn from us, but ever abides with us, in death as in life. In Thy wisdom, Thou has laid upon us this heavy burden. Mayest Thou also in Thy mercy, give us strength to bear it. Guide and sustain us, lest we stray from Thy paths. Give us that strength of faith which shall keep us from murmuring against the justice of Thy dispensation, even when Thou dost afflict us. Grant us, we pray Thee, the understanding which shall enable us to recognize that the hand that woundeth is the hand that bindeth up again. Thou art the Life of all life.[2]

For Reform Judaism, the soul is the repository of personhood, as the funeral service emphasizes in the *El Male Rahamim* prayer which is recited by the congregation:

> O God, full of compassion, Thou who dwellest on high!
> Grant perfect rest unto the soul of _____, who hast de-
> parted from this world. Lord of mercy, bring him (her) into
> Thy presence and let his (her) soul be bound up in the bond
> of eternal life. Be Thou his (her) possession, and may his (her)
> response be peace.[3]

In the cemetery, the rabbi leads the service, emphasizing that
the dead will live beyond the grave:

> Eternal is Thy power, O Lord, Thou art mighty to save. In
> lovingkindness Thou sustainest the living: in the multitude
> of Thy mercies, Thou preservest all. Thou upholdest the fall-
> ing and healest the sick, freest the captives and keepest faith
> with Thy children in death as in life. Who is like unto Thee,
> Almighty God, Author of life and death, Source of salvation?
> Praised be Thou, O Lord, who hast implanated within us
> eternal life.[4]

A further prayer stresses the eternal life:

> The dust returns to the earth as it was; the spirit returns to
> God who gave it. It is only the house of the spirit which we
> now lay in the bosom of the earth. The spirit itself cannot die.
> Here, too, our dear ones continue in the loving remembrance
> of those to whom they were precious. Receive in mercy, O
> God, the soul of our departed _____. Grant him (her)
> that everlasting peace which Thou hast laid up for us in the
> world to come. Though no human eye has seen, nor ear has
> heard, nor mind has compassed it, it is still our sure inheri-
> tance and our everlasting portion.[5]

The prayers prior to the *Kaddish* similarly stress the belief in
the soul:

All flesh is grass, and the goodliness thereof as the flower of the field. The grass withers, the flower fades. The body dies, and is laid in the earth. Dust returns to dust, but the spirit returns unto God who gave it.

May our Heavenly Father spread the sheltering tabernacle of His peace over _____. May He send His comfort unto you who mourn. May His love be with you and bring peace to your sorrowing hearts. Lift up hour hearts unto Him who is the source of all light and all joy. He wounds and He heals; He causes death and He gives life. In His hands are the souls of all the living and the spirits of all flesh. Let us praise His name in the words sanctified by memory and glorified by hope.[6]

The Hereafter

Even though there is no explicit reference to life after death in the Hebrew Bible, a number of expressions are used to refer to the realm of the dead. In Psalm 28:1 ("To Thee, O Lord, I call; my rock, be not deaf to me, lest, if thou be silent to me, I become like those who go down to the pit") *bor* refers refers to a subterranean pit. In Psalm 6:5, the term *sheol* is used in a similar sense: "For in death there is no remembrance of thee; in *sheol* who can give thee praise." Again, in Psalm 22:15, the term *afar mavet* refers to the dust of death: "my strength is dried up like a potsherd, and my tongue cleaves to my jaws; thou dost lay me in the dust of death." In Exodus 15:12, the earth is described as swallowing up the dead: "Thou didst stretch out thy right hand, the earth swallowed them." In addition, the words *ge ben hinnom, ge hinnom* and *ge* are used to refer to a cursed valley associated with fire and death where, according to Jeremiah, children were sacrificied as burnt offerings to Moloch and Baal. In later rabbinic literature the word normally used for hell (*Gehinnom)* is derived from these terms.

Though these passages point to a biblical notion of an afterlife, there is no indication of a clearly defined concept. It was only later in the Greco-Roman period that such an idea began to materialize. The concept of a future world in which the righteous will be compensated for the ills they have suffered in this life was prompted by a failure to justify God's ways by any other means. According to Scripture, individuals were promised rewards for obeying God's law and punishments were threatened for disobedience. As time passed, however, it became clear that life does not operate in accordance with such a tidy scheme. In response to this problem, the sages developed a doctrine of reward and punishment in the hereafter. Such a belief helped Jews to cope with suffering in this life and it also explained—if not the presence of evil in the world—then at least the value of creation despite the world's ills.

Given that there is no explicit belief in eternal salvation in the Bible, rabbinic scholars of the post-biblical period were faced with the difficulty of proving that the doctrine of resurrection of the dead is based on Scripture. To do this they used methods of exegesis which were based on the assumption that every word in the Torah was given by God to Moses on Mount Sinai. Thus, for example, Eleazar, the son of R. Jose who lived in the second century, claimed to have refuted the sectarians who maintained that resurrection is not a biblical doctrine:

> I said to them, "You have falsified your Torah.... For you maintain that resurrection is not a biblical doctrine, but it is written (in Numbers 15:31), "Because he has despised the word of the Lord, and has broken his commandment, that person shall be utterly cut off; his iniquity shall be upon him." Now seeing that he shall be utterly cut off in this world, when shall his iniquity be upon him? Surely in the next world.[7]

According to rabbinic sources, the World to Come is divided into several stages. First, there is the time of messianic redemption. According to the Talmud the *Yemot Hamashiah* (Days of the Messiah) is to take place on earth after a period of decline and calamity. This will result in a complete fulfilment of every human desire. Peace will reign throughout nature; Jerusalem will be rebuilt and, at the close of this era, the dead will be resurrected and rejoined to their souls. Then a final judgment will take place, and the deeds of all human beings will be assessed. The righteous will enter into heaven (*Gan Eden)* which is portrayed in various ways in rabbinic texts. One of the earliest descriptions is found in the *midrash Konen:*

> The Gan Eden at the east measures 800,000 years (at ten miles per day or 3650 miles per year). There are five chambers of various classes of the righteous. The first is built of cedar, with a ceiling of transparent crystal. This is the habitation of non-Jews who become true and devoted converts to Judaism. They are headed by Obadiah the prophet and Onkelos the proselyte, who teach them the Law. The second is built of cedar, with a ceiling of fine silver. This is the habitation of the penitents, headed by Manasseh, King of Israel, who teaches the law. The third chamber is built of silver and gold ornamented with pearls. It is very spacious, and contains the best of heaven and earth, with spices, fragrance, and sweet odors.... The fourth chamber is made of olive-wood and is inhabited by those who have suffered for the sake of their religion.... The fifth chamber is built of precious stones, gold and silver, surrounded by myrrh and aloes.... This chamber is inhabited by the Messiah of David, Elijah, and the Messiah of Ephraim.[8]

Conversely, those who are judged wicked are condemned to eternal punishment. In one of the most elaborate descriptions of this place of punishment, Moses is depicted as guided by an angel through Hell:

> When Moses and the Angel of Hell entered Hell together, they saw men being tortured by the Angels of Destruction. Some sinners were suspended by their eyelids, some by their ears, some by their hands, and some by their tongues.... In another

place.... Moses saw sinners suspended by their heads downward and their bodies covered with long black worms. These
sinners were punished in this way because they swore falsely,
profaned the Sabbath and the Holy Days, despised the sages,
called their neighbors by unseemly nicknames, wronged the
orphan and the widow and bore false witness.[9]

In another section Moses saw sinners prone on their faces with
2,000 scorpions lashing, stinging, and tormenting them. Each of
these scorpions had 70,000 heads, each head 70,000 mouths,
each mouth 70,000 stings, and each sting 70,000 pouches of
poison and venom. So great was the pain they inflicted that the
eyes of the sinners melted in their sockets. These sinners were
punished in this way because they had robbed other Jews, were
arrogant in the community, put their neighbors to shame in
public, delivered their fellow Jews into the hands of the gentiles,
denied the Torah, and maintained that God is not the creator of
the world.

On the basis of this scheme of eternal salvation and damna-
tion, which was at the center of rabbinic theology throughout
the centuries, it might be expected that modern Jewish thinkers
would seek to interpret contemporary Jewish history in the context of traditional eschatology.

This, however, has not occurred. Instead, many Jewish writers have set aside doctrines concerning messianic redemption,
resurrection, and final judgment (reward for the righteous and
punishment for the wicked). This shift in emphasis is in part
due to the fact that the views expressed in the narrative sections
of the *midrashim* and the Talmud are not binding. Although all
Jews are obliged to accept the divine origin of the Law, this is
not so with regard to theological theories expounded by the rabbis. Thus it is possible for a Jew to be pious without embracing
all the central beliefs of mainstream Judaism.

Indeed throughout Jewish history there has been widespread
confusion as to what these beliefs are. In the first century B.C.E.,
for example, the sage Hillel stated that the quintessence of

Judaism could be formulated in a single principle: "That which is hateful to you, do not do to your neighbor. This is the whole of the Law; all the rest is commentary."[10] Similarly, in the second century C.E., the Council of Lydda ruled that, under certain circumstances, the laws of the Torah may be transgressed in order to save one's life, with the exception of idolatry, murder, and unchastity.[11]

In both of these early formulations, the center of gravity was in the ethical rather than the religious sphere. However, in the medieval period, Maimonides formulated what he considered to be the thirteen theological principles of the Jewish faith. Other thinkers though challenged this formulation. Hasdai Crescas, Simon ben Zemah Duran, Jospeh Albo and Isaac Arami elaborated different creeds, and some thinkers argued that it is impossibe to isolate from the whole Torah essential principles of the Jewish faith. Thus, when formulations of the central theological tenets of Judaism were propounded, they were not universally accepted since they were simply the opinions of individual teachers. Without a central authority whose opinion in theological matters is binding on all Jews, it has been impossible for any particular group to establish its views as the foundational beliefs of the Jewish faith.

Given that there is no authoritative bedrock of Jewish theology, many modern thinkers have felt fully justified in abandoning the various elements of traditional rabbinic eschatology, which they regard as untenable: the doctrine of the resurrection of the dead has in modern times been largely replaced in both Orthodox and non-Orthodox Judaism by the belief in the immortality of the soul. The original belief in resurrection was an eschatological hope bound up with the rebirth of the nation in the Days of the Messiah. However, as messianic hopes faded into the background, so also did this doctrine. For most Jews the physical resurrection is simply inconceivable in the light of a scientific understanding of the world. The late Chief Rabbi of Britain, Dr. Joseph Herman Hertz, for example, argued that what really matters is the doctrine of the immortality of the soul—not the belief in the resurrection of the dead:

> Many and various are the folk beliefs and poetical fancies in
> the rabbinic writings concerning Heaven, *Gan Eden* and Hell,
> *Gehinnom.* Our most authoritative religious guides, however,
> proclaim that no eye hath seen, nor can mortal fathom, what
> awaiteth us in the Hereafter; but that even the tarnished soul
> will not forever be denied spiritual bliss.[12]

The belief in eternal punishment has also been discarded by
a large number of Jews partly because of the interest in penal
reform during the past century. Punishment as retaliation in a
vindictive sense has been generally rejected. As Louis Jacobs
noted in *Principles of the Jewish Faith* :

> the value of punishment as a deterrent and for the protection
> of society is widely recognized. But all the stress today is on the
> reformatory aspects of punishment. Against such a background
> the whole question of reward and punishment in the theologi-
> cal sphere is approached in a more questioning spirit.[13]

Further, the rabbinic view of Hell is seen by many as morally
repugnant. Jewish theologians have stressed that it is a delusion
to believe that a God of love could have created a place of eternal
punishment. In his commentary on the prayerbook, Hertz cat-
egorically declared, "Judaism rejects the doctrine of eternal dam-
nation."[14] And the Reform rabbi, Kaufmann Kohler argued that
the question whether the tortures of Hell are reconciliable with
Divine mercy "is for us superfluous and superseded. Our modern
conceptions of time and space admit neither a place or a world-
period for the reward and punishment of souls, nor the intolerable
conception of eternal joy without useful action and eternal agony
without any moral purpose."[15]

Traditional Jewish eschatology has thus lost its force for a large
number of Jews in the modern period, and in consequence there
has been a gradual this-worldly emphasis in Jewish thought. We

can see therefore that the wheel has come full circle from the faint allusions to immortality in the biblical period that led to an elaborate development of the concept of the Hereafter in rabbinic Judaism. Whereas the rabbis put the belief in an afterlife at the center of their religous system, modern Jewish thinkers, both Orthodox and non-Orthodox, have abandoned such an otherworldly outlook, even to the point of denying the existence of such doctrines.

Reflections on Life after Death

For most Jews physical resurrection is simply inconceivable in the light of a scientific understanding of the nature of the world. In its place, Jewish theologians have embraced the doctrine of the immortality of the soul. This has become a central feature of contemporary Judaism in which frequent reference is made to the state of eternal bliss that awaits each individual soul.

Proponents of such a view insist that there are strong precedents for this concept. Citing Maimonides, they point out that the idea of a disembodied soul has been a central element of Jewish theology through the ages. Here reference is made to Maimonides' formulation of this doctrine in the *Mishneh Torah*:

There are neither bodies nor bodily forms in the World to Come but only the disembodied souls of the righteous who have become like ministering angels. Since there are no bodies there is no eating or drinking there nor is there anything which the human body needs in this world. Nor do there occur there any of the events which occur to the human body in this world such as sitting, standing, sleep, death, distress, laughter and so forth...You may be repelled by this, imagining that the only worthwhile reward for keeping the commandments and for a man being perfect in the ways of truth is for him to eat and drink well and have beautiful women and wear garments of fine linen and embroidery and live in marble palaces and have vessels of silver and gold...But the sages and intellectuals know that these things are vain, stupid and valueless and only are greatly attractive to us in this world where we do have bodies and bodily forms. All these things have to do with the needs of the body. The soul only longs for them because the body needs them if it is to remain healthy and thus perform its function. But all these things cease when the body no longer enjoys existence.[16]

Increasingly, however, theologians have emphasized the logical inadeqacies of such a belief. The concept of disembodied personal survival after death, they argue, is internally inconsistent. Personal words—personal pronouns, names, and so on—are used to designate creatures of flesh and blood. Hence, in the ordinary, everyday understanding of personhood, the notion of incorporeal persons makes no sense. Continuity of selfhood presupposes bodily continuity. Further, critics of the concept of an incorporeal soul point out that words that describe mental operations apply to human behaviour which is dependent on the existence of a physical body—only observable human beings are capable of the kinds of actions attributed to the soul. Human beings, on this view, are creatures with bodies who behave in characteristic ways rather than nonphysical entities.

The lack of evidence of bodily resurrection and the conceptual dilemmas connected with the notion of disembodied existence pose serious challenges for traditional Judaism. Faced with the problem of human suffering, rabbinic sages of the past appealed to the doctrine of life after death to explain God's ways. Today, however, Jews have largely rejected such eschatological theories, retaining only a vague sense of spiritual continuity after death. A new vision of Judaism demands a recognition of such a fundamental change of consciousness. No longer does it make sense for Jews to long for messianic deliverance, the resurrection of the dead, miraculous return from exile, the rebuilding of the Temple, the advent of the messianic age, and final judgment for all humankind. The longing for eternal life as a solution to life's difficulties could be recognized as a pious illusion.

Instead, Jews might accept that human beings are responsible for their own destiny. No longer does it make sense in my opinion to appeal to a miraculous divine intervention in history to solve the problems of immorality and injustice. Rather, earthly life can be viewed as the sole arena for human action. Such a shift from an other-worldly to a this-worldly perspective should not be viewed as a rejection of Jewish values. On the contrary, biblical Judaism similarly emphasized the importance of earthly existence. God had established a covenant with Israel: sin was conceived as a failure to follow the divine commands, and reward or punishment was to take place in this life rather than the next. It was only with the emergence of Pharisaic Judaism that the concept of the World to Come became a central feature of Jewish theology.

A new vision of Judaism suggests a reversal of perspective. Today Jews can return to their biblical roots in accepting the finality of death. The Jewish heritage provides a framework for ethical responsibility and humanitarian concern; the moral life can be lived for its own sake, rather than out of a desire for future reward. No longer dependent on supernaturalism, modern Jews have the option of embracing the highest principles of their faith in seeking to build a better world. If the utopian conception of the messianic age is thereby demythologized, it can still animate Jews to create a society in which human beings are treated with concern and compassion. In ancient times, the prophets served as the moral conscience of the nation; their words can still stir the spirit of twenty-first century Jews, calling them to a recognition of the centrality of moral responsibility in the life of the nation.

PART III

WRESTLING WITH THE WORLD

Chapter 13.

JEWISH COMMUNITY

Through the centuries, the Jewish people have seen themselves as a separate people. Chosen by God, they were to serve as a light to the nations. Such religious conviction served as a unifying force, drawing the nation together during times of persecution and oppression. Despite the emergence of different sects that occurred throughout history, Jewry was bound together through common ancestry, ethnic ties, and experience. In the modern world, Jews continue to see themselves as the congregation of Israel, yet today the community is divided into sub-groups with fundamentally different and conflicting ideologies. If Jewry is to have a future, what is now now required is a new spirit of tolerance of the divisions that currently exist within the Jewish world.

Reform Judaism and Jewry

In my hometown I was aware of the various divisions within the Jewish community. Strictly Orthodox Jews lived on the West side of the city—there they followed ancient patterns of Jewish observance. On the East side there were also Orthodox synagogues, but of a modernist character. Instead of isolating themselves into self-imposed ghettos, these Neo-Orthodox Jews mixed freely with the outside world despite their determination to follow Jewish law. There were also Conservative congregations and a small Reconstructionist synagogue. The largest congregation, however, was Reform, and it was there that I was exposed to the Jewish way of life.

From its origin in the early nineteenth century, Reform Judaism pressed for a reevaluation of the Jewish faith, advocating major alterations to both belief and practice. Preeminent among early reformers, Israel Jacobson sought to revolutionize Jewish education by founding schools in which Jewish teachers gave lessons about Judaism, and secular subjects were taught by Christians. In 1817 the Hamburg Temple was opened—this new institution made a number of changes to the liturgy, including prayers and sermons in German, choral singing, and organ music. Later a series of synods took place that sought to formulate a coherent policy for the movement.

In the United States, European reformers who had immigrated to the New World established a series of Reform institutions including the Central Conference of American Reform Rabbis and the Union of American Hebrew Congregations. In 1875 the Hebrew Union College, the first Reform rabbinical seminary, was created in Cincinnati, Ohio. Ten years later a gathering of Reform leaders in Pittsburgh, Pennsylvania, set out the basic principles of the movement. Fifty years following this historical meeting, the Jewish world had undergone major changes: America was the center of the Diaspora; Zionism had become a vital force in Jewish life; Hitler was in power. The Columbus Platform of the Reform movement of 1937 reflected a new approach to Reform Judaism, and the views expressed in this Platform served as the background to the tenets of Reform Judaism expressed in the Union Prayerbook:

1. Nature of Judaism: Judaism is the historical religious experience of the Jewish people. Though growing out of Jewish life, its message is universal, aiming at the union and perfection of mankind under the sovereignty of God. Reform Judaism recognizes the principle of progressive development in religion and consciously applies this principle to spiritual as well as to cultural and social life....

2. God: The heart of Judaism and its chief contribution to religion is the doctrine of the One, living God, who rules the world through law and love. In him all existence has its creative source and mankind its ideal of conduct. Though transcending time and space, He is the indwelling Presence of the world....

3. Man: Judaism affirms that man is created in the divine image. His spirit is immortal. He is an active co-worker with God. As a child of God, he is endowed with moral freedom and is charged with the responsibility of overcoming evil and striving after ideal ends.

4. Torah: God reveals himself not only in the majesty, beauty and orderliness of nature, but also in the vision and moral striving of the human spirit. Revelation is a continuous process, confined to no one group and to no one age. Yet the people of Israel, through its prophets and sages, achieved unique insight in the realm of religious truth. The Torah, both written and oral, enshrines Israel's ever-growing consciousness of God and

of the moral law.... Each age has the obligation to adapt the teachings of the Torah to its basic needs in consonance with the genius of Judaism.

5. Israel: Judaism is the soul of which Israel is the body. Living in all parts of the world, Israel has been held together by the ties of a common history, and above all, by the heritage of faith.... The non-Jews who accept our faith are welcomed as full members of the Jewish community.... In the rehabilitation of Palestine, the land hallowed by memories and hopes, we behold the promise of renewed life for many of our brethern. We affirm the obligation of all Jewry to aid in its upbuilding as a Jewish homeland by endeavoring to make it not only a haven of refuge for the oppressed but also a center of Jewish culture and spiritual life.... We regard it as our historic task to co-operate with all men in the establishment of the kingdom of God, of universal brotherhood, justice, truth and peace on earth. This is our messianic goal.

6. Ethics and Religion: In Judaism religion and morality blend into an insoluble unity. Seeking God means to strive after holiness, righteousness and goodness. The love of God is incomplete without the love of one's fellow men....

7. Social Justice: Judaism seeks the attainment of a just society by the application of its teachings to the economic order, to industry and commerce, and to national and international affairs. It aims at the elimination of man-made misery and suffering, of poverty and degradation, of tyranny and slavery, of social inequality and prejudice, of ill-will and strife....

8. Peace: Judaism, from the days of the prophets, had proclaimed to mankind the ideal of universal peace. The spiritual and physical disarmament of all nations has been one of its essential teachings....

9. The Religious Life: Jewish life is marked by consecration to these ideals of Judaism. It calls for faithful participation in the life of the Jewish community as it finds expression in home, synagogue and school, and in all other agencies that enrich Jewish life and promote its welfare....[1]

Although distancing itself from the other branches of the faith, Reform Judaism insisted on seeing itself as part of the community. Anxious to disseminate the highest values of the tradition, it nonetheless viewed the body of Israel as an indissoluble whole. Growing up with a sense of such communal ties, I regarded myself as bound together with all Jews regardless of their ideological commitments. We were one family, drawn together by history and religion into *klal Israel* (the community of Israel).

Community Life

Through the centuries, Jewry has been organized as a distinct group. In ancient times they were the Hebrew clan. Later as they changed from a nomadic to an agricultural existence, they became an urban people. As a result, their leadership was urbanized. Elders were responsible for administering justice, and towns were arranged in territorial or tribal units. During the Babylonian exile, the emergence of Jewish institutions established the pattern for later communal development throughout the Diaspora. As early as the second century B.C.E. Jews in Alexandria formed their own corporation with a council that conducted its affairs in conformity with Jewish practice. In addition, these bodies built synagogues and sent taxes collected for the Temple to Jerusalem. In the Roman Empire, Jews were judged by their own courts according to Jewish law, and this system established the basis for legal autonomy that characterized Jewish life for the next two thousand years.

With the destruction of the Second Temple in 70 C.E., Jewish life underwent a major change. In Israel the patriarchate together with the Sanhedrin constituted the central authority.

In Babylonia, the *exilarch* (ruler of the exile) was the leader of the community along with the heads of the rabbinic academies. In its daily life Jewry was bound by *halakhah* (Jewish law), and synagogues, law courts, schools, philanthropic institutions, and ritual baths formed the framework for communal life. In North Africa and Spain, the *nagid* (prince) was the head of the community. Later during the Middle Ages, communal leadership in the Franco-German region was exercised by rabbinic authorities, and daily existence was regulated by the *halakhah*. As in Babylonia, a wide range of institutions dealt with the aspects of the community as a whole, and taxes were raised to provide for a wide range of needs such as ransoming captives, providing hospitality to Jewish visitors, visiting the sick, caring for the elderly, collecting dowries for poor brides, maintaining widows, and supervising baths. As elsewhere in the Jewish world, the focus of the Jewish community was the synagogue, which served as the center for Jewish worship and study.

To regulate Jewish life, *takkanot ha-kahal* (communal statutes) were stipulated by the community's constitution. These were amplified by special ordinances and enactments. To ensure their enforcement, a *bet din* (court) was presided over by a *dayyanim* (panel of judges). In certain cases they excommunicated individuals or, in the case of Jews who informed on fellow Jews, they passed sentences of death. The community's *parnas* (head) was recognized by secular or Church authorities as the representative of the Jewish people. He and the local rabbi were frequently designated as *Magister Judaeorum* (Master of the Jews) or *Judenbischof* (Bishop of the Jews).

From the fourteenth century, Polish Jewry gained dominance in Eastern Europe, and communal autonomy was often invested in the Jewish community of a central town which had responsibility for smaller communities in the region. In Poland-Lithuania the Council of the Four Lands functioned as a Jewish parliament. By contrast, in the Ottoman Empire, authority was vested in a chief rabbi, who was recognized as the Jewish community's representative. Each province of the Empire had its own chief rabbi, and in Egypt this office replaced the *nagid*.

With the advent of the *Haskalah* (Enlightenment) in the nineteenth century, the traditional pattern of Jewish life was transformed. Previously Jews had been unable to opt out of the community. However, with full civil rights, Jews became members of the wider society and membership in the Jewish community was voluntary. In modern times Jews adjusted communal life to contemporary demands throughout the Diaspora, and in Israel new forms of association emerged. In contrast with previous centuries, in which Jewish religious life was uniform in character, the community has fragmented into a number of differing religious groupings, each with its own character.

At the far right of the religious spectrum, traditional Orthodoxy has attempted to preserve the religious beliefs and practices of the Jewish faith. From the late eighteenth century, Orthodox Judaism opposed religious reforms brought about by the Enlightenment and the innovations advanced by Reform Judaism. In essence, Orthodoxy is synonymous with rabbinic Judaism as it evolved through the ages. Orthodox Jewry accepts the doctrine of *Torah MiSinai* (the belief that God revealed the Torah to Moses on Mount Sinai), and the process of rabbinic expansion of biblical law as guided by God's will.

From the very beginning of the modern period, Orthodox Jews rejected the values of the *Haskalah* and proclaimed a ban of excommunication against reformers. Such an approach was advocated by Mosheh Sofer of Pressburg and was characteristic of Hungarian Orthodoxy as well as Eastern European Jewry. In addition, it found expression in the anti-Zionist *Agudat Israel* movement. Other Orthodox leaders, however, sought to integrate traditional Judaism and modern values. Such figures as Samson Raphael Hirsch, Azriel Hildesheimer, and members of the Breuer and Carlebach families formed the Neo-Orthodox movement from which centrist Orthodoxy subsequently emerged in the West. A similar development occurred in Eastern Europe and can be traced from Elijah Gaon of Vilna, Hayyim of Volozhin, and the Berlin and Soloveichik families to Isaac Jacob

Reines and Abraham Isaac Kook.

In the United States the Orthodox movement underwent enormous growth with the arrival of Orthodox scholars, heads of *yeshivot* and Hasidic leaders during the first half of the twentieth century. From 1944 *Torah Umesorah* organized a network of Hebrew day schools and *yeshivot* throughout the country. Today there are about forty *yeshivot* for advanced talmudic studies. The most important Orthodox rabbinic institutions are Yeshivah University in New York and the Hebrew Theological College in Chicago. The largest Orthodox synagogue body is the Union of Orthodox Jewish Congregations of America. As elsewhere, Orthodoxy in the United States is divided into two distinct groups: traditionalists and modernists.

The institutions of Orthodox traditionalists include: the Union of Orthodox Rabbis, the Rabbinic Alliance, and *Agudat Israel*. Modern Orthodoxy's religious leadership, on the other hand, is found in the Rabbinical Council of America. Elsewhere in the Diaspora Orthodox Judaism constitutes the largest religious body. In France, for example, several traditional *yeshivot* have emerged alongside the old-fashioned Ecole Rabbinique. In Great Britain a large network of congregations is maintained by the United Synagogue. Parallel with this body is the Federation of Synagogues and the Spanish and Portuguese Jews Congregation. On the traditional right is the Union of Orthodox Hebrew Congregations and the *yeshivah* community of Gateshead.

In Israel, Orthodoxy is the formally recognized religious body of the State. Rabbinical courts exercise exclusive jurisdiction in matters of personal status and Orthodox religious judges are presided over by the two Chief Rabbis. At the local level Orthodox religious councils cater to religious needs: the provision of ritual baths, burial facilities, registration of marriages, care of synagogues, and the promotion of religious education. In addition, a state religious school system run on Orthodox lines exists alongside the state school system. Within the government Orthodox religious parties represent both religious Zionists and the non-Zionist *Agudat* camp.

Within the Orthodox establishment, Hasidism plays an important role. Founded by the Baal Shem Tov (Israel ben Eleazer) in the eighteenth century as a reaction against arid rabbinism, the Hasidic movement spread to Southern Poland, the Ukraine, and Lithuania. This popular mystical movement was initially condemned by Orthodox leaders such as the Gaon of Vilna. Eventually, however, it became a major force in Jewish life. Prior to World War II hundreds of Hasidic dynasties flourished in Eastern Europe, but after the Holocaust most of the remaining leaders escaped to Israel and the United States. Today the best known groups are (named after their towns of origin): Belz, Bobova, Gur, Klausenburg-Zanz, Lubavich, Satmar and Vizhnits. Each of these groups preserves its traditions, including a distinctive type of dress worn by noblemen in the eighteenth century. Like the Orthodox generally, the Hasidim rigidly adhere to traditional Jewish observances as contained in the *Code of Jewish Law.*

Moving to the center of the religious spectrum, Conservative Judaism constitutes one of the major developments in modern Jewish life. Founded by Zacharias Frankel in the middle of the nineteenth century, it advocates a middle of the road stance in which traditional Jewish law is observed, but modified according to contemporary needs. According to Frankel, Judaism should be understood as an evolving religious system. In the United States this ideology was propounded by the Jewish Theological Seminary. Later its president, Solomon Schechter, founded the United Synagogue as the movement's lay organization.

From 1940–72 the Seminary was headed by Louis Finkelstein; during this time a West Coast affiliate of the Seminary (The University of Judaism) was established in Los Angeles. Through its rabbinical body and its synagogual association, the movement grew in strength and founded a variety of innovative institutions including a camping program, radio and TV programs, Solomon Schechter Day Schools, and New York's Jewish Museum. In 1972 Finkelstein was succeeded by Gerson D. Cohen who

introduced far reaching changes, including the ordination of
women. By 1985, 830 congregations were affiliated to the United
Synagogue of America, which had a membership of 1,250,000.
Elsewhere, the movement is represented by the World Council
of Synagogues.

An offshoot of the Conservative movement, Reconstructionist
Judaism, has also made an important impact on Jewish life. This
new religious body was founded by Mordecai Kaplan who rejected
supernaturalism and instead propounded a new view of Judaism.
Currently, Reconstructionist Judaism has its headquarters at the
Rabbinical College in Pennsylvania; affiliated congregations are
organized in the Federation of Reconstructionist Congregations.

On the left of the religious spectrum is Reform Judaism. At the
beginning of the nineteenth century, the communal leader Israel
Jacobson initiated a program of educational and liturgical reform.
Following this initiative, Reform Temples were established in
Germany and elsewhere. The central aim of the early Reformers
was to adapt Jewish worship to contemporary aesthetic standards.
For these innovators, the informality of the traditional service
seemed foreign and undignified, and they therefore insisted on
greater decorum, more participation in prayer, a choir and hymns
as well as alterations in prayers and the length of the service.
Despite the criticisms of the Orthodox, the Reform movement
underwent considerable growth and, during the nineteenth century, a series of Reform synods took place in Europe.

In the United States Reform Judaism first appeared in
Charleston, South Carolina, in 1824; in subsequent years
German immigrants founded a number of congregations
throughout the country. Under the leadership of Isaac Mayer
Wise the first Conference of American Reform Rabbis took
place in Philadelphia in 1869; this was followed in 1873 by the
founding of the Union of American Hebrew Congregations.
Two years later Wise established the Hebrew Union College,
the first American rabbinical seminary. In 1885 the principles of
the first Reform movement were formulated by a group of rabbis in the Pittsburgh Platform. In 1889 the Central Conference

of American Rabbis was established with Isaac Mayer Wise as president. Dissatisfaction with the Pittsburgh Platform led to the adoption of a more traditionalist position (the Columbus Platform) in 1937. In recent years Reform Judaism has undergone further development: by 1980, 739 congregations were affiliated with the Union of American Hebrew Congregations; during the latter half of the twentieth century the Jewish Institute of Religion in New York combined with the Hebrew Union College and branches were established in Los Angeles and Jerusalem. Elsewhere Reform Judaism is represented in Africa, Asia, Australia, and Europe; these congregations are affiliated with the World Union for Progressive Judaism.

A more radical branch of contemporary Jewish life—Humanistic Judaism—was founded in Detroit, Michigan, in the 1960s by Sherwin Wine, a Reform rabbi. This new movement now numbers about 40,000 members in the United States, Israel, Europe and beyond. Distancing itself from all other branches of Judaism, the movement extols the humanistic dimensions of the faith. On the basis of this ideology, Jewish holidays and life-cycle events have been reinterpreted so as to emphasize their humanistic characteristics. In addition, Humanistic Jews insist that traditional Jewish beliefs must be reformulated in the light of scientific knowledge. Promoting a secular life style, this new conception of Judaism seeks to adjust the Jewish tradition to modernity.

Open Judaism

As we have seen, the contemporary Jewish community is deeply divided into a variety of sub-groups with different and competing ideologies. Arguably, a vibrant approach to communal relations for the twenty-first century should acknowledge the nature of such pluralism and encourage tolerance across religious lines. In contrast with the rigid authoritarianism of the past, such an attitude would grant each member of the Jewish community an inalienable right to religious autonomy. In other words, the freedom of each individual Jew would end only where another person's freedom began. The central feature of this new approach is the principle of personal liberty. Such a concept of Jewish existence would grant all Jews the right to select those elements of the tradition which they find religiously significant. No one—no rabbi or rabbinical body—should seek to decide which observances are acceptable.

This notion of Judaism as an amorphous religious system can perhaps best be illustrated by the analogy of the supermarket. If we imagine Jewish civilization as a vast emporium with articles from the past arranged in long aisles and individual Jews with shopping carts, this new concept of Judaism would encourage all Jews to select from the shelves those items they wish to possess. Orthodox Jews would leave with overflowing carts; Conservative and Reconstructionist Jews would depart with less; Reform and Humanistic Jews with even fewer commodities; and non-affili-ated Jews with hardly any. The image of the supermarket em-phasizes the non-judgmental character of such an approach to Jewish existence.

Just as when shopping each person is able to make selections without the fear of coercion or criticism, so within this open model of Judaism individuals would be allowed to decide for themselves which features of the Jewish heritage they desire to incorporate. Shoppers in such a Jewish market-place would be free agents, charting their own personal paths through the tradition.

Such openness as a solution to Jewish living in the twenty-first century is not conceived as an alternative denomination along-side the various branches of contemporary Judaism. It is rather an ideology which can be embraced by members of all religious groupings as well as the unaffiliated. Traditionally-minded Jews, for example, who are supporters of Orthodox or Hasidic Judaism could be advocates of this model of Judaism as long as they were willing to grant legitimacy to all modes of Jewish living, includ-ing the most lax. For such individuals, traditional Judaism would provide the most satisfactory and religiously compelling form of Judaism. But as followers of this new philosophy they would ac-cept that alternative forms of the faith could be equally satisfying for others. Hence, there would be a conscious recognition of the validity of all Jewish options.

Turning to non-Orthodox alternatives, those who accept this new vision of Judaism would similarly acknowledge the validity of patterns of belief and practice other than their own. Thus Reform Jews, while not concurring with Orthodox, Conservative, Reconstructionist or Humanistic interpretations of the faith would respect the choices of those who subscribe to these systems. Conversely the same would apply to Conservative, Reconstructionist, and Humanistic Jews when confronted with the views of others. And as far as non-affiliated Jews are concerned, the members of the various non-Orthodox movements who accept this vision would be committed to a policy of tolerance of those who had deliberately sought to distance themselves from organized religion.

What is needed, in my opinion, is a revolution in Jewish thinking. From post-Enlightenment times to the present the various religious subgroups in the community have been anxious to stress that they are the legitimate heirs of biblical and rabbinic Judaism. As far as Orthodoxy is concerned, traditionalists have subscribed to the belief that Orthodox Judaism constitutes the only true form of Judaism. Orthodoxy is thus perceived as the only legitimate expression of the Jewish faith—it constitutes the true center of Jewish religiosity whereas the various non-Orthodox movements are viewed as heretical.

Non-Orthodox movements, however, are less exclusivist in orientation—they generally do not condemn other expressions of Judaism. Rather, they propose an inclusivist conception of the different forms of post-Enlightenment Judaism in which other Jewish religious systems are included but as less suitable for the modern age than their own. This new vision of Judaism, however, calls for a reversal of this conceptualization. Instead of placing any particular movement at the center of the various Jewish subgroups, they are all arranged inside the circle of Judaism without any differentiation made about their respective claims. All are perceived as valid for contemporary Jews.

Such an altered vision of the various religious groupings is based on a revised understanding of Divine Reality. In the past, Jewish theologians and philosophers stressed that God is unknowable: He is the Infinite, who lies beyond human conceptualization. Such philosophers as Moses Maimonides formulated the doctrine of negative attributes to explain such a theory. In his view, God as He is in Himself cannot be known. Scripture reveals God's actions rather than his essence. For the kabbalists, God is the *Ayn Sof,* who lies beyond human comprehension. The unknowable source of all, He manifests himself in the cosmos through a series of divine emanations. Drawing on these insights, this new conceptualization of Judaism emphasizes the total unknowability of the Divine. Yet, like previous Jewish theories, this new philosophy of Judaism is theologically non-dogmatic in character.

Such a reconstruction of Judaism acknowledges the fact that each branch of the Jewish faith affirms its own superiority—all rival claims are viewed as misapprehensions. From a pluralistic perspective, however, this new vision of Judaism asserts that there is simply no means by which it is possible to ascertain which, if any, of these spiritual Jewish paths reflect the true nature of Ultimate Reality. In the end, the varied truth-claims of Orthodox, Conservative, Reform, Reconstructionist, and Humanistic Judaism must be regarded as human icons that are constructed within specific social and cultural contexts. In the light of a theological shift from absolutism to religious pluralism, it no longer makes sense for the various branches of the tradition to champion their interpretations of the Jewish religion. Instead, they should be respectful of the opinions of others. As a remedy for the bitter divisions that beset contemporary Jewish life, this new approach to the tradition offers the hope of unity beyond diversity for the next millennium.

Chapter 14.

WORSHIP

Throughout the history of the nation, Jews have turned to God for comfort and support. For the Jewish people, prayer has served as the means by which they have expressed their joys, sorrows, and hopes. In ancient times the Tabernacle and the Temple served as the focus of religious life; subsequently the synagogue became the central place for public worship. Throughout the year believers gathered together to recite the traditional liturgy. In the modern world Jews continue to worship God, yet there has been a concerted attempt to reinterpret the nature of Jewish spirituality.

Reform Worship

As a child I attended religious services every week. On the

Sabbath, my classmates and I worshipped in the Sanctuary of the Temple where the rabbi led us in prayer. In addition, my parents took me to Temple for the High Holiday services. On Rosh Hashanah (New Year), I attended services only in the morning, but on Yom Kippur (Day of Atonement) I stayed at the Temple in the afternoon as well. These religious services were supplemented by worship services for numerous festivals including *Passover, Sukkot, Shavuot, Purim*, and *Hanukkah*. The Jewish calendar thus served as the framework for Jewish prayer in Reform Judaism.

The movement, however, stressed the importance of prayer in other religious contexts. The circumcision ceremony, for example, includes numerous prayers to be recited by those in attendance. At the beginning of the service the rabbi prays for the life of the child:

> Our God and God of our fathers, sustain this child in life and health and let him be known in the household of Israel by the name…. Cause the parents to rejoice in the child whom Thou hast entrusted to their care. As he has been brought into the covenant of Abraham, so may he be led to the study of Thy Torah, enter into a marriage worthy of Thy blessing, and live a life enriched with good deeds.[1]

The prayer for naming a child expresses thanksgiving for God's graciousness:

> O Lord, how bountiful are Thy mercies unto us! Strength and sustenance, joy and contentment, love and companionship come from Thee and Thou dost crown our happiness with the supreme gift of parenthood.[2]

Other life-cycle events are similarly marked by communal worship. On the occasion of a betrothal, the rabbi prays:

> Loving Father, grant Thy blessing to…and…, who come into

Thy sanctuary to thank Thee for the gift of their love. They seek Thee, O God, in joy, and they pray that Thou wilt look with favor upon their union. Hopefully they look forward to the day when, under Thy protection, they may establish a home within the Jewish community.[3]

During the marriage service, the rabbi recites the traditional seven blessings in the presence of those assembled:

Blessed art Thou, O Lord our God, Ruler of the Universe, Who hast created all things for Thy glory.

Blessed art Thou, O Lord our God, Ruler of the Universe, Creator of man.

Blessed art Thou, O Lord our God, Ruler of the Universe, Who hast fashioned us in Thine image and hast established marriage for the fulfillment and perpetuation of life in accordance with Thy holy purpose. Blessed art Thou, O Lord, Creator of man.

Blessed art Thou, O Lord our God, Ruler of the Universe, Who art the source of all gladness and joy. Through Thy grace we attain affection, companionship, and peace. Grant, O Lord, that the love which unites this bridegroom and bride may grow in abiding happiness. May their family life be ennobled through their devotion to the faith of Israel. May there be peace in their home, quietness and confidence in their hearts. May they be sustained by Thy comforting presence in the midst of our people and by Thy promise of salvation for all mankind. Blessed art Thou, O Lord, Who dost unite bridegroom and bride in holy joy.[4]

At silver and golden wedding anniversaries, the rabbi publicly thanks God for his mercies:

Eternal God and Father! In the fullness of this day's joy, we turn our hearts in praise and gratitude to Thee. We thank Thee for Thy favor which has preserved and sustained this happy couple and permitted them to reach this hour.[5]

The Reform liturgy also contains prayers for the sick. Here the rabbi prays for their return to health:

> Heavenly Father, source of all blessings and mankind's ever firm support, we turn to Thee in prayer as our hearts are filled with concern for the welfare of…for whose recovery his (her) dear ones yearn. May it be Thy will, Fount of strength and healing, that he (she) be restored to health and be enabled to return to the circle of family life and love.[6]

Finally, at funeral services the congregation prays:

> O God, full of compassion. Thou who dwellest on high! Grant perfect rest unto the soul of… who has departed from this world. Lord of mercy, bring him (her) into Thy presence and let his (her) soul be bound up in the bond of eternal life. Be Thou his (her) possession, and may his (her) repose be peace.[7]

These few examples illustrate the centrality of worship in the life of the Reform Jewish community. On Sabbaths, holidays and life-cycle commemorations, Jews gather together to celebrate these events and ask God for his providential care. Reform Judaism has therefore continued the ancient pattern of communal worship, frequently including prayers from the traditional prayer book. For believers, God is a past and present reality whose intervention into daily life is a source of comfort and hope.

Prayer

From biblical times, prayer has served a central role in the life of the Jewish nation. In the Torah the patriarchs frequently turned to God for assistance. Abraham, for example, begged God to spare Sodom since he knew that by destroying the entire population He would destroy the righteous as well as the guilty. (Gen. 18:23–33) At Beth-el, Jacob vowed: "If God will be with me, and will keep me in this way that I go, and will give me bread to eat, and raiment to put on...then shall the Lord be my God." (Gen. 28:20–1). Later Moses, too, prayed to God. After Israel had made a golden calf to worship, he begged God to forgive them for this sin. (Exod. 32:31–2)

Joshua also turned to God for help. When the Israelites went to conquer the city of Ai, their attack was repulsed; in desperation Joshua prayed to God for help in defeating Israel's enemies. (Jos. 7:7) Later, in the prophetic books the prophets also offered prayers to God, as did the Psalmists and others. This tradition of prayer continued after the canonization of Scripture, and as a consequence prayer has constantly animated the Jewish spirit—through personal encounter with the Divine, Jews have been consoled, sustained, and uplifted.

Scripture relates that Moses made a portable shrine (sanctuary) following God's instructions. (Exod. 25–7) This structure traveled with the ancient Israelites in the desert and it was placed in the centre of the camp in an open courtyard 1000 cubits by 50 cubits in size. The fence surrounding it consisted of wooden pillars from which a cloth curtain was suspended. Located in the eastern half of the courtyard, the sanctuary measured 30 cubits by 10 cubits. At its end stood the Holy of Holies, which was separated by a veil hanging on five wooden pillars on which were woven images of the cherubim. Inside the Holy of Holies was the Ark of the Covenant, the table on which the shewbread (twelve loaves) was placed, the incense altar, and the *menorah* (candelabrum).

Eventually this structure was superseded by the Temple, which was built by Solomon in Jerusalem in the tenth century B.C.E. Standing within a royal compound, it also consisted of the palace, a Hall of Judgment, the Hall of Cedars, and a house for Solomon's wife. The Temple was 60 cubits long, 20 cubits wide, and 30 cubits high. The main part of the Temple was surrounded by a three-storey building divided into chambers with

storeys connected by trapdoors. These were probably storerooms
for Temple treasures. The main building consisted of an inner
room—the Holy of Holies—on the west, and an outer room
measuring 20 by 40 cubits on the east. Within the Holy of
Holies stood the Ark which contained the Two Tablets of the
Covenant with the Ten Commandments. In the outer room
stood an incense altar, the table for the shewbread, and ten
lampstands made of gold. In front of the Temple stood a bronze
basin supported by twelve bronze cattle. A bronze altar also
stood in the courtyard, which was used for various sacrifices.

From the time of Solomon's reign, the Temple served as the
site for prayer and the offering of sacrifices. Twice daily—in the
morning and afternoon—the priests offered prescribed sacrifices
while Levites chanted psalms. On Sabbaths and festivals additional services were added to this daily ritual. At some stage it
became customary to include other prayers along with the recitation of the Ten Commandments and the *Shema* (Deut 6:4–9,
11, 13–21; Numb. 15:37–41) in the Temple service.

With the destruction of the Second Temple in 70 C.E., sacrificial offerings were replaced by the prayer service in the synagogue,
referred to by the rabbis as *avodah she-ba-lev* (service of the heart).
To enhance uniformity, they introduced fixed periods for daily
prayer which corresponded with the times sacrifices had been offered in the Temple: the morning prayer *(shaharit)* and afternoon
prayer *(minhah)* correspond with the daily and afternoon sacrifice;
evening prayer *(maariv)* corresponds with the nightly burning
of fats and limbs. By the completion of the *Talmud* in the sixth
century, the essential features of the synagogue service were established, but it was only in the eighth century that the first prayer
book was composed by Rav Amram, Gaon of Sura.

In the order of service, the first central feature is the *Shema*. In
accordance with the commandment: "You shall talk of them when
you lie down and when you rise" (Deut. 6:7), Jews are obliged to
recite this prayer during the morning and evening service. The
first section (Deut. 6:4–9) begins with the phrase *Shema Yisrael*
("Hear, O Israel"). This verse teaches the unity of God, and the

paragraph emphasizes the duty to love God, meditate on his commandments, and impress them on one's children.

In addition, it contains laws regarding the *tefillin* and the *mezuzah*. The *tefillin* consists of two black leather straps on the arm and forehead with boxes on them containing scriptural passages, in accordance with the commandment requiring that "You shall bind them as a sign upon your hand, and they shall be as frontlets between your eyes" (Deut. 6:8) They are worn by men during morning prayer except on the Sabbath and festivals. The *mezuzah* consists of a piece of parchment containing two paragraphs of the *Shema* which are placed into a case and put on the right-hand side of an entrance. Male Jews wear an undergarment with fringes (the smaller *tallit*) and a larger *tallit* (prayer shawl) for morning services. The prayer shawl is customarily made of silk or wool with black or blue stripes with fringes (*tzitzit*) at each of the four corners.

The second major feature of the synagogue service is the *Shemoneh Esreh* (Eighteen Benedictions or *Amidah*). These prayers were composed over a long period of time and received their full form in the second century. They consist of eighteen benedictions plus an additional prayer dealing with heretics. These benedictions consist of the following:

1. Praise for God who remembers the deeds of the patriarchs on behalf of the community.

2. Acknowledgement of God's power in sustaining the living and his ability to revive the dead.

3. Praise of God's holiness.

4. Request for understanding and knowledge.

5. Plea for God's assistance to return to him in perfect repentance.

6. Supplication for forgiveness for sin.

7. Request for deliverance from affliction and persecution.

8. Petition for bodily health.

9. Request for God to bless agricultural produce so as to relieve want.

10. Supplication for the ingathering of the exiles.

11. Plea for the rule of justice under righteous leaders.

12. Request for the reward of the righteous and the pious.

13. Plea for the rebuilding of Jerusalem.

14. Supplication for the restoration of the dynasty of David.

15. Plea for God to accept prayer in mercy and favor.

16. Supplication for the restoration of the divine service in the Temple.

17. Thanksgiving for God's mercies.

18. Request for granting the blessing of peace to Israel.

On some occasions a number of additional prayers are added to these benedictions.

From the earliest times, the Torah was read in public gatherings; later regular readings of the Torah on Sabbaths and festivals were instituted. In Babylonia the entire Torah was read during a yearly cycle; in Palestine it was completed once every three years. The Torah itself is divided into fifty-four sections, each of which is known as the "order" or "section" (*sidrah*). Each section is subdivided into portions. Before the reading of the Torah in the synagogue, the Ark is opened. The number of men who participate in the reading of the Torah varies. In former times those who were called up to read the Torah read a section of the weekly portion; subsequently an expert in Torah reading was appointed to recite the entire *sidrah*, and those called up recited blessings instead. The first three people to be called up are: *Cohen* (priest), *Levi* (priest), and *Yisrael* (member of the congregation).

After a reading of the Torah, a section from the prophetic books (*Haftarah*) is recited. The person who is called up for the last *parashah* of the *sidrah* reads the *Haftarah*; he is known as the *maftir*. The section from the Prophets parallels the content of the *sidrah*. Once the Torah scroll is replaced in the Ark, a sermon is delivered it is usually based on the *sidrah* of the week.

Another important feature of the synagogue service is the *kaddish* prayer. Written in Aramaic, it takes several forms in the prayer book and expresses the hope for universal peace under the

Kingdom of God. There are five main forms:

1. Half *kaddish,* recited by the reader between sections of the service.
2. Full *kaddish,* recited by the reader at the end of a major section of the service.
3. Mourners' *kaddish,* recited by mourners after the service.
4. Scholar's *kaddish,* recited after the reading of talmudic midrashic passages in the presence of a *minyan* (quorum).
5. Expanded form of the mourners' *kaddish,* recited at the cemetery after a burial.

Since the thirteenth century the three daily services have concluded with the recitation of the *Alenu* prayer which proclaims God as king over humankind. In all likelihood it was introduced by Rav in the third century as an introduction to the *Malhuyot,* the section recited as part of the *musaf* service for Rosh Hashanah. During the Middle Ages this prayer was the death-song of Jewish martyrs. The first part proclaims God as king of Israel; the second anticipates the time when idolatry will disappear and all human beings will acknowledge God as king of the universe.

The traditional liturgy remained essentially the same until the Enlightenment. At this time reformers in Central Europe altered the worship service and introduced new prayers into the liturgy in conformity with current cultural and spiritual developments. Influenced by Protestant Christianity, these innovators decreed that the service should be shortened and conducted in the vernacular as well as in Hebrew. In addition they introduced Western melodies to the accompaniment of a choir and organ and replaced the chanting of the Torah with the reading of the Torah portion. Prayers viewed as anachronistic were eliminated, and prayers of a particularistic nature were changed so that they were more universalistic in scope.

The Conservative Movement also produced prayer books in line with its ideology. In general the Conservative liturgy follows the traditional *siddur* (prayer book) except for several differences:

(1) prayers for the restoration of sacrifice were changed; (2) the early morning benediction thanking God that the worshipper was not made a woman was altered; (3) prayers for peace were changed to include all humanity; (4) in general the *yekum purkah* prayer for schools and scholars in Babylonia was omitted; (5) priests did not usually recite the priestly benediction; (6) the *Amidah* was not usually repeated except on the High Holy Days. Amongst Reconstructionists Jews, revision to the traditional *siddur* was similarly made to reflect the ideology of the movement. Humanistic Judaism, however, has radically altered the nature of the Jewish liturgy, eliminating the use of God language altogether. Even though Humanistic Jews celebrate the major festivals, they do so without any reference to a supernatural Deity.

In recent times all groups across the Jewish spectrum have produced new liturgies (such as those that commemorate Holocaust Remembrance Day, Israel Independence Day, and Jerusalem Reunification Day). Moreover, a wide range of occasional liturgies exist for camps, youth groups, and *havurot* (informal prayer groups). Among non-Orthodox denominations there is a growing emphasis on more egalitarian liturgies with gender-free language and an increasing democratic sense of responsibility. Thus prayer and worship continue to be of vital importance to the Jewish people, yet there have occurred a variety of alterations to its nature within all branches of the Jewish faith.

Reflections on Jewish Worship

As we have seen, prayer and worship have played a fundamental role in the life of the Jewish nation. From biblical times to the present, Jews have expressed their deepest longings and desires in prayer. In times of distress, they have turned to God for comfort and help. Yet, there are serious questions that need to be raised about the nature of such prayer. In the light of the tragedies of the twentieth century, does it make sense to pray to

God for divine assistance as Jews did in ancient times? In the Book of Exodus, for example, the Jewish people turned to God for deliverance from the hand of Pharaoh. In response to Moses' supplication, God assured him that the Jewish people would be delivered from oppression and would eventually inherit the Promised Land.

Is the notion of divine causality, on which such a conception is based, plausible? In recent years a number of Jewish theologians have stressed that the concept of divine intervention is no longer viable. Deeply disturbed by God's seeming inaction during the Holocaust, they argue that it is a mistake to believe in a God who acts in history. In his theological study of the Holocaust, *Tremendum*, Arthur A. Cohen argued that God does not directly act in history. In his view, it is a mistake to long for an interruptive God who can intervene magically in the course of human affairs. If there were such a God, he stated, the created order would be an extension of God's will rather than an independent domain brought about by God's creative love.

Arguing along similar lines, the Reform rabbi Steven Jacobs outlined a number of central areas which need to be considered in light of the Nazi onslaught of the Jews. In his view, Jewish theology must be reformulated in a radically new fashion:

> What is now demanded in the realm of theological integrity is a notion of a Deity compatible with the reality of radical evil at work and at play in our world, a notion which, also, admits of human freedom for good or evil because he or she could not act. To continue to affirm the historically traditional notions of faith in God as presented by both biblical and rabbinic traditions...is to ignore those who, like myself, continue to feel the pain of family loss, yet want to remain committed to Jewish survival...a possible source of divine affirmation, to the degree to which such affirmation is either desired or acknowledged as desired, lies in the concept of "limited Deity" who could neither choose nor reject action during the dark years of 1933 (39)-1945, who could not have responded to those humanly created and crafted processes of destruction....[8]

According to Jacobs and others, God is not a causal agent—yet it would be an error to think that he is aloof from the created order. Rather, God is present in human history to inspire those who seek his guidance.

For these writers, God continues to be the focus of human aspiration, yet He does not directly intervene in response to his people's prayers. Rather, He is there to inspire the faithful. In the light of this altered understanding of God's actions, Jewish prayer can still be relevant in the modern world. Even if God does not directly answer supplications that are addressed to Him, He can still animate the human spirit. Acting in this way, He allows full scope of human potential. This new religious understanding of Divine Presence can serve an essential feature of Judaism for the twenty-first century. In place of dogmatic formulations of the nature of the Godhead, this conception of Deity would allow Jews to continue to worship God without assuming that the course of history can be influenced through intercessory prayer.

Chapter 15.

EDUCATION

Through the centuries, Jewish education has been paramount in the lives of the Jewish people. Scripture decrees that God's precepts should be taught to the nation, especially children. The religious revival introduced by Ezra in the fifth century B.C.E. centered on the regular reading of the Torah. During the rabbinic period, there was a comprehensive education system for Jewish boys. In the Babylonian academies Jewish scholarship reached great heights; subsequently *yeshivot* were created throughout the Jewish world which carried on the traditions of Jewish study. In modern times the traditional pattern of Jewish education has been radically altered. Yet, despite such changes, all religious movements are committed to perpetuating Jewish learning.

Reform Religion School

In the Temple I attended as a child, religious education began at a very early age. Once a week, I was taken to classes on Sunday morning; there Jewish children from Reform homes throughout the city were divided into groups. In the first-year class we were told about biblical heroes. We were given crayons and paper and told to draw pictures of Abraham, Isaac, and Jacob, as well as Moses and the kings of Israel. The biblical stories were supplemented by information about the major Jewish festivals. Again, we were told to create pictures or make objects connected with these holidays. Before Hanukkah, for example, we made *menorahs* out of clay and painted them vivid colors.

Children's services were also conducted on Sunday, led by the rabbi. After class we flooded into the sanctuary, where a shortened version of the worship service was held; the rabbi read the prayers and preached a brief sermon, emphasizing the importance of loyalty to the tradition. Our teachers' aim was to encourage us to be proud of our Jewish heritage and to commit ourselves to the Jewish faith. Judaism, they stressed, extolled the highest ethical ideals. Repeatedly they encouraged us to integrate such moral standards into our everyday lives.

At the age of thirteen, a significant number of boys prepared for their *bar mitzvah*. Prior to this event, they were given lessons by a Hebrew teacher—they practiced reading their Torah portion as well as various prayers and memorized their *bar mitzvah* speech. Several years later, confirmation took place. This process of formal education was designed to provide a basis for an understanding of Judaism, as interpreted within the Reform movement. Given the emphasis on the prophetic tradition combined with universalistic ideals, Reform Judaism was conceived as a religious system emphasizing ethical standards. Worship services were intended to reinforce the commitment to moral ideals within a monotheistic framework.

As a supplement to religion school, summer camp similarly sought to guide campers to an appreciation of the Jewish heritage. At every meal prayers were recited, and on the Sabbath a service was held outdoors. Assisted by camp counselors, the director of the camp sought to instill an attachment to the Jewish way of life. Around the camp fire we sang Jewish songs. Many of the evening events had Jewish themes. Occasionally the rabbi came to conduct Sabbath services.

For many children, weekend religion school as well as summer camp had little impact. Compared with ordinary school, religion classes were of minimal significance. Attending worship services was nothing more than a duty to be performed. Parents deposited their children at the Temple, and collected them several hours later without any curiosity about its impact. *Bar mitzvah* and confirmation were formal *rites de passage,* lacking spiritual significance for either children or parents.

In short, for most students the Reform educational process was devoid of meaning.

There were some students, however, who were deeply affected by what they learned in religion school. For them, Reform Jewish education provided the first steps toward an appreciation of Judaism as it had developed through the ages. At the Hebrew Union College, there were students who had come to Judaism through Reform religion school as well as summer camp. Often, they had served as student officers in regional Jewish youth groups. Their determination to enter the rabbinate was based on these early experiences. Yet, it must be stressed that such individuals were unusual. The vast majority of students in Reform religion schools viewed their exposure to Judaism as a peripheral activity.

Critics of Reform religion school emphasize the insignificance of this exposure to Judaism, arguing that only an intensive Jewish education offers the basis for living a religiously Jewish life style. In their view, the study of the Bible, the Jewish liturgy, rabbinic sources, and the Talmud can prepare Jewish children for a Jewish lifestyle. Particularly among Orthodox Jews, the Reform educational system is bitterly denounced; in their view, it distorts the true nature of the Jewish faith and provides a rationalization for neglect of the tradition. From the Reform side, the traditional system of education is criticized for its irrelevance and antiquarian character. What is needed, reformers argue, is modernization, providing means of determining which elements of the past continue to have spiritual significance. Championing the principles of the *Haskalah*, Reform educators (from Israel Jacobson in the nineteenth century to the present) have insisted that an adequate school curriculum must include secular as well as Jewish subjects. The aim of Reform education is therefore to supplement secular education with religious instruction.

Jewish Education

According to Scripture, it is the responsibility of parents to educate their children. Thus Deuteronomy 6:7 proclaims: "And you shall teach them diligently to your children, and shall talk of them when you sit in your house, and when you walk by the way and when you lie down and when you rise." Further, the Hebrew Bible repeatedly refers to a father's obligation to tell his children about the Exodus:

> you may tell in the hearing of your son and of your son's son how I have made sport of the Egyptians and what signs I have done among them (Exod. 10:2)

> When your son asks you in the time to come, "What is the meaning of the statutes and the ordinances which the Lord our God has commanded you?" then you shall say to your son, "We were Pharaoh's slaves in Egypt, and the Lord brought us out of Egypt with a mighty hand." (Deut. 6:20–21)

Thus from the earliest period of Israelite history, the study of the Jewish heritage was of fundamental significance. For this reason Scripture contains frequent references to the process of study. The Book of Joshua, for example, declares: "This book of the law shall not depart out of your mouth, but you shall meditate on it day and night, that you may be careful to do according to all that is written in it." (Joshua 1:8) Again, the Book of Proverbs contains numerous references to education: "He who spares the rod hates his son" (Prov. 13:24); "Train up a child in the way he should go, and when he is old he will not depart from it." (Prov. 22:6)

When the Israelites returned from Babylonian exile, the Bible records that Ezra gathered the people and taught them the law (Neh. 8). When the nation heard his message, they were deeply moved and vowed to keep the religious practices and festivals of their ancestors, including the pilgrim festivals, the New Year celebrations, and the Day of Atonement. As the rabbis explained, it was Ezra who instituted the Torah reading on Monday and Thursday when the people went to local markets.

During the rabbinic period, sages continued this process of education. As Judah ben Tema stated: "Five years old [is the age] for [the study of] the Bible, ten years old for the Mishnah, thirteen for [the obligation to keep] the commandments, fifteen years old for *Gemara* (rabbinic commentary on the Mishnah)."[1] According to Jewish law, parents are obliged to begin a child's education at the earliest moment; as soon as a child begins to speak he must be taught the verse: "Moses commanded us a law, as a possession for the assembly of Jacob." (Deut. 33:4) In the first century C.E. Simeon ben Shetah founded schools and urged parents to send their sons to them.

However, it was Joshua ben Gamla in the first century C.E. who is credited with creating a formal system of education. About him the Talmud states: "May Joshua ben Gamla be remembered for good, for had it not been for him, the Torah would have been forgotten in Israel."[2] Prior to Joshua ben Gamla, only those with fathers were taught the tradition, whereas those without fathers were deprived of instruction. To remedy this situation, Joshua ben Gamla stated that teachers had to be engaged in each locality at the community's expense and that all children were to be given education. Later the Talmud stipulated the size of classes: one teacher was permitted to handle up to twenty-five students. If students exceeded this number, an assistant was to be hired. More than forty students required two teachers.

Even though the Talmud does not provide a comprehensive and systematic program of study, it emphasizes the importance of parental instructions: "One who does not teach his son an occupation, teaches him to be a brigand." Among the duties imposed on fathers is the obligation to teach their sons the Torah. As in Babylonia, such teaching occurred in the Palestinian academy. According to tradition, Johanan ben Zakkai arranged to have himself smuggled out of the city in a coffin. He was then brought before the Roman commander and requested permission to found a center of learning. This institution took the place of the Great Sanhedrin; subsequently other academies flourished under Johanan ben Zakkai's disciples. In the second century following the devastation of central and southern Palestine during the Bar Kochba revolt, many scholars emigrated and the Javneh academy was moved to Galilee.

In Babylonia, schools of higher learning were created in the first century C.E. In the next century, under the leadership of Rav Shila and Abba bar Abba, the academy of Nehardea became the Babylonian spiritual centre, maintaining contact with the Palestinian Jewish community. When Rav returned to Babylonia from Palestine, he founded another academy at Sura in 220 C.E. In 259 C.E. the Nehardea academy was destroyed; under Judah ben Ezekiel it was transferred to Pumbedita where it remained for the next five hundred years. From then it functioned in Baghdad until the thirteenth century. These academies attracted students from throughout the Jewish world. Twice a year, during the months of *Adar* and *Elul,* individual study sessions *(kallah)* were held for large audiences.

During the period between the completion of the *Talmud* in the sixth century C.E. and the Enlightenment, the majority of male Jews received some sort of education. This was generally limited to the study of sacred texts; however, in some periods secular subjects were also included. In twelfth- and thirteenth-century Spain, for example, Jewish scholars engaged in secular learning. In this context, the talmudist Joseph Ibn Aknin contended that there is no contradiction between studying sacred texts and such subjects as logic, rhetoric, arithmetic, geometry, astronomy, music, science, and philosophy.

Prior to Jewish emancipation, the typical pattern of Jewish education involved a teacher with a number of students who studied religious sources—this was known as a *heder*. Even though these study circles were not schools in the modern sense, they did have some parallels. Students were able to graduate from one teacher to another as they advanced in their education. In some areas there was a formally structured *Talmud Torah*, which had several classes. Here, too, the subjects of study were exclusively religious. Most students were exposed to several years of formal education before they went to work. Only a few were able to have an extensive educational training.

In the nineteenth century organized *yeshivot* (rabbinic academies) were established in Eastern Europe in such centers as Tels, Ponevezh, and Slobodka as well as at Hasidic centers. In these colleges students progressed from one level to another—the best students often went on to a lifetime of Torah study. Throughout the subject matter was the Talmud and Jewish law—secular studies were not allowed. With the emancipation of Jewry in the modern period, however, many Jews became proficient in other fields of study, including languages, mathematics, and the sciences.

In Western Europe new schools were founded which combined religious and secular learning. The Neo-Orthodox thinker Samson Raphael Hirsch formulated the principles of such an educational system in his *Torah im Derekh Erets*. Eventually even Eastern European *yeshivot* broadened their curriculum to include ethics as a result of the influence of the *Musar* (moral instruction) movement. The Alliance Israélite Francaise championed the combination of religious and secular studies in new schools in North Africa and the Middle East.

Once Jews were allowed to study at secular schools, there was a growing need for supplementary Jewish education. In most cases *heders* or *Talmud Torah* schools were held in the afternoon or on Sundays. In some cases Jewish day schools were created to provide a more extensive Jewish education. By the middle of the twentieth century, there was an increasing awareness that such supplementary Jewish education was insufficient, and the number of day schools proliferated. In the United States the Orthodox Torah-Meshorah day school network expanded from 100 schools prior to the Second World War to more than 600. In addition, both the Conservative and Reform movements established religious day schools. In other countries day schools have been encouraged by the Zionist movement. In Yiddish circles day schools were also founded, but most have either closed or amalgamated with other schools.

During the period of Emancipation, Non-Orthodox rabbinical seminaries were founded in the United States. Thus, in the last quarter of the nineteenth century, the Reform seminary, the Hebrew Union College, and the Conservative Jewish Theological Seminary were created on the pattern of their predecessors in Berlin and Breslau. At this time New York's Yeshiva University was founded on neo-Orthodox lines; its curriculum combines religious with secular studies. Eventually all these seminaries developed graduate schools in a wide range of fields including Jewish education, communal services, sacred music, biblical studies, and rabbinics. More recently, the Reconstructionist Seminary was founded in the 1960s, and at the end of the twentieth century the Humanistic rabbinical seminary was established. The Jewish Renewal movement has also ordained rabbis to serve its members.

Until the period of the Enlightenment, Jewish education was limited to the education of male Jews. However, as Jews assimilated into Western society, the education of women became a priority. Thus in 1917 Sara Schnirer, with the encouragement of a number of Orthodox rabbis, established the Beth Jacob Orthodox system, in which women were provided with an official educational program, although these institutions refused to teach Mishnah and Talmud. By contrast, the Stern College for Women in Yeshiva University provides a wide range of courses, including talmudic study. In the Conservative, Reconstructionist, Reform, Humanist, and Jewish Renewal movements, the education of women has been a fundamental principle and in the last few decades, all these religious bodies have ordained women as rabbis.

In recent years there has also been a large growth in traditional *yeshivot* for post-high school students, particularly in Israel and the United States. In addition, a considerable number of *yeshivah* graduates have gone on to spend several years studying in *kollels* (advanced institutes for Talmud study). In addition, Jewish studies have become an integral part of university and college studies since World War II. Throughout the world, Jewish studies departments have been established in which thousands of Jewish as well as non-Jewish students are able to take courses on a wide range of Jewish subjects.

Judaism in the Modern World

In previous centuries the aim of Jewish education was to indoctrinate children into the faith. In particular, boys and young men received a rigorous training in Hebraic study. At the earliest age male children learned the rudiments of Hebrew; they were then exposed to the Hebrew Scriptures. This was followed by study of the Mishnah, *midrash* and Talmud. In ancient times, Jewish study took place in academies in Palestine and Babylonia. Later *yeshivot* were established throughout the Jewish world. Today the Orthodox support rabbinic academies modeled on similar lines, in which young men follow the traditional course of Jewish study. In Israel, the United States, Europe, and elsewhere distinguished Orthodox scholars uphold the educational standards of the past.

Despite such an adherence to traditional ways, there has been a revolution in Jewish education. No longer are girls and young women segregated from their male counterparts. In addition, the vast majority of Jewish youth attend secular schools—their exposure to Judaism is therefore limited to weekend religion school and bar and bat mitzvah training. This shift in emphasis has resulted in widespread ignorance of the Jewish heritage, and in reaction some Jewish educators have pressed for the establishment of Jewish day schools. In Israel Jewish youth attend mixed public schools, but emphasis is also given to traditional Jewish sources.

This shift in orientation calls for a new conception of Jewish education for the modern world. No longer do Jews live in self-imposed ghettos with limited exposure to outside influences. Even the strictly Orthodox are unable to isolate themselves entirely from the non-Jewish world. In such changed circumstances, it is unproductive to separate Jewish learning from secular knowledge. Instead—as is the case amongst non-Orthodox families as well as the unaffiliated—there is a universal recognition that Jewish children must be exposed to a broad curriculum, and that young men and women must receive an education that trains them for employment.

In such a context, knowledge about Judaism must be supplementary in character, providing resources to enrich one's spiritual life. No longer does the rabbinical establishment have the power to enforce its rulings. All Jews are free to decide for themselves which aspects of the Jewish heritage are religiously significant. Such liberty imposes new responsibilities on Jewish education. Rather than seek to indoctrinate children into the faith, rabbis and teachers could see themselves as transmitters of a rich heritage whose duty is to inform children so that they can make sensible choices about the ways in which they can incorporate Judaism into their everyday lives.

Today, this task is made easier than ever before by the proliferation of educational resources. Not only is there a wealth of books published on all aspects of Judaism, the internet provides a means of finding information about the entire tradition. Search engines enable students to locate millions of websites dealing with every aspect of Jewish life. It makes no difference where one lives, the internet offers the opportunity to discover information about every feature of the Jewish religion.

With a computer containing a CD drive, it is possible to gain access to classical reference works such as the *Encyclopedia*

Judaica, the Talmud, the *Zohar*, midrashic sources, and general introductions to Judaism. The internet also provides free access to various on-line resources such as the *Jewish Encyclopedia* as well as the Wikipedia. The advent of the internet also has profound implications for the way in which Judaism can be studied and taught in colleges, universities, and religion schools. The internet has opened up the possibility of gaining information about the Jewish faith and the Jewish people. There are millions of sites dealing with Jewish history, belief, *kashrut*, conversion, law and custom, ethics, life-cycle events, family and personal matters, prayer, God and Messiah, ritual objects, synagogues, history, Torah, Talmud, *kabbalah*, and so on. In addition, Jewish newspapers and magazines are available on line. It is even possible, on the internet, to ask rabbis questions on any aspect of Jewish life.

What this means is that Jewish education on all levels is open to anyone. No longer is it necessary to belong to a synagogue, attend classes, or have a teacher. Instead, Jewish knowledge is accessible to everyone no matter where they live. Such openness is to be welcomed in a pluralistic, multi-cultural world. As indicated previously, contemporary Judaism is multi-faceted and amorphous. In secular society Jewish authoritarianism has been eroded, and instead all Jews are at liberty to chart their way through the tradition. Modern educationalists should recognize this revolution in Jewish life, and accept the inevitable subjectivity involved in personal decision-making about the relevance of the Jewish past.

The role of Jewish educators is in my opinion to impart knowledge about Judaism with the hope of inspiring those they teach. Informed about the tradition, students should be able to discover ways in which the Jewish heritage can feature in their lives. As a consequence, the Sabbath, Jewish festivals, ritual law, ethics, legends, and history can become spiritually inspiring and meaningful. With the vast resources available, the Jewish faith can be presented as a living religion, offering to its adherents means of elevating their daily lives. Yet, such a new vision of

Judaism must be based on a spirit of tolerance and acceptance in which each person's choices are regarded as inviolable and sacrosanct.

Chapter 16.

THE SABBATH

According to Scripture, God rested on the Sabbath day; as a consequence, the Jewish people are to rest from all forms of labor on *Shabbat* (the Sabbath). During the rabbinic era, Jewish sages formulated thirty-nine categories of work that were later interpreted by scholars as forbidding a wide range of activities. For Orthodox Jews these regulations are authoritative and binding. Within the Reform community, however, these manifold prescriptions have lost their force. Instead, Reform Jews stress that the Sabbath should be regarded as a holy day set aside from the rest of the week. This theme is repeatedly emphasized in the liturgy, which extols the Sabbath as a time of personal reflection.

Reform Judaism and the Sabbath

At home my mother recited the prayer for lighting candles on the Sabbath:

> Come, let us welcome the Sabbath. May its radiance illumine our hearts as we kindle these tapers. Light is the symbol of the divine. The Lord is my light and my salvation.
>
> Light is the symbol of the divine in man. The spirit of man is the light of the Lord.
>
> Light is the symbol of the divine law. For the commandment is a lamp and the law is a light.
>
> Light is the symbol of Israel's mission. I, the Lord, have set thee for a covenant of the people, for a light unto the nations.
>
> Therefore, in the spirit of our ancient tradition that hallows and unites Israel in all lands and all ages, do we know kindle the Sabbath lights.
>
> Blessed art Thou, O Lord our God, King of the universe, who hast sanctified us by Thy laws and commanded us to kindle the Sabbath light.[1]

This was followed by the recitation of the *Kiddush* prayer recited by my father:

> Let us praise God with this symbol of joy, and thank Him for the blessings of the past week, for life and strength, for home and love and friendship, for the discipline of our trials and temptations, for the happiness that has come to us out of our labors. Thou hast ennobled us, O God, by the blessings of work, and in love hast sanctified us by Sabbath rest and worship as ordained in the Torah: Six days shalt thou labor and do all thy work, but the seventh day is the Sabbath to be hallowed unto the Lord, thy God.
>
> Praised be Thou, O Lord our God, King of the universe, who hast created the fruit of the vine.[2]

On Friday night I accompanied my parents to services. In the Union Prayer Book, the Sabbath is extolled as a day of rest and rejoicing. This theme was reiterated throughout the worship service. Early in the service, the choir sang: "The children of Israel shall keep the Sabbath, to observe the Sabbath throughout their generations as a perpetual covenant. It is a sign between Me and the children of Israel forever."[3]

This was followed by several traditional prayers and an extensive recitation by the rabbi concerning the spiritual significance of the Sabbath:

> Heavenly Father, we rejoice that amid the ceaseless cares and anxieties, the vain desires and wearisome struggles of our earthly life, Thy holy Sabbath has been given us as a day of rest and refreshment of soul. We thank Thee for all Thy mercies unto us during the past week, for the preservation of our lives, of our health, and our strength; for the blessings of home, of love, of friendship, and for all good influences which support us in the hour of trial and temptation. Thou sendest us the joys that brighten our days; from Thy hand also come the sorrows that cast their shadows over them. In all our experiences we recognize Thy guidance and praise Thy wisdom. O may this Sabbath bring rest to every disquieted heart and be a healing balm of every wounded soul.[4]

The Sabbath is thus a time of spiritual refreshment. But it also should be reserved as a day of rest. Later in the evening service, the rabbi emphasized that the Sabbath must be differentiated from other days of the week:

> God and Father, we have entered Thy sanctuary on the Sabbath to hallow Thy name and to offer unto Thee prayers of thanksgiving. The week of toil is ended, the day of rest has come. Thou, Creator of all, hast given us the blessing of labor, so that by our work we may fashion things of use and beauty. May the fruit of our labor be acceptable unto Thee. May each

new Sabbath find us going from strength to strength, so that by Thy grace we may be helped to even worthier work. Make us conscious of our obligation to Thee and of the opportunities for service which Thou hast put within our reach. Help us to use our powers for the benefit of our fellowmen, so that the hearts of Thy children may be gladdened by the work of our hands.[5]

The morning service echoes such sentiments. Again, various prayers emphasize the spiritual significance of Sabbath rest. Early in the service, the rabbi stressed that the Sabbath day is a time to set aside the problems of the past week:

Again has come the day which bids us lay aside the burden of care and the anxiety of the daily task. Thou hast commanded us to work, that we may free ourselves from that bondage of nature in which all other creatures on earth are held. But in the struggle for the mastery over things material, we often forget the divine purpose of our life, Driven by the desire for gain or the longing for pleasure, we become enslaved, fettered by new wants, oppressed by new burdens. Therefore hast Thou, O Father, in Thy love appointed for us a day of rest, that in Thy presence we may regain that freedom of the soul which comes through obedience to Thy commandments. Quickened by Thy spirit, may we learn how to ennoble the things of earth by sanctifying them to Thy service.[6]

Such sentiments about the sacredness of the Sabbath and its special place in Jewish consciousness conform to the traditional understanding of Sabbath rest and peace. Yet, for us in religion school it was difficult to reconcile such a conception with the realities of Sabbath observance. Even though we attended worship services on the Sabbath as part of our religious instruction, the rest of the Sabbath was spent in a normal way. We were picked up from the Temple by our parents, taken home to lunch, and afternoon activities were no different from what took place on Sunday. We played games, went shopping, or did homework.

The Sabbath, we were told in services, was a sacred time, but there seemed no indication of it once we left the Temple.

Sabbath Worship

The Book of Genesis declares:

the heavens and the earth were finished and all the host of them. And on the seventh day God finished his work which He had done, and He rested on the seventh day from all his work which He had done. So God blessed the seventh day and hallowed it, because on it God rested from all his work which He had done in creation. (Gen. 2:1–3)

This passage serves as the basis for the decree that no work should be done on the Sabbath. During their sojourn in the wilderness of Zin, the Israelites were first commanded to observe the Sabbath. They were told to work on five days of the week when they should collect a single portion of manna; on the sixth day the were instructed to collect a double portion for the following day was to be "a day of solemn rest, a holy sabbath of the Lord." (Exod. 16:23) On the seventh day when several individuals made a search for manna, the Lord stated: "How long do you refuse to keep my commandments and my laws? See! The Lord has given you the sabbath, therefore on the sixth day He gives you bread for two days; remain every man of you in his place, let no man go out of his place on the seventh day." (Exod. 16:28–9)

Some time later God revealed the Ten Commandments, including prescriptions concerning the Sabbath day:

Remember the sabbath day, to keep it holy. Six days you shall labor, and do all your work, but the seventh day is a sabbath to the Lord your God; in it you shall not do any work, you, or your son, or your daughter, your manservant, or your maid-servant, or your cattle, or the sojourner who is within your gates; for in six days the Lord made heaven and earth, the sea, and all that is

in them, and rested the seventh day; therefore the Lord blessed
the sabbath day and hallowed it. (Exod. 20:8-11)

The Book of Deuteronomy contains a different version, emphasizing the exodus from Egypt:

> Observe the sabbath day, to keep it holy, as the Lord your
> God commanded you. Six days you shall labor, and do all your
> work; but the seventh day is a sabbath to the Lord your God;
> in it you shall not do any work.... You shall remember that
> you were a servant in the land of Egypt, and the Lord your
> God brought you out thence with a mighty hand and an out-
> stretched arm; therefore the Lord your God commanded you
> to keep the sabbath day. (Deut. 5:12-15)

According to the Book of Exodus, the Sabbath is a covenant
between Israel and God:

> Say to the people of Israel, "You shall keep my sabbaths,
> for this is a sign between me and you throughout your gen-
> erations, that you may know that I, the Lord, sanctify you....
> Therefore the people of Israel shall keep the sabbath, observ-
> ing the sabbath throughout their generations as a perpetual
> covenant." (Exod. 31:12–16)

By the time the Sanhedrin began to function, the observance
of the Sabbath was regulated by Jewish law. Following the in-
junction in Exodus 20:10, the primary aim was to refrain from
work. In the Torah only a few provisions are delineated; kindling
a fire (Exod. 35:3); ploughing and harvesting (Exod. 23:12);
carrying from one place to another (Exod. 16:29). Such regulations were expanded by rabbinic sages who listed thirty-nine
categories of work (which were involved in the building of the
Tabernacle). According to the Mishnah, they are:

1. sowing; 2. ploughing; 3. reaping; 4. binding sheaves; 5.

threshing; 6. winnowing; 7. sorting; 8. grinding; 9. sifting; 10. kneading; 11. baking; 12. shearing sheep; 13. washing wool; 14. beating wool; 15. dyeing wool; 16. spinning; 17. sieving; 18. making two loops; 19. weaving two threads; 20. separating two threads; 21. tying; 22. loosening; 23. sewing two stitches; 24. tearing in order to sew two stitches; 25. hunting a deer; 26. slaughtering; 27. flaying; 28. salting; 29. curing a skin; 30. scraping the hide; 31. cutting; 32. writing two letters; 33. erasing in order to write two letters; 34. building; 35. pulling down a structure; 36. extinguishing a fire; 37. lighting a fire; 38. striking with a hammer; 39. moving something.[7]

In the Talmud these categories are discussed and expanded to include within each category a range of actions. In order to ensure that individuals do not transgress these prescriptions, the rabbis enacted further legislation which serves as a fence around the Law. Yet despite such ordinances, there are certain situations which take precedence over Sabbath prohibitions. Witnesses of the New Moon, for example, who were to inform the Sanhedrin or Bet Din of this occurrence, were permitted to do so on the Sabbath. Other instances include circumcision on the Sabbath; dangerous animals may be killed; persons are permitted to fight in self-defense; anything may be done to save a life or assist a woman in childbirth.

The Sabbath itself commences on Friday at sunset. About twenty minutes before sunset, candles are traditionally lit by the woman of the house, who recites the blessing: "Blessed are you, O Lord our God, King of the universe, who has hallowed us by your commandments and commanded us to kindle the Sabbath light." In the synagogue, the service preceding Friday *maariv* (evening service) takes place at twilight. Known as *Kabbalat Shabbat*, it is a late addition, dating back to the sixteenth century, when kabbalists in Safed went out to the fields on Friday afternoon to greet the Sabbath queen. In kabbalistic lore the Sabbath represents the *Shekhinah* (divine presence). This ritual is rooted in the custom of the first century sage Hanina who, after preparing himself for the Sabbath, stood at sunset and declared: "Come, let us go forth to welcome the Sabbath," and that of the third century scholar Yannai who said: "Come bride! Come bride!!" On the basis of such sentiments Solomon Alkabets in the sixteenth century composed the Sabbath hymn *Lekhah Dodi*, which has become a major feature of the liturgy.

In the Sephardic rite Psalm 29 and *Lekhah Dodi* are recited, whereas the Ashkenazi rite is comprised of Psalms 95–99, *Lekhah Dodi* and Psalms 92–3. The Reform prayer book offers a variety of alternative services including abridged versions of these psalms and the entire *Lekhah Dodi*. The Reconstructionist service commences with biblical passages, continues with an invocation and meditation on the Sabbath, and then moves on to an invocation and mediation on the Sabbath, and proceeds to a reading of psalms and *Lekhah Dodi*.

Traditionally, when the father returns home from the synagogue, he blesses the children. With both hands placed on the head of a boy, he says: "May God make you like Ephraim and Manasseh"; for a girl: "May God make you like Sarah, Rebekah, Rachel and Leah." In addition, he recites the priestly blessing. Those assembled then sing *Shalom Aleikhem* which welcomes the Sabbath angels. At the Sabbath table the father recites the *kiddush* prayer over a cup of wine. This is followed by the washing of the hands and the blessing of the bread. The meal is followed by the singing of *zemirot* (table hymns), and concludes with the *Birkhat ha-Mazon* (Grace After Meals). This, which Jews are obligated to recite after every meal, originally consisted of three paragraphs in which worshippers thank God for sustenance, the land, and the Torah, and a prayer for the restoration of the Temple. Subsequently a fourth paragraph was added, which contains the words: "Who is good and does good." Subsequently short prayers beginning with "the All Merciful" were added. On the Sabbath an additional prayer is included dealing with the Sabbath day.

On Sabbath morning the liturgy consists of a morning service, a reading of the Torah and the *Haftarah*, and the additional service. In the service itself, introductory prayers prior to the

Shema differ from those of weekdays, and the *Amidah* (Eighteen Benedictions) is also different. Seven individuals are called to the reading of the Law, and an eighth for a reading from the prophets. In the Reform movement worship is abridged and has no additional service. On returning home, the morning *kiddush* and the blessing over bread are recited followed by the Sabbath meal and the Grace after Meals. In the afternoon service the Torah is read prior to the *Amidah*; three persons are called to the Torah, and the first portion of the reading of the Law for the following week is recited. Customarily three meals are to be eaten on the Sabbath day. The third meal is known as the *Seudah Shelishit* which should take place just in time for the evening service. At the end of the Sabbath, the evening service takes place and is followed the *Havdalah* service.

The *Havdalah* ceremony marks the conclusion of the Sabbath period—it is divided and consists of four blessings. Three are recited over wine, spices and lights:

> Behold. God is my deliverance. I am confident and unafraid. The Lord is my strength, my might, my deliverance.

> With joy shall you draw water from the wells of deliverance. Deliverance is the Lord's; He will bless His people. *Adonai tzeva'ot* is with us; the God of Jacob is our fortress. *Adonai tzeva'ot*, blessed the one who trusts in You. Help us, Lord; answer us, O King, when we call.

> Grant us the blessings of light, of gladness, and of honor which the miracle of deliverance brought to our ancestors. I lift up my cup of deliverance and call upon the Lord. Praised are You, Lord our God, King of the universe who creates the fruit of the vine. Praised are You, Lord our God, King of the universe who creates fragrant spices. Praised are You, Lord our God, King of the universe who creates the lights of fire.[8]

The service concludes with the *Havdalah* blessing:

Praised are You, Lord our God, King of the universe who has endowed all creation with distinctive qualities, distinguishing between sacred and secular time, between light and darkness, between the people Israel and other people, between the seventh day and the six working days of the week. Praised are You, Lord who distinguishes between sacred and secular time.

God of Abraham, of Isaac and of Jacob, protect Your people Israel in their need, as the holy beloved *Shabbes* takes its leave. May the good week come to us with health and life, good fortune and blessing, prosperity and dignity, graciousness and lovingkindness, sustenance and success, with all good blessings and with forgiveness of sin.

He separates sacred and profane; May He forgive our sins from on high. Our families and means (and our peace) may He increase like grains of sand, like stars up in the sky. May we have a good week.[9]

The hymn *Ha-Mavdil* follows the *Havdalah* ceremony and asks for forgiveness for sins and for the granting of a large number of children. A number of customs including filling a cup and extinguishing the *Havdalah* candle in wine poured from it are associated with the ceremony. Within Reform Judaism an alternative *Havdalah* service incorporates additional readings with traditional blessings.

Sabbath Rest

Today most Jews no longer live a ghetto existence. As a result, Sabbath observance has become voluntary in many communities. Amongst the strictly Orthodox, Sabbath regulations are rigorously followed. However for the majority of Jews, the voluminous strictures regulating Sabbath rest have been largely neglected. Thus, in this sphere of religious activity there is the same freedom of interpretation as in all other aspects of the Jewish heritage. Although the various religious establishments—from the Orthodox to the most liberal—seek to impose their understanding of the Sabbath on their adherents, all Jews are free to select from the tradition those features they find spiritually meaningful. What I believe is required in the modern world, therefore, is an acknowledgement of such individual decision-making. The authoritarianism of the past could be replaced by an acceptance of personal liberty.

A new vision of Judaism for the twenty-first century could be based on an acknowledgement of such individualized decision-making. Yet, there is every reason for the Sabbath to continue to occupy a central place in the religious life of modern Jews. As we have seen, the Sabbath is the most frequent Jewish holiday, occurring once a week. Totally independent of the calendar, it celebrates the completion of creation and is conceived as a day of abstinence from work. Drawing on biblical precedent, rabbinic sages categorized all activities that were forbidden. In their place, Jews were to focus on worship and study.

In modern times, the Sabbath day can still function as a reminder of the importance of contemplation, reflection, and meditation. Even though the vast majority of Jews do not follow the multifarious legal strictures concerning Sabbath observance, the holiday can be reconstructed to highlight its religious significance. As the demands of work increase, the Sabbath bears testimony to the importance of non-material concerns. As the *Havdalah* ceremony emphasizes, it is spiritually beneficial to differentiate between weekly labor and Sabbath rest. How this is to be done will vary from person to person, but the principle of establishing an occasion for spiritual deliberation is vital. Human beings need to reflect on the meaning and direction of their lives.

Seen in this way, the Sabbath day can operate as a time to take stock of the most important aspects of one's life. Most importantly, it can serve as a weekly break to consider one's ultimate goals. What really matters: is it work? or family? or possessions? The Sabbath provides an oasis of time to consider the balance between the various dimensions of one's daily life. Have work concerns crowded out other important areas? Is there enough time for one's spouse and children? Has the quest for money or success become burdensome? In seeking to answer these questions, the Sabbath can serve as an occasion to reflect on the purpose of one's life.

A weekly day of rest can also offer the opportunity to take stock of oneself. Who are you? Most people answer this question by responding with a name or a job description. Even though our common identity includes our job, or role, or some facts about each of us such as our age, sex or physical appearance, there are other hidden features which constitute the underlying elements of our character. The Sabbath can serve as a moment to reflect on the patterns of one's life and the critical events that have shaped one's nature. To discover one's true self, one needs to ask oneself a variety of questions about one's past: What have been the turning points in one's life? Have they to do with work, or family, or money? What sorts of events constituted crises? How did one respond? What were peak experiences? What kinds of risks did one take? What does all this tell one about the sort of person one is?

Another area of self-evaluation concerns the networks that surround a person. The Sabbath can also provide an occasion for considering one's relations with other people. Imagine life as a web of such connections. Put yourself in the center of it, and then draw the lines that connect you to all the other people in your life. If they are special, they should be close; if they are not particularly important, they should be placed at a distance. Join together those that are interrelated. Each of these relationships is a blend of love, fear, worries and hopes. You will have a view of each person at the end of one of these lines as well as an expectation of what they should do for you or with you. There are unwritten contracts with all of these individuals. The Sabbath offers an opportunity to reflect on this web of relationships and your expectations of others. What kind of web surrounds you? Is it what you want? What do you expect from others? Are the unwritten contracts the sort you desire? Do you desire a different kind of social network? What do you really want from other people?

In previous centuries the Sabbath day was conceptualized religiously in terms of obedience to law. As we have noted, such rigorous legalism is no longer relevant to many in the contemporary Jewish world. Today all Jews are free to choose those elements of the tradition which they find spiritually significant. Yet no matter how the Sabbath is observed, it can still function as a time for personal reflection about the meaning and purpose of one's life. Interpreted in this way, Sabbath observance can retain its centrality in the life of the modern Jew.

Chapter 17.

PASSOVER, SUKKOT, AND SHAVUOT

According to Scripture, male Israelites were commanded to make a pilgrimage to Jerusalem on the festivals of Passover, *Shavuot*, and *Sukkot*—these festivals were therefore known as "pilgrim festivals." All pilgrims were to offer a sacrifice and give the second tithe of their produce to the Temple. Later special prayers were recited in the synagogue, and each festival has its own special liturgical charcteristics, ceremonies and customs. Today these festivals continue to be celebrated in the various branches of the faith according to different patterns of worship.

The Pilgrim Festivals

When I was young, Passover (a spring festival which begins on the fifteenth of the Hebrew month *Nisan*) was a time when my family gathered together. Led by my father, the seder (home Passover service) commemorated the Exodus from Egypt and stressed the liberation of the Jewish people from Egyptian bondage. Repeatedly, it was emphasized that it was not only the redemption of the Jewish people that is important, but the redemption of the entire world. The *Haggadah* (Passover prayer book), reflecting the historical experience of the Jewish nation, recognizes that slavery is not limited to human bondage, but that social degradation and spiritual enslavement are evils that must be eradicated from modern society.

In the morning service for Passover, the theme of Israel's deliverance from oppression and God's concern for all humankind is repeated:

> Gratefully we lift up our hearts to Thee, O God, and thank thee for Thy never-ending goodness to the house of Israel. Our ancestors languished in Egyptian slavery; they ate the bread of affliction; the lash of the taskmaster drove them to their daily toil; but Thou wast mindful of the descendants of Abraham, Isaac and Jacob, Thy faithful servants. In the fulness of time Thou didst raise up a deliverer who, in Thy name, brought the message of redemption to the enslaved. Thou didst lead Israel from bondage to freedom, from darkness to light, from despair to hope…. We pray unto Thee on this day of our feast that, as Thou hast protected the children of Israel throughout the past, so mayest Thou deliver them wherever they are still bowed beneath the oppressor's yoke. May all persecution cease, and every trace of bondage disappear from among men, so that at last a universal feast of freedom shall be celebrated in Thy name, God of Freedom, Father of mankind.[1]

Passover is followed by the festival of *Shavuot* (an early summer festival which begins on the sixth of the Hebrew month *Sivan*) commemorates the revelation on Mount Sinai. On *Shavuot*, the Jewish people celebrate their covenantal relationship with God and reaffirm their commitment to a Jewish life. The significance of the events at Sinai derives not only from the Jews receiving the commandments, but also from their acceptance of the law. Recalling these events, the worship service contains responsive readings extolling the law:

> Happy are they that are upright in the way,
> Who walk in the law of the Lord.
> Happy are they that keep His testimonies,
> That seek Him with the whole heart;
> With my whole heart have I sought Thee;
> O let me not err from Thy commandments,
> Unless Thy law had been my delight,
> I should then have perished in mine affliction.
> Thy word is a lamp unto my feet, and a light unto my path.
> I will delight in Thy statutes, I will not forget Thy word.[2]

The festival of *Sukkot*, an autumn festival, begins on the fifteenth of the Hebrew month of *Tishri* and concludes on the twenty second. More than any of the other pilgrim festivals, it has retained its agricultural character, commemorating the journey through the wilderness toward the Land of Israel. According to the Torah, the ancient Israelites lived in *sukkot* (temporary dwellings) during their sojourn in the desert. In the Temple I attended as a child, a *sukkah* was constructed covered with fruit. During the worship service, the rabbi emphasized God's providential care of his people:

> On this Feast of Tabernacles, O God, we recall with grateful hearts the loving care with which Thou didst watch over our fathers in the wilderness. When wearied by sultry sun and violent storm, they found shelter and refreshment in the booth of Thy protecting love. In drought Thou didst sustain them,

in famine Thou didst preserve them. With a father's tender care Thou didst guide and shield them, and didst make them bearers of Thy truth, champions of Thy law.[3]

Celebrating the Pilgrim Festivals

According to Scripture, Jews are to celebrate Passover, *Sukkot* and *Shavuot* each year: "Three times each year shall all your males appear before the Lord your God at the place which he will choose, at the feast of unleavened bread, at the feast of weeks, and at the feast of booths." (Deut. 16:16) On the basis of this decree, large numbers of pilgrims traveled to Jerusalem from throughout the Holy Land as well as Babylonia. There they worshiped in the Temple, offering sacrifices and praying to God.

The first of these festivals, Passover, is celebrated for eight days from the 15th through the 22d of *Nisan*. The various names for this festival illustrate its various dimensions:

1. *Pesah* (Passover). This term is derived from the narrative of the tenth plague in Egypt, when first-born Egyptians were killed, whereas God "passed over" the houses of the Israelites (whose door-posts and lintels were sprinkled with the blood of the paschal lamb). This term also refers to the Passover sacrifice (symbolic of the paschal lamb) which occurred on the 15th of *Nisan*—its flesh was roasted and eaten together with unleavened bread (*matzah*) and bitter herbs (*marror*).

2. *Hag ha-Matzot* (The Festival of Unleavened Bread). This term refers to the unleavend bread (*matzah*) baked by the Israelites when they fled from Egypt. In accordance with God's instructions to Moses and Aaron while the people were in Egypt, no leaven was to be consumed during Passover celebrations, nor was it to be stored in the house. All vessels used for leavening were to be put aside, and their place taken by a complete set of utensils used only for Passover. Even though no leaven may be eaten during this period, the obligation to eat unleavened bread applies only to the first two nights during the seder service.

3. *Zeman Herutenu* (The Season of our Freedom). This term des-
ignates the deliverance of the Jewish people from Egyptian slavery
and the emergence of the Jewish people as a separate nation.

4. *Hag ha-Aviv* (The Festival of Spring). This term is used because the month of *Nisan* is described in the Bible as the month of
Aviv, when ears of barley began to ripen. In accordance with the
biblical commandment, a measure of barley (*omer*) was brought
to the Temple on the second day of Passover. Only when this was
done could bread be made from the new barley harvest.

In preparation for Passover, Jewish law stipulates that all
leaven must be removed from the house. On the 14th of *Nisan* a
formal search is to be made for any remains of leaven. Before the
search, the following prayer is recited: "Blessed art thou, O Lord
our God, king of the universe, who has commanded us concerning the removal of leaven." After the search, the following prayer
is said: "May all leaven in my possession both that which I have
seen and that which I have not seen or not removed be annulled
and deemed as dust of the earth."

This is then put aside and burned on the following morning.
The first night of Passover is celebrated in a home ceremony: the
seder. This is done to fulfill the biblical commandment to tell the
story of the Passover to one's son: "And you shall tell thy son on
the day, saying: 'It is because of what the Lord did for me when I
came out of Egypt.'" (Exod. 13:8) The order of the service dates
back to Temple times. During the ceremony celebrants traditionally lean on their left sides—this was the custom of freemen
in ancient times.

The symbols placed on the seder table serve to remind those
present of Egyptian bondage, God's redemption, and the celebration in Temple times. They consist of:

1. Three *matzot*: These three pieces of unleavened bread are
placed on top of one another, usually in a special cover. The upper and lower *matzot* symbolize the double portion of manna
provided for the Israelites in the wilderness. The middle *matzah*

(which is broken in two at the beginning of the seder) represents the "bread of affliction." The smaller portion is eaten to comply with the commandment to eat unleavened bread. The larger part is set aside for the *afikoman* (part of the middle *matzah*) which recalls Temple times when the meal was completed with the eating of the paschal lamb. These three pieces of unleavened bread also symbolize the three divisions of the Jewish people—Cohen, Levi, and Israel.

2. Four cups of wine. It is traditional for each Jew to drink four cups of wine at the seder. The first is linked to the recital of *kiddush*; the second with the narrative of the Exodus and the Blessing for Redemption; the third with the Grace after Meals; and the fourth with the *Hallel* and prayers for thanksgiving. These cups also symbolize four expressions of redemption in Exodus 6:6–7.

3. The cup of Elijah: This cup symbolizes the hospitality awaiting the passer-by and the wayfarer. According to tradition, the Messiah will reveal himself at Passover, and the prophet Malachi declared that he will be preceded by Elijah. The cup of Elijah was also introduced because of the doubt as to whether five cups of wine should be drunk rather than four.

4. Bitter Herbs: These symbolize the bitterness of Egyptian slavery.

5. Parsley: This is dipped in salt water and eaten after the *kiddush*. It is associated with spring.

6. *Haroset*: This is a mixture of apples, nuts, cinnamon and wine. It is a reminder of the bricks and mortars that Jews were forced to use in Egypt.

7. Roasted Shankbone: This symbolizes the *paschal* offering.

8. Roasted egg: This commemorates the festival sacrifice in the Temple.

9. Salt water: This recalls that salt was offered with all sacrifices. It also symbolizes the salt water of the tears of the Israelites.

At the seder, the *Haggadah* details the order of service:

1. The *kiddush* is recited.
2. The celebrant washes his hands.
3. The parsley is dipped in salt water.
4. The celebrant divides the middle *matzah* and sets aside the *afikoman*.
5. The celebrant recites the *Haggadah* narration.
6. The participants wash their hands.
7. The blessing over bread is recited.
8. The blessing over *matzah* is recited.
9. Bitter herbs are eaten.
10. The *matzah* and *marror* are combined.
11. The meal is eaten.
12. The *afikoman* is eaten.
13. Grace after Meals is recited.
14. The *Hallel* is recited.
15. The service is concluded.
16. Hymns and songs are sung.

The second festival—*Shavuot*—is celebrated for two days on the 6th and 7th of *Sivan*. The word *shavuot* means "weeks." Seven weeks are counted from the bringing of the *omer* on the second day of *Pesah* (Lev. 23:15). The festival is also referred to as Pentecost, a Greek word meaning "fiftieth," since it was celebrated on the fiftieth day. Symbolically the day begins with the culmination of the process of emancipation, which commenced with the Exodus at Passover. It is concluded with the proclamation of the Law at Mount Sinai. Liturgically, the festival is also called *Zeman Mattan Toratentu* (The Season of the Giving of our Torah). This name relates to events depicted in Exodus 19–20.

During the Temple period, farmers set out for Jerusalem to offer a selection of first ripe fruits as a thanksgiving-offering. In post-Temple times, the emphasis shifted to the festival's identification as the anniversary of the giving of the Law on Mount Sinai. In some communities it is a practice to remain awake during *Shavuot* night. In the sixteenth century Solomon Alkabets and other kabbalists began the custom of *tikkun,* in which an anthology of biblical and rabbinic material was recited. Today in those communities where this custom is still observed, this lectionary has been replaced by a passage of the Talmud or other rabbinic sources. Some congregations in the Diaspora read a book of psalms on the second night. Synagogues themselves are decorated with flowers or plants, and dairy food is eaten during the festival. The liturgical readings for the festival include the Ten Commandments preceded by the liturgical poem *Akdamut Millin* on the first day, and *Yetsiv Pitgam* before the *Haftarah* on the second day. The Book of Ruth is also recited. In some communities this festival marks the graduation of young people from formal synagogue education (or confirmation in Reform synagogues). In Israel, agricultural settlements celebrate a First Fruits ceremony on *Shavuot*.

Sukkot is also prescribed in the Bible: "On the fifteenth day of this seventh month and for seven days is the feast of tabernacles to the Lord. (Lev. 23:34) Beginning on the 15th of *Tishri*, it commemorates God's protection of the Israelites during their sojourn in the desert. Leviticus decrees that Jews are to construct *sukkot* during this period as a reminder that the people of Israel dwelt in booths when they fled from Egypt. (Lev. 23:42–3)

During this festival a *sukkah* is constructed and its roof is covered with branches of trees and plants. The following prayer is recited in the *sukkah* on the first night:

> May it be thy will, O Lord my God and God of my fathers, to let thy divine presence abide among us. Spread over us the tabernacle of thy peace in recognition of the precept of the Tabernacle which we are now fulfiling, and whereby we establish in fear and love the unity of thy holy blessed name. O surround us with the pure and holy radiance of thy glory, that is spread over our heads as the eagle over the nest he stirreth up: and thence bid the stream of life flow in upon thy servant.[4]

Meals are to be eaten inside the *sukkah*. Leviticus also states that various agricultural species should play a part in the observance of *Sukkot*: "And you shall take on the first day the fruit of goodly trees, branches of palm trees, and boughs of leafy trees, and willows of the brook; and you shall rejoice before the Lord your God seven days." (Lev. 23:40) In compliance with this prescription the four species are used in the liturgy: palm, myrtle, willow and citron. On each day of the festival the *lulav* (palm branch) is waved in every direction—this symbolizes God's presence throughout the world. Holding the four species Jews make one circuit around the Torah which is carried on the *bimah* (platform) on each of the first six days. During this circuit, *hoshanah* prayers are recited. On the seventh day of *Sukkot (Hoshanah Rabba)* seven circuits are made around the Torah while reciting *hoshanah* prayers. During the service the reader wears a white *kittel* (robe).

In conformity with Leviticus 23:36 ("On the eighth day you shall hold a holy convocation…it is a solemn assembly"), *Shemini Atseret* and *Simhat Torah* are celebrated on the same day (or on separate days in the Diaspora). No work is permitted at this time. On *Shemini Atseret* a prayer for rain is recited, and the reader wears a *kittel*. Ecclesiastes is recited at the end of the morning service on *Shabbat Hol Hamoed* (or on *Shemini Atseret* if it falls on the Sabbath). The ninth day of *Sukkot* is *Simhat Torah*. On this joyous day the reading of the Torah is completed and recommenced. The Torah scrolls are taken out of the Ark, and members of the congregation carry them in a procession around the synagogue.

Liberation and the Heritage

The Passover celebration is a symbolic exaltation of freedom. Jews are to rejoice in God's liberation of their ancestors, in which each of them takes part. Throughout the history of the Jewish people, this festival has awakened the spirit of the people to the significance of human liberation. The biblical account of the Exodus, embodied in the liturgy of the *Haggadah*, has played a central role in the Jewish quest for human dignity. In post-biblical literature the Exodus continued to be a source of hope and inspiration even during the darkest hours of Jewish history. The lessons of the *Haggadah* were taught repeatedly by Jewish sages in the *midrash* and Talmud through commentary, interpretation, and legend.

Just as rabbinic sources of the Tannaitic and Amoraic period frequently alluded to the Exodus event as central in the life of the nation, so too in Jewish literature of the medieval period there were frequent references to this act of deliverance. Modern Jewish writers of post-Enlightenment Judaism similarly emphasized the significance of the themes of liberty, redemption, and freedom as found in the Passover festival. The Passover meal was perceived as a symbol of Israel's vocation as a people; the deliverance of the nation afforded a glimpse of its destiny.

Reflecting on the spiritual significance of the Passover, it becomes clear that Jews have found renewed strength and hope in the message of the Exodus. The Passover ceremony unites the Jewish people with their ancestors who endured slavery and oppression in Egyptian bondage. Despite the persecution of centuries, the Jewish nation remained confident of eventual deliverance and the ultimate redemption of humankind. In contemporary society, the message of the Exodus can still serve to call the Jewish people to hold steadfast to their conviction that justice and freedom will prevail throughout the world.

In this respect, *Pesach* continues to hold spiritual meaning for modern Jews. Committed to the biblical heritage and vision of the transformation of society, Jewry is united in a common hope and aspiration for the triumph of justice. Remembering the divine deliverance of the ancient Israelites, modern Jews can work together for the emancipation of the enslaved. The biblical motif therefore contains a reservoir of meaning for Jews in their struggle to create a better world. The Passover—by symbolizing the primal act of liberation—points to a future and ultimate redemption of the human family.

Similarly, *Shavuot* can function as a religiously meaningful event in the life of the nation. Although biblical scholarship has chal-

lenged the traditional belief in revelation at Sinai, modern Jews
can nonetheless envisage this festival as a validation of the Jewish
tradition. Today, what is required is an awareness and appreciation
of the Jewish heritage. *Shavuot* honours the tradition; it affirms
the religious stature of Jewish classical literature. Rooted in the
past, a new vision of Judaism could respect previous customs and
laws while striving for adaptation and change.

The symbol of the giving of the law on Mount Sinai could
therefore be perceived as a religiously significant event. Even if
there is no historical evidence to support this occurrence, it remains a potent image for the present. Human beings need order
and structure; society must be governed by law. The festival of
Shavuot consciously recognizes this crucial dimension of human life and celebrates the achievements of Jewish scholars and
sages. A new conception of Judaism for the modern age could
treasure the riches of the Jewish tradition while at the same time
respecting the personal choices and lifestyles of individual Jews.
A modern celebration of *Shavuot* could celebrate the intellectual,
moral, and spiritual achievements of the Jewish past combined
with a recognition of the need for religious progress.

Sukkot, too, has spiritual significance for the modern age.
According to legend, the ancient Israelites dwelt in temporary
booths during their sojourn in the desert. For forty years they
wandered in search of the Promised Land. Although the biblical
account lacks historical support, the festival of *Sukkot* is a powerful symbol of hope. The biblical narrative portrays the Jewish
people as resolute in their determination to survive against all
odds. Despite their waywardness and disobedience, Moses encouraged them to remain faithful to God who had delivered
them from bondage.

In a post-Holocaust world, such determination is of paramount importance. Today, Jewry is united in its conviction that
the Jewish people must survive. In this regard, the Jewish theologian Emil Fackenheim argues that, just as the root experience
of God's presence at Mount Sinai resulted in a series of divine
commands, so in the death camps God revealed a further com-

mandment to his people. This 614th commandment—added to the 613 commandments contained in the Torah—is directed to the post-Holocaust Jewish community. According to Fackenheim, Jews must not grant Hitler a posthumous victory:

> They are commanded to survive as Jews lest the Jewish people perish. They are commanded to remember the victims of Auschwitz lest their memory perish. They are forbidden to despair of man and his world, and to escape into either cynicism or otherworldliness, lest they cooperate in delivering the world over to forces of Auschwitz. Finally, they are forbidden to despair of the God of Israel, lest Judaism perish.[5]

Although most Jews are not persuaded by the theological presuppositions of Fackenheim's argument, they are determined that Jewish survival is the paramount goal of modern Jewish existence. Like Fackenheim, they are committed to the continuation of the Jewish people, and such dedication underlies the universal Jewish support for the State of Israel. For modern Jews, Jewish survival is an ultimate goal: in the light of such a conviction, the festival of *Sukkot* can serve as a symbol of faith in the future.

Chapter 18.

HIGH HOLY DAYS

The Jewish New Year begins in the autumn on the first day of *Tishri* and marks the start of the Ten Days of Penitence, which end on the Day of Atonement. In the Bible Rosh Hashanah is referred to as falling on the first day of the seventh month. (Lev. 23:24) During the rabbinic period, it came to be regarded as a day of judgment for the entire world, on which each person's fate is inscribed in the Book of Life. Today, the High Holy Days can continue to serve as the focus for reflection and introspection.

Reform Observance

Every year my parents took me to Temple for the Rosh Hashanah service. Over a thousand congregants crowded into the sanctuary to listen to the rabbi's sermon and hear the piercing sound of the *shofar* (ram's horn). In the evening of Rosh Hashanah, the congregation stood to recite the *Avinu Malkenu* prayer for forgiveness:

> Our Father, our King, hear our prayer.
> Our Father, our King, we have sinned before Thee.
> Our Father, our King, have mercy upon us and upon our children.
> Our Father, our King, keep far from our country pestilence, war and famine.
> Our father, Our King, cause all hate and oppression to vanish from the earth.
> Our Father, our King, inscribe us for blessing in the book of life.
> Our Father, our King, grant unto us a year of happiness.[1]

Continuing this theme, the Rosh Hashanah morning service explains the religious significance of the sounding of the *shofar*:

> The stirring sound of the *shofar* proclaimed the covenant at Mount Sinai which bound Israel to God as a kingdom of priests and a holy people. Ever since that distant day, the voice of the *shofar* has resounded through the habitations of Israel awakening high allegiance to God and His commandments. At the new moon, on joyous festivals as well as on solemn days of fasting and repentance, and in the Jubilee year when liberty was proclaimed throughout the land, our fathers hearkened to the tones of the ram's horn and recalled their obligation to serve the Lord with all their heart and with all their strength. Thus do we, their children, prepare to hearken now to the solemn sound of the *shofar*. May it summon us to struggle against the forces of evil within our hearts and in the world. Let it arouse within us the will to righteousness and strengthen our trust in God's justice and love. May it direct our thoughts to the day when the *shofar* will sound for the redemption of all mankind.[2]

On Yom Kippur we confessed our sins in the *Al Het* prayer. At the end of the service, the rabbi prayed for God to grant his people a year of blessing and peace:

> And now, at the close of this day's service, we implore Thee, O Lord our God:
> Let the year upon which we have entered be for us, for Israel, and for all mankind:
> A year of blessing and of prosperity.
> A year of salvation and comfort.
> A year of peace and contentment, of joy and of spiritual welfare.
> A year of virtue and of fear of God.
> A year which finds the hearts of parents united with the hearts of the children.
> A year of Thy pardon and favor.
> May the Lord bless thy going out and thy coming in from this time forth and forever.[3]

Following tradition, the Reform prayer book emphasizes the sinfulness of the nation, and sets out the path of repentance and forgiveness. Worship services during the High Holy Days depicted God as a loving father anxious for those who had fallen by the way, and ready to forgive those who sought his pardon. Stirred by the sound of the *shofar*, we were to search our hearts and turn to God as penitent sinners, seeking his mercy and compassion.

Rosh Hashanah and Yom Kippur

In biblical times Rosh Hashanah (the Jewish New Year) occurred on one day; it is presently observed for two days on the 1st and 2d of *Tishri*, marking the beginning of the Ten Days of Penitence. The term *Rosh Hashanah* occurs only once in the Bible. (Ezek. 40:1) Yet, this festival has three other biblical designations: (1) *Shabbaton*—a day of solemn rest to be observed on the first day of the seventh month; (2) *Zikhron Teruah*—a memorial proclaimed with the blast of a horn (Lev. 23:24); and (3) *Yom Teruah*—a day of blowing the horn (Num. 29:1). Subsequently rabbinic scholars referred to the New Year as *Yom ha-Din* (The Day of Judgement) and *Yom ha-Zikkaron* (the Day of Remembrance).

The Mishnah states that all human beings will pass before God on the New Year; the Talmud expands this notion by stressing the need for self-examination. In rabbinic sources every person stands before the throne of God, and judgment on every person is entered on the New Year and sealed on the Day of Atonement. In the Talmud the tractate *Rosh Hashanah* states that:

> there are three ledgers opened in heaven: one for the completely righteous who are immediately inscribed and sealed in the Book of Life; another for the thoroughly wicked who are recorded in the Book of Death; and a third for the intermediate, ordinary type of person whose fate hangs in the balance and is suspended until the Day of Atonement.

In this light, Rosh Hashanah and Yom Kippur are also called *Yamim Noraim* (Days of Awe).

On Rosh Hashanah the Ark curtain, reading desk, and Torah scroll mantles are covered in white, and the rabbi, cantor, and person who blows the shofar all wear a white *kittel*. In the synagogue service the *Amidah* of the *musaf* service contains three sections relating to God's sovereignty, providence, and revelation. The *Malkhuyyot*, introduced by the *Alenu* prayer, deals with God's rule; *Zikhronot* portrays God's remembrance of the ancestors of the Jewish nation when he judges every generation; *Shofarot* contains verses regarding the *shofar* and deals with the revelation on Mount Sinai as well as the messianic age. Each introductory section is followed by three verses from the Torah, three from the Writings, three from the Prophets, and a final verse from the Torah. On the first and second day of Rosh Hashanah the Torah readings concern the birth of Isaac (Gen 21:1-34) and the binding of Isaac or *Akedah* (Gen. 22:1-24). The *Haftarah* for the first day is 1 Samuel 1:9–2:10, which describes the birth of Samuel, who later dedicated his life to God's service. On the second day the *Haftarah* deals with Jeremiah's prophecy (Jer 31:2–20) concerning the restoration of Israel.

During both days of Rosh Hashanah—except when the first is on the Sabbath—the *shofar* is sounded at three points during the service: thirty times after the reading of the Law; thirty times during *musaf* (ten at the end of each of the three main sections); thirty times after *musaf,* and ten times before *Alenu.* In the liturgy, there are three variants of the blowing of the *shofar: tekiah* (a long note); *shevarim* (three tremulous notes), and *turot* (nine short notes). As Maimonides explained: the *shofar* is blown to call sinners to repent. In the *Mishneh Torah,* he wrote: "Awake you sinners, and ponder your deeds; remember your creator, forsake your evil ways, and return to God." In the Ashkenazi rite, the *U-Netanneh Tokef* prayer concludes the service on a hopeful note as congregants declare that, "Repentance, prayer and charity can avert the evil decree."

Traditionally it is a custom to go to the seaside or the banks of a river on the afternoon of the first day or on the second day if the first falls on a Sabbath. The ceremony of *Tashlikh* symbolizes the casting of one's sins into a body of water. The prayers for *Tashlikh* and three verses from the Book of Micah (Mic. 7:18–20) express assurance that God will forgive sinners. In the home, following *kiddush,* a piece of bread is dipped in honey; this is followed by a piece of apple, and a prayer is recited that the year ahead may be good and sweet. It is also customary to eat the new season's fruit on the second night of Rosh Hashanah to justify reciting the *Sheheheyanu* benediction on enjoying new things. The *hallah* loaves baked for this festival are normally round and have a plaited crust shaped like a ladder—this represents hopes for a good round year, or the effort to direct one's life upward to God.

The Ten Days of Penitence commence with the New Year and last until the Day of Atonement. This is viewed as the most solemn time of the year, when all individuals are judged and their fate determined for the ensuing year. During the Ten Days various additions are made to the liturgy, especially in the morning service.

Selihot (penitential prayers) are recited during the morning service, and various additions are made to the *Amidah* and the reader's repetition of the *Amidah*. The reader's repetition is followed by the *Avinu Malkenu* prayer. In some synagogues it is customary to recite Psalm 130:1 in the morning service. It is also traditional to visit the graves of close relatives. The Sabbath between the New Year and the Day of Atonement is *Shabbut Shuvah*.

The most holy day of the Jewish calendar is the Day of Atonement, which occurs on the 10th of *Tishri*. Like other major festivals, its observance is prescribed in Scripture: "On the tenth day of this seventh month is the Day of Atonement; and you shall afflict yourselves. It shall be to you a sabbath of solemn rest, and you shall afflict yourselves; on the ninth day of the month beginning at evening, from evening to evening." (Lev. 23:27,32) According to the rabbis, afflicting one's soul involved abstaining from food and drink. Thus every male over the age of thirteen and every female over twelve is obliged to fast from sunset until nightfall the next evening. Sick people, however, may take medicine and small amounts of food and drink. Similarly, those who are ill may be forbidden to fast.

During the day, normal Sabbath prohibitions apply, but worshippers are also to abstain from food and drink, marital relations, wearing leather shoes, using cosmetics and lotions, and washing the body except for fingers and eyes. The rabbis stress that the Day of Atonement enables human beings to atone for sins against God. However, regarding transgressions committed against others, pardon cannot be obtained unless forgiveness has been sought from the persons injured. As a result, it is customary for Jews to seek reconciliation with anyone they might have offended during the past year. Previously lashes (*malkot*) were administered in the synagogue to impart a feeling of repentance, but this custom has largely disappeared. The *kapparot* ritual still takes place before the Day of Atonement among Sephardi and Eastern communities as well as among some Ashkenazim. During this ceremony a fowl is slaughtered and either eaten before the fast or sold for money which is given to charity. Its death symbolizes the transfer of guilt from the people to the bird that has been killed. In many congregations Jews substitute coins for the fowl, and charity boxes are used in the morning and after-noon services before Yom Kippur.

Customarily Jews were able to absolve vows on the eve of Yom Kippur. In addition, afternoon prayers are recited earlier than normal, and the *Amidah* is extended by two formulas of confession (*Ashammu* and *Al Het*). Some devout Jews immerse themselves in a *mikveh* (ritual bath) in order to undergo purification before the fast. In the home a final meal (*seudah mafseket*) is eaten and, prior to lighting the festival candles, a memorial candle is kindled to burn throughout the day. Further, leather shoes are replaced by non-leather shoes or slippers. The *tallit* (prayer shawl) is worn throughout all the services, and a *parokhet* (white curtain) adorns the synagogue Ark and the scrolls of the Law. The reader's desk and other furnishings are also covered in white. Among Ashkenazim, rabbis, cantors and other officiants also wear a white *kittel*.

On Yom Kippur five services are conducted. The first, *Kol Nidre*, commences with a release of vows:

> By authority of the court on high and by the authority of this court below, with divine consent and with the consent of this congregation, we hereby declare that it is permitted to pray with those who have transgressed.
>
> All vows and oaths we take, all promises and obligations we make to God between this *Yom Kippur* and the next we hereby publicly retract in the event that we should forget them, and hereby declare our intention to be absolved of them.[4]

This service ends with the concluding service (*neilah*). Except for the extended *Amidah*, each service has its own characteristic liturgy. In all of them, however, the confession of sins (*viddui*) is pronounced—shorter confessions as well as longer ones are in the first person plural to emphasize collective responsibility.

Typical is this prayer for forgiveness for transgressions:

> We have sinned against you unwillingly and willingly, And
> we have sinned against you by misusing our minds. We have
> sinned against you through sexual immorality, And we have
> sinned against you knowingly and deceitfully. We have sinned
> against you by wronging others, And we have sinned against
> you through prostitution. We have sinned against you by de-
> riding parents and teachers.
>
> And we have sinned against you by using violence. We have
> sinned against you by not resisting the impulse to evil. For all
> these sins, forgiving God, forgive us, pardon us, grant atone-
> ment.[5]

In some liturgies there are also confessions of personal transgressions. Of special importance in the liturgy is the *Avinu
Malkenu* prayer, in which individuals confess their sins and pray
for forgiveness.

In most congregations the *Kol Nidre* (declaration of annul-
ment of vows) is recited on the eve of Yom Kippur. Among the
Orthodox it is a custom to spend the night in the synagogue
reciting the entire book of Psalms as well as other readings.
Among Sephardim and Reform Jews the memorial prayer is
recited on *Kol Nidre*. In addition to *selihot* and other hymns, the
morning service includes a Torah reading (Leviticus chapter 16)
describing the Day of Atonement ritual in the Sanctuary, and
a *maftir* (additional) reading (Num. 29:7-11), concerning the
festival sacrifices. The *Haftarah* (Isa. 57:14–58:14) depicts the
fast that is required. Ashkenazim (excluding Reform Jews) then
recite *yizkor* (memorial prayers). Among Sephardic Jewry and
Eastern communities, the *Hashkavah* service is repeated.

Before the *musaf* service, a special prayer (*Hineni He-Ani
Mi-Maas*) is recited. A number of liturgical hymns are also
included in the reader's repetition of the *Amidah*, including the
U-Netanneh Tokef passage. Interpolated in among the *selihot*

and confessions toward the end of *musaf* is the *Elleh Ezkerah* martyrology. Based on a medieval *midrash*, this martyrology describes the plight of the Ten Martyrs, who were persecuted for defying Hadrian's ban on the study of Torah. In some rites this part of the service has been expanded to include readings from Holocaust sources. In the afternoon service Leviticus chapter 18 is read, dealing with prohibited marriages and sexual offenses. The *Haftarah* is the book of Jonah.

Before the concluding service, the hymn *El Nora Alilah* is chanted among Sephardim. This part of the worship service is recited as twilight approaches. During this time hymns such as *Petah Lanu Shaar* serve to remind congregants the the period for repentance is nearly over. In many congregations the Ark remains open and worshippers stand throughout the service. Worshippers ask God to inscribe each person for a good life and to seal them for a favourable fate. *Neilah* concludes with the chanting of *Avinu Malkenu*. This is followed by the *Shema*, the threefold recital of *Barukh Shem Kevod Malkhuto*, and a sevenfold acknowledgement that the Lord is God. The *shofar* is then blown, and the congregants recite *La-Shanah ha-Baah Bi-Yerushalayim* (Next Year in Jerusalem). After the service concludes, it is customary to begin the construction of the booth (*sukkah*).

Sin and Forgiveness

The High Holidays are traditionally understood as a time for spiritual reflection. The entire community is to consider past deeds and seek forgiveness from sin. Repeatedly throughout the Rosh Hashanah and Yom Kippur services, prayers are recited in which believers recount their misdeeds and turn to God for pardon. A typical example is the prayer in the Yom Kippur service in which the congregation confesses its moral failures:

> We have sinned against you by being heartless, And we have sinned against you by speaking recklessly. We have sinned against you openly and in secret, And we have sinned

against you through offensive talk. We have sinned against you through impure thoughts, And we have sinned against you through empty confession. We have sinned against you purposely and by mistake. And we have sinned against you by public desecration of your name.

We have sinned against you through foolish talk, and we have sinned against you wittingly land unwittingly. For all these sins, forgiving God, forgive us, pardon us, grant us atonement. We have sinned against you through bribery. And we have sinned against you through slander. We have sinned against you through gluttony. And we have sinned against you through arrogance. We have sinned against you through wanton glances, And we have sinned against you by rashly judging others. We have sinned against you through stubbornness. And we have sinned against you through gossip. We have sinned against you through baseless hatred, And we have sinned against you by succumbing to dismay. For all these sins, forgiving God, pardon us, grant us atonement.[6]

A central presupposition of such prayers is that God listens to supplications addressed to him and, through his mercy and compassion, forgives sin. Yet, various theological difficulties are connected with this belief. First, if God is omniscient it is difficult to see how prayers could convey information to him about our transgressions. Surely if God knows everything, then there is no need for us to tell him about our sins since He already possesses such knowledge. Further, if God is outside time as traditional Judaism affirms, He is conscious of our transgressions even before we commit them. Finally, the notion that God pardons sinners is difficult to comprehend, given that God knows eternally both our actions and their consequences. Given God's omniscience, it appears that our actions are predetermined in any case: if God knows what we will do before we act, then surely we cannot do otherwise. Hence, we could argue there is no need to seek forgiveness for our actions.

These theological perplexities arise from the traditional Jewish understanding of God's nature. Through the centuries Jewish philosophers have wrestled with such dilemmas. Yet, despite the seemingly intractable problems associated with intercessory prayers directed to God during the High Holy Days, there is no doubt that such supplications are of enormous psychological benefit. The Ten Days of Penitence provide an opportunity for all Jews to reflect on their actions during the past year. Through the recitation of communal sins, each Jew is afforded the opportunity to consider past transgressions. Such a process of internal examination and moral evaluation can serve as a means of ethical improvement and a redirection of one's life.

Both the traditional *siddur* and the prayerbooks used in non-Orthodox communities highlight this central feature of the High Holy Day period. *Gates of the Seasons*, for example, a guide to the Jewish year published by the Reform movement, emphasizes that human beings are free moral agents who are called to account during this season:

> Rabbinic tradition identifies *Rosh Hashanah* as *Yom Hadin*, Judgment Day, and in this spirit a Talmudic parable pictures God as sitting in judgment of the world and each individual on *Rosh Hashanah*. The image of God as judge, about to inscribe human beings according to their deeds in the appropriate Book of Life, underscores the Jewish concept of human beings as moral free agents responsible for the choices which they make. We are further encouraged to believe that our fate, and indeed the fate of the entire world, depends upon every act.

> Following from the theme of divine judgement is the concept of making amends for the past and beginning the year with a clean slate. According to Judaic tradition, repentance, prayer, and charity temper judgment's severe decree. Through these *mitzvot* Jews seek to re-establish their relationship with God and with other human beings and accomplish reconciliation with God.[7]

For modern Jews such an awareness of the centrality of the moral life is of vital significance. As in the past, Rosh Hashanah and Yom Kippur can continue to recall Jews to an awareness of their moral failings and the necessity of embracing the highest ethical values in their daily lives. This yearly reminder still retains its spiritual significance for the contemporary Jewish community. By focusing on prayer, repentance, and charity, the High Holy Days function as a reminder of the highest moral principles of the faith.

Chapter 19.

DAYS OF JOY

Throughout the Jewish year, the community celebrates a number of days of joy, including Hanukkah, Purim, Rosh Hodesh, the New Year for Trees, the Fifteenth of *Av*, and Israel Independence Day. During these celebrations, Jews remember joyous historical events as well as times of the year when thanks are due to God for his blessings. In the modern world these festivities can retain their spiritual significance even if there is considerable uncertainty about the historical basis of these occasions.

Reform Celebration

At the Temple I attended as a child, festivities on these joyous days were a central feature of the religion school program. During the spring festival of Purim we were encouraged to wear costumes based on the characters in the Book of Esther. In the religious service, the *Megillah* was read and noisily we booed Haman whenever his name was mentioned. Repeatedly we were reminded of the victory of the Jewish people over their enemies: this ancient story, we were told, has symbolic significance in every generation when Jews are faced with oppression and persecution:

> We bless Thee, O Lord, our God, that Thou hast sustained us in life and preserved the house of Israel unto this day. Thou didst work miracles for our fathers in the days of old, and hast enabled us to survive the enemies of Thy truth. When Haman rose up against us, Thou didst cause the devotion of Mordecai and the lovingkindness of Esther to triumph over unjust wrath and hate. The righteous were delivered out of the hand of the wicked, and those who sought to destroy were themselves destroyed. Thou hast ever been Israel's salvation, our hope in every generation. None that trusts in Thee shall be put to shame.

> We pray, Thee, O Father, that in the presence of cruelty and wrong our hearts remain steadfast and true. When evil men plot against us and seek to uproot us, let not despair drain our strength nor fear chill our faith. Teach us to meet adversity with resolute will and unyielding self-possession. Keep alive within us the vision of our higher purposes and nobler destiny, and renew our zeal for the divine tasks of life. Open our hearts to the cry of the persecuted and the despoiled. Hasten the day when strife shall cease from the family of men, and justice and love reign supreme in the world.[1]

This theme of triumph over oppression was echoed in the winter festival of Hanukkah. This celebration commemorates the victory of the Jews over the Hellenizers who sought to pollute Jewish life in Judaea. During the second century B.C.E., a guerrilla band led by the priest Mattathias and his sons engaged in armed revolt against the Seleucids. After Mattathias' death, this movement was spearheaded by his son Judas. After the Seleucids were defeated, the Temple was restored and re-dedicated on 24 *Kislev*—an event subsequently commemorated by Hanukkah, the festival of lights.

During Hanukkah, the *menorah* candles were kindled for eight days, and prayers were said at home. On the first evening one light was lit, and blessings were recited:

> Praised be Thou, O Lord our God, Ruler of the world, who hast sanctified us by Thy commandments and bidden us kindle the Hanukkah lights.
>
> Praised be Thou, O Lord our God, Ruler of the world, who didst wonderous things for our fathers at this season in those days.
>
> Praised be Thou, O Lord our God, Ruler of the world, who has granted us life, sustained us and permitted us to celebrate this joyous festival.

After kindling the lights, the following prayers were said emphasizing the spiritual significance of this ancient festival: for modern Jewry, Hanukkah should serve as an inspiration and encouragement:

> Praised be Thou, O Lord our God, King of the universe, for the inspiring truths of which we are reminded by these *Hanukkah* lights.
>
> We kindle them to recall the great and wonderful deeds wrought through the zeal with which God filled the hearts of the heroic Maccabees. These lights remind us that we should ever look unto God, whence comes our help.
>
> As their brightness increases from night to night, let us more fervently give praise to God for the ever-present help He has been to our fathers in the gloomy nights of trouble and oppression.
>
> The sages and heroes of all generations made every sacrifice

to keep the light of God's truth burning brightly. May we and our children be inspired by their example, so that at last Israel may be a guide to all men on the way of righteousness and peace.[2]

In religion school these two joyous festivals were linked, emphasizing the ancient triumph of the Jewish people over their enemies and providing a basis for hope in a post-Holocaust world. In the years following the Second World War, when millions of Jews had lost their lives at the hands of the Nazis, the stories of Purim and Hanukkah were reminders that God does not forsake his people. The creation of a Jewish homeland in the Middle East, we were told, was a sign of his abiding concern, and a potent symbol of the Jewish determination to survive in the face of the most virulent hatred in the history of the nation.

Joyous Ceremonies

Throughout the Jewish year, the community celebrates a number of joyous occasions:

1. Hanukkah. This festival (meaning "dedication") is celebrated for eight days beginning on 25th *Kislev*; it commemorates the victory of the Maccabees over the Seleucids in the second century B.C.E. The Seleucids had desecrated the Temple in Jerusalem, an act which provoked a military struggle. After three years of conflict (165-163 B.C.E.), the Maccabees under Judah Maccabee conquered Jerusalem and rebuilt the altar. According to tradition, one day's worth of oil miraculously kept the menorah burning in the Temple for eight days. Hanukkah commemorates this miracle.

The central observance of this festival is the kindling of the festive lamp on each of the eight nights. This practice gave this festival the additional name of *Hag ha-Urim* (Festival of Lights). In ancient times, this lamp was placed in the doorway or in the street outside; later the lamp was placed inside the house. The lighting occurs after dark (except on Friday evenings, when it must be done before the kindling of the Sabbath lights). The procedure for lighting the Hanukkah candles is to light one candle on the first night, and an additional candle each night until the last night when all eight candles are lit. The kindling should go from left to right. An alternative tradition prescribes that the eight candles are lit on the first night, seven on the second night, and so forth. These candles are it by an additional candle called the *shammash* (serving light). In addition to this home ceremony, candles are lit in the synagogue.

After the proper number of lights have been kindled, the hymn *Maoz Tzur* is chanted:

> O mighty Rock of my Salvation, to praise You is a delight. Restore my House of Prayer and there we will bring a thanksgiving offering. When You will have prepared the slaughter for the blaspheming foe, Then I shall complete with a song of hymn the dedication of the Altar.
>
> Troubles sated my soul, when with grief my strength was consumed. They had embittered my life with hardship with the calf-like kingdom's bondage.
>
> But with His great power
> He brought forth the treasured ones,
> Pharaoh's army and all his offspring
> went down like a stone into the deep.
>
> To the abode of His holiness He brought me
> But there, too, I had no rest
> And an oppressor came and exiled me.
> For I had served aliens
> And had drunk benumbing wine.
> Scarcely had I departed (my land)
> When at Babylonia's demise Zerubabel came—
> At the end of seventy years I was saved.
> To sever the towering cypres sought the Aggagite, son of

Hammedatha, But it became a snare and a stumbling block to
him and his arrogance was stilled.

The head of the Benjaminite You lifted and the enemy, his
name You blotted out His numerous progeny—his possessions—on the gallows You hanged.

Greeks gathered against me
then in Hasmonean days.
They breached the walls of my towers
and they defiled all the oils;
And from the one remnant of the flasks
a miracle was wrought for the roses.
Men of insight—eight days
established for song and jubilation....[3]

In the synagogue liturgy Hanukkah is commemorated by the
recitation of the *Al ha-Nissim* prayer in the *Amidah*, and Grace
after Meals. In the morning service the *Hallel* is recited, and a
special reading of the Law takes place on each day of the holiday.
During Hanukkah, it is customary to hold parties which include
games and singing. The most well-known game involves a *dreydel*
(spinning top). The *dreydel* is inscribed with four Hebrew letters
on its side (*nun, gimmel, he shin*)—this is an acrostic for the phrase
'*nes gadol hayah sham*' (a great miracle happened here). During
Hanukkah it is customary to eat latkes (potato pancakes) and
sufganiyot (doughnuts). In Israel the festival is associated with
national heroism, and a torch is carried from the traditional burial
site of the Maccabees at Modiin to various parts of the country.

2. Purim is celebrated on the 14th of *Adar* to commemorate
the deliverance of Persian Jewry from Haman, the chief minister
of King Ahasureus. The name of this festival is derived from the
Akkadian word '*pur*' (lots) which refers to Haman's casting lots
to determine a date to destroy the Jewish people (Esther 3:7–14).
In remembrance of this date, the Fast of Esther is observed

on 13th of Adar—on this day Queen Esther proclaimed a fast before she interceded with the king. On the next day Purim is celebrated as the Feast of Lots which Mordecai, Esther's cousin. inaugurated to remember the deliverance of the Jewish people (Esth. 9:20ff) The 15th of Adar is *Purim Shoshan* since the conflict between the Jews and Haman's supporters in ancient Susa did not cease until the 14th, and Ahasureus allowed the Jews an extra day to overcome their foes. This means that the deliverance could only be celebrated a day later. (Esth. 9:13–18)

The laws regarding the observance of Purim are specified in the tractate *Megillah* in the Talmud. In the evening and morning service the Esther scroll is chanted to a traditional melody. In most congregations Purim resembles a carnival—children often attend the reading of the *megillah* in fancy dress, and whenever Haman's name is mentioned, worshippers stamp their feet and whirl noisemakers (*greggers*). In the *Amidah* and Grace after Meals a prayer of thanksgiving is included:

> In the days of Mordecai and Esther, in Shushan the capital, when Haman, the wicked, rose up against them and sought to destroy, to slay, and to exterminate all the Jews, young and old, infants and women, on the same day, on the thirteenth of the twelfth month which is the month of *Adar*, and to plunder their possessions. But You, in Your abundant mercy, nullified his counsel and frustrated his intention and caused his design to return upon his own head and they hanged him and his sons on the gallows.[4]

During the afternoon, a special festival meal takes place including such traditional dishes as *Hamentashen* (Haman's hats)— triangular buns or pastries filled with poppyseeds, prunes, dates, and the like. It is usual for parents and relatives to give children money (Purim gelt). On Purim it is customary to stage plays, and in *yeshivot* students mimic their teachers. In Israel parades take place with revellers dressed in Purim costumes.

3. *Rosh Hodesh* is another festival of joy which takes place with
the New Moon each month. Since the Jewish calendar is lunar,
each month lasts a little more than twenty-nine days. Because it
was not possible to arrange the calendar with months of alternative length the Sanhedrin declared whether a month had twenty-
nine or thirty days. If the outgoing month had twenty-nine days,
the next day was *Rosh Hodesh*. When a month had thirty days, the
last day of the outgoing month and the first day of the new month
constituted *Rosh Hodesh*. In early rabbinic times, the Sanhedrin
was responsible for determining the day of the New Moon on the
basis of eye witnesses who had claimed to see the new moon. Only
in the fourth century was a permanent calendar fixed by Hillel II.

During the period of the First Temple, *Rosh Hodesh* was observed with the offering of special sacrifices, the blowing of the
ram's horn, feasting and rest from work. By the end of the sixth
century B.C.E., *Rosh Hodesh* became a semi-holiday. Eventually
even this status disappeared, and *Rosh Hodesh* became a normal
working day except for various liturgical changes. The liturgy for
Rosh Hodesh includes the *Yaaleh Ve-Yavo* prayer, the *Amidah,* and
the Grace After Meals, which ask God to remember his people
for good, for blessing and for life:

> Our God and God of our forefathers, may there rise, come,
> reach, be noted, be favoured, be heard, be considered, and be
> remembered—the remembrance and consideration of our-
> selves; the remembrance of our forefathers, the remembrance
> of Messiah, son of David, Your servant, the remembrance
> of Jerusalem, the City of Your Holiness; the remembrance
> of Your entire people the Family of Israel—before You for
> deliverance, for goodness, for grace, for kindness, and for
> compassion, for life, and for peace on this day of *Rosh Hodesh*.
> Remember us on it, *Hashem*, our God, for goodness; consider
> us on it for blessing; and help us on it for life. In the matter of
> salvation and compassion, pity, be gracious and compassionate
> with us and help us, for our eyes are turned to You, because
> You are God, the gracious, and compassionate.[5]

In the morning service the *Hallel* psalms of praise are recited. The Bible reading is from Numbers chapter 28 which describes the Temple service for the New Moon. An additional service is also included, corresponding to the additional sacrifice which was offered on the New Moon.

4. A further joyous spring festival is the New Year for Trees (*Tu Bi-Shevat*) which takes place on 15th of *Shevat*. Even though this festival is not mentioned in the Bible, it appeared in the Second Temple period as a fixed cut-off date for determining the tithe levied on the produce of fruit trees. Once the Temple was destroyed, the laws of tithing were no longer applicable. As a result, this festival took on a new character. Wherever Jews resided, it reminded them of their connection with the Holy Land. During the fifteenth century, a number of new ceremonies and rituals were instituted by the mystics of Safed. Due to the influence of Isaac Luria, it became customary to celebrate the festival with gatherings where special fruits were eaten and hymns and readings from Scripture were recited. Among the fruits eaten on *Tu Bi-Shevat* were those of the Holy Land. In modern Israel, new trees are planted during this festival.

5. Another joyous occasion is the 15th of *Av*, which was a summer folk festival in the Second Temple period. At this time bachelors selected their wives from unmarried maidens. According to the Mishnah, on both this day and the Day of Atonement, young girls in Jerusalem dressed in white garments and danced in the vineyards where young men selected their brides. In modern times this festival is marked only by a ban on eulogies or fasting. In the liturgy the *Tanannun* prayer is not recited after the *Amidah*.

6. The final festival is Israel Independence Day—this is Israel's national day, which commemorates the proclamation of its independence on May 14, 1948. The Chief Rabbinate of Israel declared it a religious holiday, and established a special order of service for the evening and morning worship. This service includes

the *Hallel* and a reading from Isaiah (Isa. 10:32-11:12). The rabbinate also suspended any fast which occurs on the day, the recital of the *Tahanun* prayer, and mourning restrictions of the *omer* period. In Israel the preceding day is set aside as a day of remembrance for soldiers who died in battle. *Yizkor* prayers are recited then, and next-of-kin visit the military cemeteries. At home memorial candles are lit, and Psalm 9 is recited in many synagogues:

> I will give thanks to the Lord with my whole heart;
> I will tell of all thy wonderful deeds.
> I will be glad and exult in thee,
> I will sing praise to thy name, O Most High.

> When my enemies turned back, they stumbled and perished before thee. For thou hast maintained my just cause; thou hast sat on the throne giving right.

> Thou hast rebuked the nations, thou hast destroyed the wicked; thou hast blotted out their name for ever and ever. The enemy have vanished in everlasting ruins; their cities thou hast rooted out; the very memory of them has perished. (Ps. 9:1–6)

Jewish History and Freedom

As we have seen, the Bible records hostility to the Jews from the beginnings of the Hebrew nation. According to Scripture, Pharaoh feared the Jews and sought their destruction. On his instruction, first-born sons were to be killed. Every year at the Passover festival meal, Jews recount the narrative of the exodus from Egypt. During this ceremony, unleavened bread (*matzah*) serves to symbolize persecution and oppression. Other Passover symbols further stress the suffering of the Jewish people. The bitter herb, for example, is eaten because "the Egyptians embittered the life of our ancestors in Egypt. And they made their lives bitter with hard bondage." In such passages, the myth of

Jewish oppression is paramount, and this theme integrates the events that allegedly took place in ancient Egypt.

Another important day in the Jewish calendar which emphasizes victory over Israel's enemies is the Purim festival. As we noted, the Book of Esther deals with the Jewish community in the town of Susa, the Persian capital during the reign of King Xerxes in the fifth century B.C.E. The Bible relates that once Esther had become the consort of King Ahasuerus, her uncle Mordecai discovered a plot to destroy the Jewish people. Haman, the chief adviser to the king, was outraged that Mordecai would not bow down to him and declared to the king:

> There is a certain people scattered abroad and dispersed among the peoples in all the provinces of your kingdom; their laws are different from those of every other people, and they do not keep the king's laws, so that it is not for the king's profit to tolerate them. If it pleases the king, let it be decreed that they be destroyed. (Esth. 3:8–9)

Here the Jews are depicted as an alien people, determined to observe their own customs. But, as the Book of Esther relates, Haman's scheming was foiled, and the Jews were protected by royal decree. At the kings's request, secretaries wrote to all the governors of all the provinces where Jews lived, granting them permission to defend themselves from attack. To commemorate this story, the festival of Purim was inaugurated. In mythological terms, Haman personifies all of Israel's enemies through the ages.

The theme of suffering and triumph is reiterated at Hanukkah. This festival is celebrated for eight days and commemorates the victory of the Maccabees over the Seleucids in the second century B.C.E. The central observance of Hanukkah is the kindling of the festival lamp or candles on each of the eight nights—symbolically this Festival of Lights represents the triumph of light over darkness. The message is that the Jewish people will ultimately overcome their enemies.

This tradition of Jewish persecution and suffering embedded

in the biblical narrative and commemorated in Jewish observances forms the background to an understanding of Jewish
consciousness concerning the origins and nature of hostility
to the Jewish people as it evolved through history. In our post-
Holocaust world, the festivals of joy can continue to remind
Jewry of the possibilities of hope in the face of oppression,
persecution, and murder. More importantly, these festivals could
encourage the Jewish community to assist those who—like the
Jews in past centuries—are currently suffering under the yoke
of oppression and exploitation. Just as Jews were liberated from
their enemies in ancient times, so the modern Jewish community could endeavor to free those who are presently enslaved.

As God's suffering servant through the ages, the Jewish people
could strive to identify with the plight of the poor. In Scripture
the prophets condemned every kind of abuse. Scripture speaks
of positive action to prevent poverty from becoming widespread.
Leviticus and Deuteronomy contain detailed legislation designed to prevent the accumulation of wealth and consequent
exploitation of the unfortunate. Jews should thus feel an obligation to take steps to eradicate poverty and suffering from the
modern world. In particular, they could address themselves to
the economic deprivation that affects certain groups: the young
who are frustrated by the lack of opportunity to obtain training
and work; manual laborers, who are frequently ill-paid and find
difficulty in defending their rights; the unemployed, who are
discarded because of the harsh exigencies of economic life; and
the old, who are often marginalized and disregarded. In all such
cases, the festivals of joy, which celebrate human freedom, serve
as a framework for reflection on the plight of the downtrodden
in modern society.

A new vision of Judaism might thus envisage the goal of
freedom from oppression as a central preoccupation. Today as
never before, Jews can become a saving remnant of the modern
world. Embodying the liberation message of Scripture, they
like Abraham can hope against hope in laboring to build a just
and more humane world. The festivals of joy that celebrate the

Jewish liberation can thus act as a clarion call to the Jewish community, awakening the people of Israel to their divinely appointed task. Jewish tradition points to God's kingdom as the hope of humankind: a world in which all peoples and nations shall turn away from iniquity and injustice. This is not the hope of bliss in a future life, but the building up of the divine kingdom of truth and peace among all peoples.

Chapter 20.

LIFE-CYCLE EVENTS

The Jewish life-cycle is marked by a series of religious events which celebrate various stages of development. Beginning with birth, a number of ceremonies mark the acceptance of the child into the Jewish community. For male infants, the act of circumcision symbolizes the child's identification as a Jew. The Redemption of the First-born recalls the ancient practice of redeeming the child from Temple service. Bar mitzvah and bat mitzvah as well as confirmation constitute steps toward Jewish adulthood. Finally, the Jewish marriage service binds the bride and groom in the presence of God.

Reform Jewish Practice

Distancing itself from Orthodox Judaism, the Reform movement has jettisoned a number of features of the traditional pattern of life-cycle events. Nonetheless, a number of the ancient traditions have been retained within a Reform context. Baby naming, for example, continues to be a common practice. At such an event, the rabbi recited prayers for both sons and daughters:

> Our God, Source of all life, we thank Thee for all the blessings Thou dost grant unto us. We thank Thee especially for the sacred joy and privilege of parenthood, which gives supreme meaning and purpose to our existence.
>
> Grateful for Thy gift of a new life, happy parents have come before Thee to render homage unto Thee, to invoke Thy blessing, and to seek Thy guidance in the upbringing of their child (children). Grant unto them wisdom, patience and devotion, that they may rear their child (children) to live in accordance with Thy law.
>
> Our God and God of our fathers, sustain this child in life and health, and let him (her) be known in the household of Israel by the name _____. May this name become honored and respected. Extend Thy sheltering arm over him (her) and give him (her) health and understanding. May he (she) so live as to bring blessing to parents, to the congregation and to mankind.[1]

Circumcision has also been regarded as a central event in the life of a child. At the circumcision ceremony, prayers are recited which emphasize the biblical background to this act. At the beginning of the circumcision service, the father declares:

> In conformity with hallowed Jewish observance, I present my son for the covenant of circumcision.
>   Blessed art Thou, O Lord our God, Ruler of the Universe, who hast sanctified us by Thy commandments and commanded us to bring our sons into the covenant of Abraham our father.

> For He established a testimony in Jacob, and appointed a law
> in Israel, which He commanded our fathers, that they should
> make them known to their children; that the generation to come
> might know them, even the children that should be born.[2]

Although Reform Judaism embraced these ancient life-cycle
events, the movement discarded the ceremony of Redemption of
the First Born. In the view of the early reformers, such a procedure is no longer relevant given that the Temple no longer exists.
Further, Reform Judaism has abolished the role of the priesthood, and therefore it makes no sense to envisage first-born sons
being handed over to serve in a priestly capacity. Some reformers
also sought to abolish bar mitzvah as a *rite de passage* to adulthood. In their view, it was preferable to institute confirmation as
an alternative: through confirmation, they believed, Jewish children could attest their dedication to the Jewish heritage. As time
passed, however, bar mitzvah was introduced as an important
element of the tradition.

In my Temple, bar mitzvah ceremonies took place during
the Sabbath services. Bar mitzvah candidates learned how to
read their Torah portions and memorized their bar mitzvah
speeches—usually the ceremony was followed by a reception in
the Temple, and often later by a party for friends and relatives.
Confirmation took place at the age of 15 for both boys and girls,
and each confirmand participated in a service in the Temple.

Turning to marriage, the Reform marriage service follows the
general outline of the traditional marriage ceremony. Nonetheless,
it has dispensed with the reading of the *ketubbah* (marriage document). The service begins with a series of blessings:

> Blessed be he that cometh in the name of the Lord.
> Serve the Lord with gladness; come before Him with singing.
> O God supremely blessed, supreme in might and glory, guide
> and bless this bridegroom and bride.

Following an address to the bridegroom and bride, the rabbi

recites the traditional seven benedictions:

> Blessed art Thou, O Lord Our God, Ruler of the Universe, Who hast created all things for Thy glory.
>
> Blessed art Thou, O Lord our God, Ruler of the Universe, Creator of man.
>
> Blessed art Thou, O Lord our God, Ruler of the Universe, Who hast fashioned us in Thine own image and hast established marriage for the fulfillment and perpetuation of life in accordance with Thy holy purpose. Blessed art Thou, O Lord, Creator of man.
>
> Blessed art Thou, O Lord our God, Ruler of the Universe, Who art the source of all gladness and joy. Through Thy grace we attain affection, companionship, and peace. Grant, O Lord, that the love which unites this bridegroom and bride may grow in abiding happiness. May their family life be ennobled through their devotion to the faith of Israel. May there be peace in their home, quietness and confidence in their hearts. May they be sustained by Thy comforting presence in the midst of our people and by Thy promise of salvation for all mankind. Blessed art Thou, O Lord, Who doest unite bridegroom and bride in holy joy.[3]

After offering wine to the bride and groom, the rabbi asks them to recite the following statements:

> (To the bridegroom): As you _____ place this ring upon the finger of your bride, speak to her these words:
>
> With this ring be thou consecrated unto me as my wife according to the law of God and the faith of Israel.
>
> (To the bride): And you say unto him these words:
>
> Be thou consecrated unto me as my husband according to the law of God and the faith of Israel.[4]

This series of life-cycle events thus constitutes a framework for Jewish living from the cradle to the marriage canopy.

The Jewish Life-Cycle

1. Childbirth. In Scripture the first commandment is to be fruitful and multiply. (Gen. 1:28) In ancient times childbirth took place in a kneeling position or sitting on a special birth-stool. Biblical law imposes various restrictions concerning ritual purity and impurity of the mother: if she gives birth to a boy she is considered ritually impure for seven days; for the next thirty-three days she is not allowed to enter the Temple precincts or handle sacred objects. For the mother of a girl, the number of days are respectively fourteen and sixty-six. According to Jewish law, if a woman in childbirth is in mortal danger, her life takes precedence over that of the fetus—only when over half of the child's body has emerged from the birth canal is it considered to be fully human.

In ancient times the birth of a child was accompanied by numerous superstitious practices, including the use of amulets to ward off the evil eye. After the birth, family and friends gathered nightly to recite prayers to ward off evil spirits. Among German Jewry, it was frequently the practice for parents of a son to cut off a strip of swaddling in which the child was wrapped during his circumcision; this is known as the wimple and it is kept until his bar mitzvah, when it is used for tying the scroll of the Law. From the medieval period Ashkenazi mothers visited the synagogue after the birth of a child to recite the *Gomel* blessing (which expresses gratitude to God), as well as other prayers. It is also the custom for the congregation to recite the *Mi She-Barakh* prayer for the welfare of the mother and the child.

2. Babynaming. The naming of a newborn child takes place on one of the two occasions: a baby boy is named at the circumcision ceremony. A baby girl is named in the synagogue the first time the Torah is read after her birth. The Hebrew form of the individual's name consists of the person's name followed by *ben* (son) or *bat* (daughter) of the father. This form is used in all Hebrew documents as well as for the call to the reading of the Torah. In modern times it is still the practice to give a child a Jewish name in addition to a secular one. Ashkenazi Jews

frequently name the child after a deceased relative; Sephardic Jews after someone who is still alive. Alternatively, a Hebrew name may be selected that is related to the secular name either in meaning or sound, or the secular name may be transliterated in Hebrew characters. Traditionally it was the custom to change the name of a person at the time of a serious illness. According to the rabbis, changing the name is a way of misleading the angel of death. On this basis, it became the custom to add a further name to the ill person's. From that point the person was known by his original name, together with the new one.

3. Redemption of the First-Born. The custom of redeeming first-born male children is based on the biblical prescription that first-born sons should be consecrated to the Temple. Just as first fruits and first-born animals had to be given to the priests, so first-born male children were dedicated to God. The obligation to redeem first-born sons from this service is referred to in Numbers 3:44–51. Redemption is to take place by payment of five shekels to a priest. Detailed laws concerning the Redemption of the First-Born are presented in the Mishnah tractate *Behorot*, and expanded in the talmudic commentary on this passage. According to this legislation, the sons of priests and Levites are exempt from redemption, as are first-born sons whose mother is the daughter of either a priest or Levite. In the geonic period, a ceremony was instituted in which the father of the child declares to the priest on the thirty-first day after its birth that the infant is the first-born son of his mother and father and that, as a father, he is obliged to redeem him. The priest then asks the father if he prefers to give his son to the priest or redeem him for five shekels. The father replies that he wants to redeem his son, and hands the priest the required amount. The father then recites a blessing concerning the fulfillment of the precept of redeeming the child, and another expressing gratitude to God. This procedure has served as the basis for the ceremony since the Middle Ages.

4. Circumcision. According to Jewish law, all male children are to undergo circumcision, in accordance with God's decree,

and as a sign of the covenant between God and Abraham's off-spring. As Genesis 17 relates: "God said to Abraham... 'This is my covenant which you shall keep between me and you and your descendants after you; every male among you shall be circumcised. You shall be circumcised in the flesh of your foreskins, and it shall be a sign of the covenant between me and you.'" (Gen. 17:9–11)

Jewish ritual circumcision involves the removal of the entire foreskin. It is to be performed on the eighth day after the birth of the child by a person who is properly qualified (*mohel*). Jewish law specifies that this ceremony can be performed even on the Sabbath, festivals, or the Day of Atonement; however, postponement is allowed if there is any danger to the child's health. The laws regulating this procedure are derived from biblical sources as well as rabbinic enactments. Traditionally the ceremony is to take place in the presence of a *minyan*, a quorum of ten adult Jewish men. On the morning of the eighth day, the infant is taken from the mother by the godmother who hands him to the *sandak*. The *sandak* then carries the child into the room where the circumcision is to take place and hands him to the individual who places the child on a chair called the Chair of Elijah. Another person then takes him from the Chair of Elijah and passes him to the child's father who puts him on the lap of the godfather who holds the boy during the ceremony. The circumcision is performed by a *mohel*; formerly blood was drawn orally by the *mohel*, but today an instrument is used. The infant is then handed to the person who will hold him during the ceremony of naming, and the ceremony concludes with a special blessing over a cup of wine, followed by the naming of the child.

5. Bar mitzvah and Bat mitzvah. At thirteen a boy attains the age of Jewish adulthood; from this point he is counted as part of a *minyan* (the quorum for prayer). According to the Mishnah, the thirteenth year is when a boy should observe the commandments. The term bar mitzvah ("the son of a commandment") occurs five times in the Babylonian Talmud, but in all cases it is used merely to refer to someone obliged to fulfil Jewish law.

The Talmud stipulates that male adolescence begins at the age of thirteen years and a day; nonetheless a boy was able to participate in religious ceremonies at an earlier age as long as he could appreciate their meaning. However, by the Middle Ages, a Jewish minor's participation in religious rituals had become limited. Ashekenazim, for example, allowed a boy to wear *tefillin* only after he was thirteen; in addition he was not allowed to be called to the reading of the Law until then. Sephardic congregations also imposed similar restrictions.

The essentials for the bar mitzvah involve prayer with *tefillin* for the first time, and a reading from the Torah. Among East European Ashekanzim, a boy was normally called to the reading of the Torah on the first Monday or Thursday after his thirteenth birthday. Then he would recite the Torah blessings and chant some verses from the weekly *sidrah*. In Western Europe on the other hand, a thirteen-year-old boy would be called to the reading at Sabbath morning services where he would recite the Torah blessings, chant a portion of the law (*maftir*) and read from the Prophets. This has now become a universally accepted practice.

Unlike bar mitzvah, there is no legal requirement for a girl to take part in a religious ceremony to mark her religious majority (at the age of twelve years and a day). Nonetheless, a ceremonial equivalent of bar mitzvah has been designed for girls. In Orthodoxy this was the innovation of Jacob Ettliner in the nineteenth century, and subsequently spread to other lands. In the late nineteenth century it was approved by Joseph Hayyim ben Elijah al-hakam of Baghdad, who formulated various regulations concerning this event.

In the early twentieth century the Conservative scholar Mordecai Kaplan pioneered the bat mitzvah ceremony in the United States as part of the synagogue service, and since then this has become widely accepted by many American communities. In non-Orthodox congregations, a twelve-year-old girl celebrates her coming of age on a Friday night or during the Sabbath morning service where she conducts the prayers, chants the *Haftarah*, and in some cases reads from the Torah and delivers an address. In Orthodox synagogues, however, the bat mitzvah's role in the services is more limited. At a women's *minyan*, however, she is called to the reading of the Torah and may chant one of the portions, together with the *Haftarah*.

Outside the United States the bat mitzvah ceremony takes various forms. In Reform congregations it is in line with the American pattern. Orthodox girls, however, do not participate in the synagogue service; rather a bat mitzvah's father is called to the Torah on the appropriate Sabbath morning and recites the *Barukh She-Petaroni* benediction. His daughter then recites the *Sheheheyanu* prayer, and the rabbi addresses her in the synagogue or at a *kiddush* reception afterwards. Alternatively, the ceremony occurs at home or in the synagogue hall on a weekday. In Britain and South Africa the procedure is different: bat mitzvah girls must pass a special examination enabling them to participate in a collective ceremony.

6. Marriage. In the Jewish faith marriage is viewed as a sacred bond as well as a means to personal fulfillment. It is more than a legal contract; it is an institution with cosmic significance, legitimized through divine authority. The purpose of marriage is to build a home, create a family, and thereby perpetuate society. Initially Jews were allowed to have more than one wife, but this was banned in Ashkenazi countries with the decree of Rabbenu Gershom in 1000.

In the Bible marriages were arranged by fathers: Abraham, for example, sent his servant to find a wife for Isaac (Gen. 24:10–53), and Judah arranged the marriage of his first-born son (Gen. 38:6). When the proposal of marriage was accepted by the girls' father (or elder brother in his absence), the nature and amount of the *mohar* (payment by the groom) was fixed. By Second Temple times, there was a degree of choice in the selection of the bride.

According to tradition, a period of engagement preceded marriage itself. The ceremony was a seven-day occasion for celebration during which love songs were sung in praise of the bride. In the talmudic period a major development occurred concerning the *mohar*—since it could be used by the father of the bride, a

wife could become penniless if her husband divorced or prede-
ceased her. As a result the *mohar* evolved into the formulation
of a marriage document (*ketubbah*) which gave protection to the
bride. In addition, the act of marriage changed from a personal
civil procedure to a public religious ceremony that required the
presence of a *minyan* and the recitation of prayers.

In biblical and talmudic times, marriage occurred in two
stages: betrothal and *nissuin*. From the Middle Ages, it became
customary for Ashkenazic Jewish communities to postpone the
betrothal ceremony until immediately prior to the *nissuin* (second stage in the marriage procedure) wedding ceremony—this
also became customary among Sephardic Jews. In Hasidic communities, however, the traditional *tenaim* (betrothal) ceremony is
still usually observed.

Prior to the wedding itself, the bride is to immerse herself in a
mikveh (ritual bath) usually on the evening before the ceremony.
To facilitate this the wedding date is determined so that it does
not take place during the time of menstruation or the following week. In some Sephardic and Eastern communities this
event is a public celebration. In most Sephardi communities a
special celebration for the bride takes place on the evening of
the wedding. On the Sabbath before the wedding in Ashkenazi
communities, the groom is called to the reading of the Law and
is showered with candies during the reading of the Torah blessings. The wedding ceremony can be held anywhere, but since the
Middle Ages the synagogue or synagogue courtyard has been
commonly used. It also became customary to hold it in the open
air to symbolize God's promise to Abraham to make his descendants as numerous as the stars.

In modern times the traditional wedding ceremony follows
a uniform pattern. Normally the groom signs the *ketubbah*.
During the ceremony the groom is led to the bride and covers
her face with a veil; the couple are led next to the *huppah* (marriage canopy) along with their parents. When the participants
are under the *huppah,* the rabbi recites the blessing over wine
and the *erusin* blessing. Then the bride and groom drink from

the cup. The groom then recites the traditional formula: "Behold you are consecrated unto me with this ring according to the law of Moses and of Israel." To demonstrate that the act of marriage consists of two ceremonies, the *ketubbah* is read prior to the *nissuin* ceremony. The seven blessings are then recited over a second cup of wine. The ceremony concludes with the groom stepping on a glass and breaking it.

Within Conservative and Reform Judaism the wedding service follows this traditional pattern with varying alterations.

Observing the Jewish Life-Cycle

As we have seen, prescriptions regulating life-cycle events are divine commands. Today Orthodox Jews continue to subscribe to the belief that these obligations are of divine origin; for this reason, they are scrupulously followed by the strictly observant. Yet, as we noted, the basis for such religious convictions is no longer credible. In the past Jews believed that the Torah was revealed on Mount Sinai, and supplemented by the Oral Law, which was also disclosed to Moses. This conviction served as the basis for adherence to the legal code found in the Bible and expanded in rabbinic sources. However, the emergence of biblical criticism in the last centuries has called into question such a conviction. As a consequence, biblical and rabbinic law have come to be viewed by some Jews as products of an earlier age. Given such a shift in perspective, most Jews have ceased to regard biblical and rabbinic law as binding.

In the modern world, therefore, Jews need not feel any sense of duty to follow those *halakhic* sanctions regarding life-cycle events—the obligation to carry out God's will as recorded in Scripture and amplified by rabbinic sages might be left to the individual's conscience. A new vision of Judaism permits such a spirit of personal liberty. Each Jew could feel free to determine which, if any, of these life-cycle events continue to have religious meaning. They might take the view that no religious body should exercise authority to coerce members of the communityinto submission. Rather, I suggest there could be a tolerant, more conservative attitude of diversity of practice.

This does not mean, however, that those various life-cycle events should be regarded as anachronistic. On the contrary, each ceremony can have spiritual meaning for contemporary Jews even if it is no longer viewed as binding. Birth ceremonies, for example, can still retain their religious significance even when stripped of what some might regard as their superstitious characteristics. No longer, I suggest, does it make sense to believe that prayers recited after the birth of a child ward off evil spirits, nor that a child's health is protected by amulets. Nonetheless, the naming of a boy or girl in the synagogue is an occasion for reinforcing the family's link with the Jewish people. In the past a distinction was made between the birth of a boy and a girl, but such gender discrimination is now undesirable—today both sexes can play an equal role in the life of the nation, and the naming ceremony can serve to reinforce such an identification with the community.

Within reform circles, the practice of redeeming the first-born has been abandoned. For more traditional parents, however, this act can still have important symbolic significance. Even though the Temple no longer exists, the procedure of redeeming a child from cultic service is a reminder of the obligation of religious dedication and duty. Just as gratitude to God for the birth of a child is expressed through ritualized prayer, so too circumcision can be understood as a means of giving thanks to God and reinforcing communal ties. The same applies to bar and bat mitzvah as well as confirmation. These religious *rites de passage* emphasize personal commitment to both Judaism and the Jewish people. Similarly, the Jewish marriage ceremony emphasizes the bond between the married couple and the Jewish community.

There are nonetheless inherent dangers in the ways in which some of these ceremonies have been celebrated within the community. Bar mitzvahs are in some cases occasions for lavish one-upmanship. Parents are willing to spend extraordinary sums of money; friends and relations come from afar to stay for weekend celebrations. They may be housed in an expensive hotel, and there may be pre-bar mitzvah dinners and post-bar mitzvah outings. The receptions after the ceremony may be a most grandiose party with professional entertainers and a special theme which has nothing to do with Judaism. Every guest is expected to bring a gift, and the bar mitzvah boy can find himself overwhelmed by presents. The same applies to Jewish weddings, which all too often become occasions for lavish expenditure and excess. The religious establishment is often embarrassed by such extravagance, and critical of the erosion of the religious significance of these occasions. Yet, traditional life-cycle events can still serve as spiritually significant stages in the life of the modern Jew.

Chapter 21.

HOME

In Judaism religious observance in the home is of central importance. According to the sages, it is a *mikdash meat* (a minor sanctuary). Like the synagogue, it continues various traditions of the ancient Temple. The Sabbath candles, for example, recall the Temple *menorah* and the dining table symbolizes the altar. Most significantly, with the home family life is sanctified. In contemporary society, the religious importance of home observance has diminished; nonetheless, Jewish life in the home continues to have spiritual meaning in the lives of modern Jews.

The Reform Home

As we have seen, Reform Judaism has reinterpreted many traditional home practices. On the Sabbath, for example, Sabbath lights are kindled, and the *kiddush* is recited. During Passover, the seder service is observed at home, connecting the Jewish family with previous generations of Jews who celebrated the Exodus from Egypt. In many Reform homes, *mezuzahs* are fixed to the front doorposts. Memorial services also often take place in the home during the period of mourning. Hence, as in Orthodox circles, Jewish homelife is viewed as of central religious importance, as symbolized by the Reform service for the consecration of the home.

Standing before a table on which are placed lighted candles, a loaf of bread, table salt, a cup of wine, a Bible and a *mezuzah*, the rabbi reads the following service:

> Our God and God of our fathers, grant that we may consecrate this new home with humble and grateful hearts. By Thy will we live and toil; by Thy grace we prosper and rejoice. We labor in vain when we labor without Thee; we build on shifting sand when Thou are not our Rock. In Thy goodness Thou dost bless us and cause us to dwell in comfort and peace. We give thanks unto Thee for Thine unfailing love and ever-watchful care.

> Blessed art Thou, O Lord, our God, Ruler of the Universe, who has granted us life, sustained us, and permitted us to celebrate this joyous occasion.

> From of old our homes have been the dwelling place of the Jewish spirit. Within their walls our fathers built altars of faith and love. There they maintained the habit of daily devotion; there they prepared a table for the stranger and the needy. Grant, O God, that this home may be hallowed with devout thoughts and kindly acts. Give us the will, we pray Thee, to keep alive the glow of simple piety and generous hospitality.

After the loaf of bread is cut into pieces, they are dipped in salt and distributed. This is followed by the blessing: "Blessed art

Thou, O Lord, our God, Ruler of all the Universe, who causest the earth to yield food for all."

The rabbi then lifts the wine cup and says:

> Wine is the symbol of joy. "Wine rejoiceth the heart of man." He who ordains life has made all the things that give us happiness. He has also established the home as the source of our deepest joys. We pray Thee, O God, that in this home love may reign and simple pleasures abound. Preserve in us devotion to virtue and simplicity, and enable us to spend our days in contentment, happiness and peace.
>
> Blessed art Thou, O Lord, our God, Ruler of the Universe, Creator of the fruit of the vine.

The rabbi then holds the Bible and proclaims:

> This is the Law by which Israel has lived. It teaches us that man doth not live by bread only, but by everything that proceedeth out of the mouth of the Lord doth man live. We thank Thee, O God, for this Book of the Law, which Thou has placed in our keeping for the good of all mankind. May it ever be a lamp unto our feet, and a light unto our path. Give us understanding, that we keep Thy law and observe it with our whole heart. Implant in us a love of Torah, that we may treasure it more than gold and silver, and take great delight in the study of its teachings.
>
> Blessed art Thou, O Lord, our God, Ruler of the Universe, who has sanctified us by Thy commandments and ordained that we occupy ourselves with the words of the Law.

The rabbi then raises the *mezuzah* and states:

> This ancient symbol of the *mezuzah* speaks, then, to us of the One God, of our need to love Him and to obey His Law. We

affix the *mezuzah* to the doorpost of this home that it may ever remind us of our divine nature and of the sacred duties of life. We have God in our hearts when our home thus bears witness to His holy presence.

Thou, O God, art our guardian and protector. Into Thy hands we commit our lives and destiny. Whatever may befall us, we shall not fear nor be dismayed; for Thou art with us. In Thee we trust; from Thee comes our strength; with Thee alone is the power to save.

The *mezuzah* is then fastened to the doorpost, as a symbol of God's presence.[1]

Jewish Home Ritual

Traditionally, as head of the family, the father is to exercise authority over his wife and children. He is obligated to circumcise his son, redeem him if he is the first-born, teach him Torah, marry him off, and teach him a craft. Further he is obliged to serve as a role model for the transmission of Jewish ideals to his children. Regarding Jewish women, the prevailing sentiment was that the role of the wife is to bear children and exercise responsibility for family life. According to the *halakhah*, womanhood is a separate status with its own specific sets of rules, obligations, and responsibilities. In terms of religious observance, women were classed with slaves and children, disqualified as witnesses, excluded from the study of the Torah, and segregated from men. Furthermore, they were regarded as ritually impure for extended periods of time.

In general, women were exempted from time-bound commandments; as a result they were not obliged to fulfill those *mitzvot* which must be followed at a particular time (such as the recitation of prayer). The purpose of these regulations was to ensure that their attention and energy be directed toward completing their domestic duties. In the contemporary period, however, a growing number of women have agitated for equal treatment.

In consequence, the role of women has undergone a major transformation. Nonetheless, there has been a universal recognition in all branches of Judaism that the Jewish wife should continue to play a central role in the home.

Children are expected to carry out the commandment to honor (Exod. 20:12) and respect (Lev. 19:3) their parents. For the rabbis, the concept of honor refers to providing parents with food, drink, clothing and transportation. Reverence requires that a child does not sit in his parents' seat, nor interrupt them, and takes their side in a dispute. The Talmud extols such treatment: "There are three partners in man, the Holy One, blessed be He, the father, and the mother. When a man honors his father and mother, the Holy One, blessed be He, says: 'I ascribe (merit) to them as though I had dwelt among them and they had honored me.'"[2]

The Jewish tradition teaches that domestic harmony is the ideal of home life. The Talmud specifies the guidelines for attaining this goal: "A man should spend less than his means on food, up to his means on clothes, and more than his means in honoring wife and children because they are dependent on him." Such harmony is to be attained through give and take on the part of all, as well as through the observance of Jewish ritual, which serves to unify the family. The Jewish home is permeated with sanctity when the family lives in accordance with God's commandments.

Symbols of the Jewish religion characterize the Jewish home, beginning with the *mezuzah* on each doorpost. In Scripture it is written that "these words" (Deut. 6:4; 11:13–21) shall be written on the doorposts (*mezuzot*) of the house.

This prescription has been understood literally: these two passages must be copied by hand on a piece of parchment, put into a case, and affixed to the doorpost of every room in the house. The first of these passages from Deuteronomy contains the *Shema* as well as the commandments to love God, study the Torah, express the unity of God, wear *tefillin*, and affix a *mezuzah*:

> Hear, O Israel: The Lord our God is one Lord, and you shall
> love the Lord your God with all your heart, and with all your

soul, and with all your might. And these words which I command you this day shall be upon your heart; and you shall
teach them diligently to your children, and you shall talk of
them when you sit in your house, and when you walk by the
way, and when you lie down, and when you rise. And you
shall bind them as a sign upon your hand, and they shall be as
frontlets between your eyes. And you shall write them on the
doorposts of your house and on your gates. (Deut. 6:4–9)

The second passage connects prosperity with the observance
of God's commandments:

And if you will obey my commandments which I command
you this day to love the Lord your God, and to serve him with
all your heart and with all your soul, he will give the rain for
your land in its season, the early rain and the later rain, that
you may gather in your grain and your wine and your oil. And
he will give grass in your fields for your cattle, and you shall eat
and be full. Take heed lest your heart be deceived, and you turn
aside and serve other gods and worship them, and the anger of
the Lord be kindled against you, and he shut up the heavens, so
that there be no rain, and the land yield no fruit, and you perish
quickly off the good land which the Lord gives you.

You shall therefore lay up these words of mine in your heart
and in your soul; and you shall bind them as a sign upon your
hand, and they shall be as frontlets between your eyes. And you
shall teach them to your children, talking of them when you
are sitting in your house, and when you are walking by the way,
and when you lie down and when you rise. And you shall write
them upon the doorposts of your house and upon your gates,
that your days and the days of your children may be multiplied
in the land which the Lord swore to your fathers to give them,
as long as the heavens are above the earth. (Deut. 11:13–21)

The *mezuzah* itself must be written by a scribe on parchment—the scroll is rolled and put into a case with a small opening through which the word *Shaddai* (Almighty) is visible. The *mezuzah* is placed on the upper part of the doorpost at the entrance in a slanting position. The following conditions should be met in placing the *mezuzah* on every right-hand entrance:

1. The room into which the doorway leads should be at least four by four cubits.

2. The doorway should have doorposts on both sides.

3. The doorway should serve as an entrance into a room with a ceiling.

4. The door should have a lintel.

5. The doorway should have doors that open as well as close.

6. The doorway should be at least forty inches high and sixteen inches wide.

7. The room must be for ordinary residence.

8. The room should be for human dwelling.

9. The room should be used as a dignified dwelling.

10. The room should be for continued habitation.

When the *mezuzah* is placed on the doorpost, a prayer is recited. Traditional Jews touch the *mezuzah* with their hand when they enter or leave the home.

Other home ritual objects are the Sabbath candles. At least two candles should be used in accordance with the commandment to remember and observe the Sabbath day (Exod. 20:8; Deut. 5: 12). This ceremony is performed before sunset on the eve of the

Sabbath, symbolizing light and joy. Lighting the candles is normally the task of the wife, but it may be done by any family member.

At the beginning of the Sabbath, the *kiddush* prayer is recited over wine prior to the evening meal. It consists of two sections: the blessing over the wine and the benediction of the day. The introductory biblical passages which precede this prayer are Genesis 1: 31: and 2:1-3. The blessing for wine is then recited, followed by the benedictions for the sanctification of the day. The blessing that follows includes the assertion that Israel was made holy through God's commandments, that it was favored by having been given the Sabbath as an inheritance in remembrance of creation, and that the Sabbath is the first of the holy convocations and commemorates the Exodus from Egypt. This is followed by a statement whose form is reminiscent of the festival *kiddush*.

The festival *kiddush*, which is also recited at home, consists of the blessing over wine as well as the blessing over the day. This is followed by the recitation of the *sheheheyanu* prayer ("Blessed are you, Lord our God, King of the universe, who has kept us alive, sustained us, and brought us to this season"). Wine goblets reserved for this occasion are frequently made of sliver and bear an inscription such as, "Observe the Sabbath day and keep it holy." It is usual for participants to wash their hands after the *kiddush* is recited.

Before meals on the Sabbath and on ordinary days, a blessing over food is made. Over food the blessing is: "Who brings forth bread from the earth"; over wine: "who creates the fruit of the vine"; over fruit: "who creates the fruit of the tree"; over vegetables: "who creates the fruit of the ground." Alternatively there is a more general blessing for things for which there are no specific blessing: "By whose word all things were brought into being."

After the meal is completed, a Grace after Meals is recited. This prayer comprises a series of blessings and prayers. Structurally the Grace consists of four benedictions interspersed with various prayers and petitions. The first blessing praises God for sustaining his creatures with food. The second is a national expression of thanks for deliverance from Egypt, God's covenant with his chosen people, and the land that he gave to them. The third asks God to provide Israel with relief from want and humiliation, and to vindicate his people by restoring Jerusalem. The fourth blessing acknowledges the benefits for which God is to be thanked. This is followed by a series of petitions which invoke "the Compassionate One."

The cycle of the year provides various opportunities for home observances. On Passover, normal dishes are replaced. Traditional law excludes the use of all domestic utensils, crockery and cutlery. As a result, sets are kept especially for this festival. The seder itself is observed on the first two nights of Passover. The purpose of this festival is to commemorate the redemption of the the Jewish people from slavery. During the service, the *Haggadah* is read, and a special seder dish is prepared which includes: a roasted hard-boiled egg symbolizing the Temple sacrifice; a roasted bone symbolizing the *paschal* lamb; bitter herbs symbolizing bitter oppression; *charoset* reminiscent of the mortar prepared by the Israelites in making brick; parsley in imitation of the hors-d'oeuvres of Roman nobility; and salt water representing the tears shed by the Israelites. During the seder participants eat *matzot* (unleavened bread) and drink four glasses of wine. Prayers and narratives are recited both before and after the meal. In recent times revised versions of the *Haggadah* have been composed by non-Orthodox communities.

On *Sukkot* it is customary to dwell in a temporary structure (*sukkah*) built for the festival in a yard, garden, or balcony. It is covered by foliage, through which the stars can be seen at night. All meals during the festival should be eaten in the *sukkah* if possible. During *Hanukkah* a festival lamp is kindled at home on each day of the festival in memory of the victory of the Maccabees over the Seleucids. In ancient times a lamp was put in the doorway or even in the street outside. In modern times it is placed within the home. The custom is to light a candle on the first night and an additional candle for each night until the last night when eight candles are kindled. On Purim families frequently exchange gifts and enjoy a festive meal.

Life cycle events also provide an occasion for special observances in the home. At the birth of a male child, a *Shalom Zakhor* gathering takes place on the Friday night after the birth; the circumcision ceremony occurs on the eight day; and the redemption of the first-born on the thirtieth day. All these occasions are times for festivity. Similarly bar and bat mitzvah are times of celebration in the home. Again, during the week after a marriage, a nightly feast is held where the Seven Benedictons are recited. Finally, at the time of mourning, friends and visitors come to the home during the *shivah* (seven days of mourning) where a *minyan* recites the morning and evening prayers.

In contemporary society Orthodox Judaism continues to carry out all these home-centered activities. Within the various branches of non-Orthodox Judaism, however, a number of modifications have been made to those traditions, and several home festivities have been eliminated because they are no longer viewed as spiritually significant. Nonetheless, there is a universal recognition among Jewry that the home is central to Jewish existence.

A Modern Jewish Home

As we have seen, the Jewish home is regarded as of central importance in Judaism—both husbands and wives occupy crucially significant roles. However, among the Orthodox the responsibilities of men and women are very different. Because of her domestic duties, a woman is not expected to perform all the positive time-bound precepts. She does not have to wear fringes or put on *tefillin* (phylacteries). She has no obligation to attend daily services; nonetheless, if she does go, her presence is not counted in the number required for a *minyan*. Her obligations are instead to care for the material needs of her family, to ensure that her children are educated, and to encourage her husband to continue his studies. Men are to love and respect their wives, and there is no doubt that, within the family sphere, women are influential.

Today, however, many Jewish women are unhappy with this

pattern. They believe that this matriarchal role was imposed on them by the male religious establishment, and they seek to make their mark beyond the home. As a consequence, the various non-Orthodox movements have pressed for a greater acceptance of women in religious life. In Reform, Conservative, Reconstructionist, and Humanistic Judaism, women are ordained as rabbis and can lead synagogue services as cantors. In the secular sphere, most parents are anxious that their daughters as well as their sons should achieve the highest educational standards. In the modern world women are gaining full rights and an equal role within the Jewish community.

The concept of the Jewish home has also been altered by an increasing acceptance of homosexuality in contemporary society. In Scripture homosexual conduct between males is condemned. As the Book of Leviticus decrees: "And if a man lie with mankind, as with womankind, both of them have committed abomination; they shall surely be put to death." (Lev. 20:13) Although the Bible is not explicit about lesbianism, rabbinic sources regard lesbian practices as forbidden as well. Yet despite such condemnation, in recent years a number of non-Orthodox religious groups have advocated a more tolerant attitude. The American Reform movement, for example, has passed a number of resolutions respecting the rights of gays and lesbians. In a statement of its principles, the Director of Congregational Relations of the Religious Action Center of the Reform movement stated:

> I stand here today on behalf of the Union of American Hebrew Congregations and the Central Conference of American Reform Rabbis, representing 1.5 million American Reform Jews, to say that we fervently believe in God and the Torah, and also to state that there is no room for discrimination against gays, lesbians, or bisexuals in our synagogues, in our communities, in our nation.[3]

Such attitudes have profoundly affected the nature of the Jewish home. In the past, the Jewish religion clearly delineated the role of parents and children. The Jewish community now includes homes in which a homosexual or lesbian couple has taken on responsibility for looking after children. Moreover, the high divorce rate among Jewish parents has resulted in an increase in the number of single-parent families. Such a reconfiguration of family life, however, has not diminished the importance of the Jewish home. Despite these changes, Jewish home observance can reinforce family ties as well as bonds to the Jewish past.

Although communal prayer is a central tenet of Jewish religious practice, it is not more important than home ritual. As we have observed, home and family are of paramount significance. Along with community and God, family life is one of the central mainstays that has enabled Jewry to survive. Home worship ranges from lighting of candles and reciting a prayer of sanctification over wine to mark the Sabbath and festivals to the building of the *sukkah*, where meals are to be eaten during *Sukkot*, to the celebration of the exodus from Egypt at Passover. When a Jew rises in the morning, he or she thanks God for preserving him through the night; and when he or she goes to sleep, he prays to God for protection. When Jews eat anything, they are to wash their hands and say the appropriate blessing. Traditionally, only kosher food is to be eaten. Afterwards, Jews are commanded to recite the Grace After Meals. In short, the Jewish heritage circumscribes all aspects of home life.

This sanctification of the home can offer spiritual resources for the modern Jewish community. Although the nature of family life has dramatically changed with the altered status and role of women, the inclusion of homosexual couples, and the increase in single-parent families, Jewish home observance can continue to bind members of the family together and reinforce allegiance to the Jewish people. Through the multifarious Jewish home observances, parents and children can see themselves as part of an ongoing tradition stretching back through centuries. As a small sanctuary, the home can symbolically link each family member to generations of Jews whose identity was inextricably linked to the community of Israel.

Chapter 22.

DEATH AND MOURNING

According to tradition, the utmost regard and consideration should be shown to the dying. Jewish law stipulates that the body must be buried as soon as possible after death. The general pattern for funerals involves the ritual rending of garments, the funeral procession, the eulogy either in a funeral chapel or beside the grave, and special memorial prayers. Once the funeral is over, it is customary for the family to return home to begin a seven-day period of mourning. Despite alterations to these customs in modern times, the process of mourning for the dead can still have spiritual significance for the bereaved.

Reform Observance

As a Reform rabbi, I was often called upon to officiate at funerals. Unlike the Orthodox, it was not unusual for Reform Jews to cremate the dead. Nor was the custom of sitting *shivah* observed. Nonetheless, the funeral itself incorporated many of the features of the traditional service. At the beginning of the funeral, I read various passages from Scripture such as the Twenty-third Psalm:

> The Lord is my shepherd, I shall not want. He maketh me to lie down in green pastures; He leadeth me beside the still waters. He restoreth my soul; He guideth me in straight paths for His name's sake. Yea, though I walk through the valley of the shadow of death I will fear no evil, for Thou art with me; Thy rod and Thy staff, they comfort me. Thou preparest a table before me in the presence of mine enemies; Thou hast anointed my head with oil, my cup runneth over. Surely goodness and mercy shall follow me all the days of my life, and I shall dwell in the house of the Lord forever.[1]

The service continued with a prayer for God's help, followed by a eulogy. The congregation then stood, and I recited the traditional prayer extolling God's compassion:

> O God, full of compassion, Thou who dwellest on high! Grant perfect rest unto the soul of _____, who has departed from this world. Lord of mercy, bring him (her) into Thy presence and let his (her) soul be bound up in the bond of eternal life. Be Thou his (her) possession, and my his (her) repose be peace.[2]

This chapel service was then followed by a procession to the cemetery. By the grave I began the service with a prayer of confidence in God's guidance:

> The Lord, His work is perfect, for all His ways are justice; a

God of faithfulness and without iniquity, just and right is He. Who can say unto Him, "What doest Thou?" He bringeth death and He giveth life. What mortal can demand of Him "What hast Thou wrought?" Thou alone, O Lord, dost righteously apportion life and death, for in Thy hand is the destiny of all souls. Thou wilt not forget us; Thy mercy will surely abide with us. Blessed art Thou, Judge of truth, who dost ordain death and summon us to life.[3]

The service continues with a recitation expressing trust in God's decree:

Even in sorrow, O Lord, we trust in Thy love. Therefore we do not complain, for we know that Thou art righteous and that Thy judgments are just. O Thou whose wisdom is infinite and whose power is supreme, Thou understandest our needs. Help us to feel Thy presence in this time of trouble, so that we may declare with perfect faith that the Lord is upright, our Rock, in whom there is no unrighteousness. The Lord hath given, and the Lord hath taken away. Blessed be the name of the Lord.[4]

The service concluded with the *kaddish* prayer for the dead. Throughout the funeral, emphasis was thus placed on God's compassion and justice. Mourners were reassured that death was not final, but that the soul of the person who had died would live on and be united with God.

Some time later, the dedication of a tombstone took place— this ceremony similarly emphasized the continuation of the person's spirit. Following an address about the departed, I recited the following prayer:

In the name of the family of our late brother (sister) _____ and in the presence of his (her) relatives and friends, we consecrate this memorial as a token of respect and love.

May his (her) soul be bound up in the bond of eternal life.[5]

Death and Burial

Concerning death, the Bible states that human beings will return to the dust of the earth. (Gen. 3:19) According to Scripture, burial—especially in a family tomb—was the normal procedure for dealing with the deceased. (Gen. 47:29–30; 49:29–31) In a number of biblical passages, human beings are portrayed as descending to a nether world where they live a shadowy existence. Only in the later books of the Bible is there any allusion to resurrection.

The rabbis of the Talmud decreed that death occurs when respiration has ceased. However, with the development of modern medical technology, this definition has been subject to alteration. Today it is now possible to resuscitate those who previously would have been viewed as dead. Thus the modern rabbinic scholar Mosheh Sofer in his *responsum* declares that death is considered to have occurred when there has been respiratory and cardiac arrest. Another Jewish legalist, Mosheh Feinstein, however, has ruled that a person is considered to have died with the death of his brain stem. Despite such disagreements, it is generally accepted that a critically ill person who hovers between life and death is alive. It is forbidden to hasten the death of such an individual by any positive action. Nonetheless, it is permitted to remove an external obstacle which may be preventing his death.

Jewish law accepts that no steps should be spared to save a dying patient; in this regard the Talmud lays down that a change of name may avert the evil decree; hence the custom developed of altering the formal name of an individual who is seriously ill. Yet despite such an attitude, traditional Judaism fosters an acceptance of death when it is inevitable. The *Tzidduk ha-Din* prayer, which is recited by mourners at the funeral service, describes God as a righteous Judge and accepts the finality of his decrees. On his deathbed, the dying person is to recite a prayer accepting God's will:

> I admit before you, God, my God and God of my ancestors,
> that my cure and my death are in your hands. May it be your

will that you heal me with a complete healing. And if I die, may my death be an atonement for the sins, transgressions, and violations which I have sinned, transgressed, and violated before you. And set my portion in the Garden of Eden, and let me merit the world to come reserved for the righteous. Hear, O Israel, the Lord our God, the Lord is One.

A dying person is not to be left alone. When informing someone who is dying of the duty to confess sins, he should be told: "many have confessed, but have not died; and many who have not confessed have died. And many who are walking outside in the market-place have confessed. By the merit of your confessing, you live. All who confess have a place in the world to come." All those who are present at the moment of death should recite the blessing: "Blessed be the true judge"; relatives are to recite the prayer, *Tzidduk ha-Din*. The arrangements for care of the body and burial are referred to as *hesed shel emet* (true kindness), because they are made on behalf of those who are unable to reciprocate.

Once death has been determined, the eyes and mouth are closed, and if necessary the mouth is tied shut. The body is then put on the floor, covered with a sheet, and a lighted candle is placed close to the head. Mirrors are covered in the home of the deceased, and any standing water is poured out. A dead body is not to be left unattended, and it is considered a *mitzvah* (good deed) to sit with the person who has died and recite psalms. An individual who watches over a person who has died is exempt from prayers and wearing *tefillin*.

The burial of the body should take place as soon as possible. No burial is allowed to take place on a Sabbath or the Day of Atonement, and in contemporary practice it is considered unacceptable for it to take place on the first and last days of pilgrim festivals. After the members of the burial society have taken care of the body, they prepare it for burial: it is washed and dressed in a white linen shroud. The corpse is then placed in a coffin or a bier before the funeral service. Traditional Jews only permit the use of a plain wooden coffin, with no metal handles or adornments. The deceased is then borne to the grave face upward; adult males are buried wearing their prayer shawls—one of the fringes having been removed or marred so as to render the prayer shawl unfit. In some Eastern communities, the dead person's *tefillin* are also buried with him. A marker should be placed on a newly-filled grave, and a tombstone should be erected and unveiled as soon as permissible. A limb severed or amputated from a person who is still alive should also be buried. This is true also of bodies on which autopsies or dissections have been carried out.

Among Reform Jews, burial practice differs from that of the Orthodox. Embalming and cremation are usually permitted, and Reform rabbis commonly officiate at crematoria. Burial may be delayed for several days, and the person who has died is usually buried in normal clothing without a prayer shawl. No special places are reserved for priests, nor is any separate arrangement made for someone who has committed suicide or married out of the faith.

Despite differences in procedure between Ashkenazi and Sephardi Jews, there are a number of common features of the burial service; in both rites mourners rend their garments, and biblical and liturgical verses are chanted by the rabbi as he leads the funeral procession to the cemetery. It is customary to stop on the way, allowing mourners to express their grief. Often a eulogy is given, either in the funeral chapel or as the coffin is lowered into the grave, which the male mourners help to fill with earth. Memorial prayers and a special mourners' *kaddish* are recited; mourners present words of comfort to the bereaved; and all wash their hands before leaving the cemetery.

The Jewish tradition provides a specific framework for mourning which applies to males over the age of thirteen and females over the age of twelve who have lost a father or mother, husband or wife, son or daughter, brother or sister. From the moment that death takes place until the burial, the mourners are exempt from positive commandments (praying, reciting grace after meals, wearing *tefillin*, etc.); in addition, a mourner is not allowed to participate in festival meals or engage in pleasurable activities. Instead, he must rend a garment—this is done, depending on the custom, on receiving the news of death, just prior to the funeral, or after the funeral. Once burial has taken place, mourners are to return to the home of the deceased or where the mourning period will be observed and consume a meal consisting of bread and a hard-boiled egg, which should be provided by others.

The period of mourning, known as *shivah* (seven), lasts for seven days beginning with the day of burial. During this time mourners sit on the floor or on low cushions or benches and are forbidden to shave, bathe, go to work, study the Torah, (except subjects relating to mourning), engage in sexual relations, wear leather shoes, greet others, cut their hair, or wear laundered clothing. Through these seven days, it is customary to visit mourners—it is the practice to bring prepared food. Those comforting mourners are not to greet them but rather offer words of consolation. On the Sabbath that falls during *shivah*, it is forbidden to make a public display of mourning; in some communities mourners do not occupy their normal seats in the synagogue. Among the Sephardim, members frequently sit near the mourners for part of the service.

Shivah concludes on the evening of the seventh day and is followed by mourning of a lesser intensity for thirty days known as *sheloshim* (thirty). At this time mourners are not permitted to cut their hair, shave, wear new clothes or attend festivities. Some traditions consider that the *sheloshim* constitute the full mourning period for relatives other than parents. Other traditions continue the period for one year for all relatives. Mourning for parents should take place for nearly a year, and mourners are not supposed to shave or cut their hair after *sheloshim*. Mourners are to recite *kaddish* daily throughout the period of mourning. In the case of those whose mourning continues for a year, it is at times customary to recite *kaddish* one month or week before the anniversary of death. If the holy days and festivals of Rosh Hashanah, Day of Atonement, *Sukkot*, Passover, or *Shavuot* intervene, the *shivah* is terminated. If a burial takes place during the middle days (*Hol Hamoed*) or *Sukkot* or Passover, the laws of *shivah* take effect once the festival ends.

If one hears of the death of a relative while other mourners are observing *shivah*, the person may end his *shivah* with these individuals. However, if news arrives within thirty days after death, *shivah* must be observed in its entirety. On the other hand, if the news arrives after thirty days, mourners are required to observe only a brief period of mourning. When news arrives of a parent's death, the mourner shall rend his garment; however, if he learns of the death of another relative after thirty days, he need not do so, although he is to recite the blessing of *Tzidduk ha-Din*. If the deceased was a violator of God's law or had committed suicide unless it was the result of insanity, the laws of mourning are not carried out. It is a general practice to mark the anniversary of the death of a relative (*yartzeit*) by reciting the *kaddish*, a memorial prayer, studying the Torah, chanting the *Haftarah*, and lighting memorial lights.

Mourning in the Modern World

In the modern world, there has been enormous variation among the different religious movements regarding Jewish mourning practices. As we have seen, the Orthodox insist that the body of the dead must be buried as soon as possible after death, ideally on the next day. After the person has drawn his final breath, the eyes and the mouth are closed and the body is placed on the floor and covered with a sheet. Mirrors throughout the house are covered, and any standing bowls of water are poured out. A lighted candle is placed near the head of the body, and close family members rend their clothes. It is a *mitzvah* to sit with the body and read from the Book of Psalms.

The body is then taken from the house to the funeral parlor where it is washed—this task is performed by a *Chevra Kadishah*, a burial society. The body is then dressed in a simple white linen or cotton shroud and placed in a simple pine coffin. The non-Orthodox do not generally follow these procedures. Many do not cover mirrors or rend their clothes, nor do they feel an obligation to sit with the body. They would be appalled by the idea of volunteer ritual washers. Some people desire to have elaborate coffins, and others insist on embalming. It is not uncommon for the dead to be cremated even though this is forbidden by Jewish law.

The various communities also observe different customs when burying the dead. The general pattern involves the ritual rending of garments, the funeral procession into the cemetery, the eulogy in the funeral chapel or by the grave and the special memorial prayers. After the coffin is lowered into the grave, each male mourner casts three shovelfuls of earth into the grave until it is covered. Each of the non-Orthodox movements has produced its own funeral service and has modified these observances.

Once the funeral is over, an Orthodox family returns home to begin the seven-day period of mourning, known as sitting *shivah*. As we noted, during this time they are forbidden to go to work, shave, have their hair cut, or wear leather shoes. It is the custom to keep the mirrors in the house covered, and to light a special memorial candle. The family sits together on low stools and ideally the whole group remains in one place for the whole *shivah* period. During this week, visitors come to the house to comfort the mourners. Once *shivah* ends, there is a time of lesser mourning for the next thirty days. For eleven months after the death of a parent, the Orthodox say *kaddish* for the deceased. Finally, every year the person who has died is remembered on the date of his or her death. Non-Orthodox Jews do not observe all these customs. Nonetheless, the practices of saying *kaddish* and lighting a memorial candle are widespread in the community.

A new vision of Judaism for contemporary Jews could accept the wide variation of mourning practices. No longer do Jews live in isolated communities where they are bound together by ancient law. Instead, as we have seen throughout this study, the Jewish community is divided into a wide range of sub-groups with conflicting ideologies and patterns of observance. Given such diversity, it is imperative in my opinion that Jewry adopts a spirit of tolerance and respect. Instead of bitterly denouncing variations in observance, religious leaders might accept that in an open, democratic society, each person will chose for him or herself which aspects of the tradition are spiritually meaningful.

Despite such differences of observance, the various Jewish mourning practices continue to have considerable significance for contemporary Jews. The tradition emphasizes that utmost regard and consideration should be shown to the dying. The central principle of dealing with those who have died is to honor them: all the religious rituals are designed with this in mind. This is the reason why the eyes and the mouth are closed and the body is washed and prepared for burial. As we observed, it is a *mitzvah* to sit with the body—indeed any action performed for the dead is regarded as especially meritorious. This is because it is doing an act of kindness to someone who has no way of returning it.

The rituals surrounding burial are also designed to pay respect and tribute to the deceased. Rending garments, reciting prayers, delivering a euology, and burying the dead are means of honoring the person who has died and comforting the bereaved. The laws of mourning are also directed to this end: sitting *shivah*, observing the period of lesser mourning, and reciting *kaddish* draw family members together to console one another and reflect on the life of the loved one who has passed away. In the Mishnah, there is a well-known story about the first-century sage Hillel. He was approached by a pagan who wished to convert, but who insisted that he should be taught the entire Torah while standing on one leg. Hillel replied: "Whatever is hateful to you, you should not do to your fellow human beings. This is the whole of the Torah and all the rest is commentary." This maxim is clearly illustrated by these mourning practices, which continue to have religious significance in modern times.

PART IV

WRESTLING WITH THE VISION

Chapter 23.

WRESTLING WITH THE VISION

In this chapter I present my evaluation of traditional Judaism and my suggestions for a new vision of Judaism. In the past Jews were compelled to live isolated, self-enclosed lives regulated by the Jewish legal tradition. In such circumstances, religious authorities were able to impose their will on the community. The rabbinical establishment dominated Jewish life and directed communal affairs. In modern times, however, such a theocratic structure has disintegrated. Today—as never before—Jews are free to select those features of the Jewish heritage that they find spiritually significant. Such a shift in perspective has profound

implications for the formulation of a viable religious framework for modern Jews. What is now required is a reconstructed
Judaism based on the central features of the past.

As I indicated in the introduction to this study, such a new
vision of Judaism should be based on a shift from inclusivism to
pluralism, in which Divine Reality is placed at the center of the
universe of faiths. This pluralistic stance would enable Jews to
affirm the uniqueness of their own faith while acknowledging
the validity of other religions. The theology underpinning this
theological reorientation is based on the distinction between the
Divine as it is in itself and the Divine as perceived. No longer
should Jews believe that they possess the one true path to God.
Rather, Judaism should be seen as simply one way among many.

Given the diversity of images of the Divine among the world's
faiths, it is not surprising that there are innumerable conflicts
between believers. In all cases the faithful maintain that the
doctrines of their traditions are true and superior to competing
claims. In this regard the Jewish people in previous centuries
believed that they are God's chosen people and the recipients of
his unique revelation. This new theological framework, however,
dismisses such absolutism. In its place, it recognizes the inevitable subjectivity of all religious traditions. Given that the Divine
as it is in itself is beyond human comprehension, this conception
of God cannot be viewed as definitive and final. Rather, it should
be seen as only one among many ways in which human beings
have sought to make sense of the Ultimate Reality.

Theological belief as well as religious observance must
therefore be reformulated for the modern age. Focusing on the
concept of divine unity, chapter 2 stressed that throughout the
history of the Jewish people, the belief in one God served as
the cardinal principle of the faith. However, given the various
notions of Reality in the world's religions, it should now be
accepted that Jewish monotheism is one among many ways of
conceptualizing the Divine. Although Judaism has traditionally
affirmed its own theological superiority to other faiths, there is
no way to ascertain which, if any, of these spiritual paths accu-

rately reflects the nature of the Real.

In the end, the varied truth-claims of the world's faiths must be understood as human images which are constructed from within particular cultural contexts. As a consequence, Jews lack any justification for believing that the Jewish tradition embodies a uniquely true and superior conception of Ultimate Reality. A new vision of Judaism demands a complete reorientation of religious apprehension—what is now required is for the Jewish community to recognize that its understanding of God is nothing more than a lens through which the Jewish people have perceived the Divine.

As we observed in chapter 3, even though Jews in the past viewed God as all-mighty and all-knowing, there are innumerable theological difficulties with this view. In the Middle Ages, Jewish theologians wrestled with the question whether it makes sense to believe that God can do everything, including impossible actions. Some thinkers argued that God can do everything; others insisted that it makes no sense to believe He can do what is logically absurd. In modern times, Jewish writers focused on the problem of evil and its religious implications. In the view of a number of Jewish theologians, the events of the Holocaust call into question the belief that God is omnipotent. In their view, what is now required is a reformulation of Jewish theology in the light of the horrors of the death camps. Yet, arguably no single theory provides an adequate explanation of God's seeming inaction during the Holocaust, and an acknowledgement of the inevitable subjectivity of belief can liberate Jewish theology from such a struggle.

Chapter 4 continued this discussion of the traditional concept of God by focusing on the doctrine of creation. Here it is noted that the Bible provides a detailed account of the stages in the creative process. Yet, as we have seen, the scientific understanding of the origins of the universe is at odds with the biblical narrative. Today there is widespread agreement among scientists that the cosmos was formed through a "big bang." The clash between these rival views illustrates the antiquated character of

Scripture. A new vision of Judaism for the modern age calls for a reevaluation of the biblical text. The Five Books of Moses are not inerrent and authoritative. Instead, they should be regarded as an ancient, and now outmoded, attempt to make sense of the cosmos. The universe was not created in six days, but rather evolved over billions of years, and we must accept that scientific methods of investigation and experimentation provide a more reliable basis for understanding the origins of the universe than a book written thousands of years ago by pious Jews who were influenced by the myths of the ancient Near East.

Continuing the discussion of God's attributes, chapter 5 examined the centrality of the belief in divine providence. According to the tradition, God not only created the universe, He sustains the cosmos and is actively involved in human history. According to Scripture, He chose the Jews, and guides their destiny to its ultimate fulfilment. Such providential care is a core theme of rabbinic theology and later Jewish thought. However, such a conception of God needs to be modified given its conceptual difficulties and in the light of contemporary Jewish history. No longer is it plausible to believe that God is actively involved in everyday events. It might appear that this shift in perception would be deeply unsettling for Jews, given its centrality in Jewish thought through the ages. Yet in a post-Holocaust world, there is a widespread recognition in the Jewish community that the religious outlook of the past must now be modified in the light of scientific discovery and the terrible events of the twentieth century.

Turning to the concept of divine revelation, chapter 6 outlined the nature of this belief and its significance in the history of the faith. As we have seen, Judaism is a revealed religion: according to tradition, Moses received the Written and Oral Torah on Mount Sinai—as a consequence, the Torah, *Neviim* and *Ketuvim* are viewed as holy books, containing God's word. For Orthodox Jews, the 613 commandments in the Five Books of Moses are binding for all time, and the theological views expressed in Holy Writ are inerrent.

Such fundamentalist notions, however, have been challenged

by the discoveries of modern biblical scholars. Over the last few centuries, scholars have argued that the Five Books of Moses are a composite work. The Torah is regarded, not as Mosaic in origin, but rather a mosaic of different elements which were later combined into a unified whole. Further, textual studies of ancient manuscripts have highlighted the improbability of the traditional view of Scripture. In addition, it is now widely accepted that the ancient Israelites were influenced by the culture of the ancient Near East in composing their religious epic: as we have noted, there are strong parallels in the Bible to the myths and legends contained in the Babylonian account of creation and the flood. Hence, the doctrine of *Torah MiSinai* is now regarded as antiquated.

As we noted in chapter 7 this change in perception has far-reaching implications for modern Jewish life. In the past the bedrock of divine disclosure provided a basis for Jewish belief and practice. Today, within the Jewish world it is widely accepted that the Pentateuch evolved over centuries and is the product of an ancient culture. As a result, the majority of Jews no longer view the *mitzvot* as authoritative. In the modern world, Jews do not regard themselves as under the yoke of the law; rather, they believe they have the freedom to select those features of the tradition that are personally significant and discard those which appear anachronistic. This new situation calls for a reevaluation of Jewish life and an acceptance of the principle of personal liberty—in modern times, a new approach is needed that allows all individuals the freedom to chart a path through the Jewish heritage. Such an open form of Judaism would encourage a spirit of tolerance concerning each Jews' choice of observance—no matter how rigorous or lenient.

Such freedom of interpretation should be reflected in a modern approach to transgression and sin. As Chapter 8 illustrated, in previous centuries, sin was understood as a violation of the divine commandments—a sinner is one who has failed to fulfil his obligations to God. Sins against God can be atoned for by repentance, prayer, and giving charity; in cases of wrongdoing against others, restitution and placation are necessary conditions for atonement. Given, however, that Jews today no longer view the Jewish legal system as obligatory, it no longer makes sense to envisage transgression as a breach of the covenant. Rather, the vast majority of Jews do not feel any sense of remorse if they violate the Jewish legal code. Yet, the notion of sinfulness has not disappeared from Jewish life. From the most Orthodox to the most liberal, Jews continue to express shame and sorrow for moral imperfection. A new vision of Judaism requires a recognition of this change of perception. Today Jews envisage religious duty largely in moral terms, and this alteration is reflected in the liturgies used on the Day of Atonement. Sinfulness, repentance, and forgiveness should be conceived in terms of ethical irresponsiblity rather than loyalty to the *mitzvot*.

In this connection, the traditional belief that the Jews are God's chosen people also needs modification. As chapter 9 explained, in the Bible the Jewish people are portrayed as a kingdom of priests and a holy nation, and the prophets taught that divine election is based on righteousness. In rabbinic literature, the role of Israel as the teacher of all nations is emphasized. Yet, given the transition from absolutism to religious pluralism, the Jewish community needs to adopt a more open stance in which the Divine—rather than the Jewish faith—is placed at the center of the universe of faiths. As we noted, such a pluralistic outlook would enable Jews to affirm the uniqueness of the Jewish faith while acknowledging the validity of other religious traditions. This new vision of Judaism provides a framework for engagement with other faith traditions in a spirit of tolerance and openness.

Believing themselves to be God's chosen people, the Jewish nation was determined to settle in the land promised to their ancestors. As we saw in chapter 10, this belief sustained Jewry through the centuries, and in modern times the creation of a Jewish homeland in the Middle East has revitalzed world Jewry. Regrettably, however, the Jewish state has been beleagured by its Arab neighbors as well as bitterly attacked by Palestinians living within its midst. In recent years attempts to establish peace in the Middle East have been continually thwarted. Today it is vital that the idealism of the early Jewish pioneers as well as the spiritual values of the tradition animate political life. What is now required is the infusion of Jewish ethical principles into the national life if a peaceful solution to the Middle East crisis is to be found.

As we have observed in chapter 11, the return from exile was linked to the coming of the Messiah. Such an eschatological notion sustained Jews through the centuries, providing a source of consolation and hope for the future. In modern times, however, this scheme of salvation has been largely discarded. With the exception of the strictly Orthodox, the vast majority of Jews no longer anticipate the coming of the Messiah. In contemporary society, it has become apparent that the traditional Jewish conception of the universe was based on a pre-scientific understanding of nature. As a result, most modern Jews do not accept biblical predictions about the end of time. Nor are they persuaded by arguments concerning messianic redemption found in rabbinic sources. A new consciousness is thus needed consonant with this change of perception: arguably what is now required is a this-worldly conception of Judaism devoid of any appeal to supernatural deliverance.

This shift from an other-worldly outlook has important implications for the traditional Jewish belief in the hereafter. As we noted in chapter 12, rabbinic sages argued that, with the coming of the Messiah, the dead would be resurrected and eventually the virtuous would be rewarded in a future life. Today, however, most Jews have abandoned the various elements of traditional rabbinic eschatology. As we noted, the doctrine of messianic redemption has been modified in the light of contemporary Jewish thought; similarly the belief in the resurrection of the dead has been largely replaced by the conviction that the soul is immortal. Yet, even this belief is beset with theological difficulties: the concept of disembodied personal survival appears to be internally inconsistent. Further, the notion of personhood seems dependent upon the existence of a physical body. Given such a change in direction, a new vision of Judaism calls for the return to the early biblical concentration on earthly life lived in accordance with the highest moral principles of the faith.

The second part of this study continues with a consideration of traditional Jewish practice. As we observed in chapter 13, in the past the Jewish community was bound together by adherence to a common tradition. Despite the emergence of various Jewish sects such as the Sadducees, Pharisees, Essenes, Karaites, Hasidim and Mitnagdim, Jews were bound together by a common ancestry and legal code. In the modern world, however, Jewry is divided into a wide range of sub-groups with radically different ideologies. Arguably what is now needed is for Jewry to acknowledge the nature of such religious pluralism and encourage tolerance across the chasms that separate these different movements. In contrast with the authoritarianism of previous centuries, such an attitude would grant each Jew an inalienable right to religious autonomy. The guiding principle of such a shift in orientation would be the notion of personal liberty. Such a concept would allow all Jews the right to select those elements of the tradition that they view as spiritually meaningful: such openness as a solution to Jewish living should not be seen as an alternative denomination, but rather a philosophy that could be embraced by all Jews no matter how observant.

Turning to Jewish worship, chapter 14 explored the nature of Jewish prayer in the modern world. Here it is recognized that, in previous centuries, Jews expressed their deepest longings and desires through the traditional liturgy. Today, many Jews continue to appeal to God for assistance in times of peril. Yet as we noted in previous chapters dealing with divine agency, there are serious difficulties with the notion of providence. Recently, a number of Jewish theologians have argued that the notion of divine action is no longer plausible in a post-Holocaust world. Deeply troubled about God's seeming absence during the Nazi era, they argue that it is a mistake to believe that God acts in the course of human history. Such writers as Arthur A. Cohen and Stephen Jacobs have pointed out that Jewish theology must be reformulated in a post-Holocaust age. For these writers, God is not a causal agent. Rather, they believe, He acts by inspiring human beings to carry out his will. Other writers see God as a source of inspiration and hope. Such a reinterpreation offers believers a framework in which worship can continue to animate Jewish life.

Chapter 15 continued this discussion about Jewish practice, by focusing on the nature of Jewish education in the contemporary world. Through the centuries, Jewish training has been paramount in the life of the nation. In modern times, however, the traditional pattern of Jewish instruction has undergone a major transformation: today, the process of indoctrination has been superseded by an effort simply to transmit knowledge of the Jewish heritage. Both boys and girls are exposed to the tradition in religion and day schools both in Israel and the Diaspora. As we noted, Jews no longer live in self-imposed ghettos with limited exposure to outside influences. As a consequence, knowledge of the tradition is imparted alongside secular learning. Jewish education has thus become supplementary in character, providing resources to enrich the student's religious life.

In such a context, the task of educating the young has been made easier by the proliferation of educational resources. Not only is there an abundance of books dealing with Judaism, the internet has provided a means of finding information about all aspects of the tradition. Today, as I have said, it makes no difference where one lives—the internet offers the opportunity to explore every facet of the Jewish religion. What this means is that Jewish education is open to anyone, providing resources designed to help the young formulate an informed response to the Jewish tradition. Without the overpowering influence of religious authorities, each individual is free to select those elements from the Jewish past that continue to animate his or her spiritual life. Modern educators must recognize this revolution in Jewish life and accept the inevitable subjectivity involved in such personal decision-making.

Preeminent among the Jewish festivals is the Sabbath.

Chapter 16 surveyed the nature of Sabbath observance. As
we observed, during the rabbinic era, Jewish sages formulated
thirty-nine categories of work which were regarded as forbidden
on this holy day. During the centuries when Jews lived a ghetto
existence, these laws rigorously regulated Jewish life. Today,
however, the overwhelming majority of Sabbath regulations
have been neglected. Even though the various Jewish movements have sought to impose their understanding of Sabbath
rest on their adherents, all Jews are free to observe the Sabbath
in their own ways. A new vision of Judaism must be based on
an acknowledgement of such individualized decision-making.
Nonetheless, in modern times the Sabbath can continue to
function as a reminder of the importance of self-reflection. As
we noted, this holiday can be reconstructed to highlight its religious significance. As the demands of modern life increase, the
Sabbath can offer an oasis of peace and an occasion to take stock
of the most important aspects of one's life. Most importantly,
it can serve as a weekly break to consider one's ultimate goals,
including the relationship between work and home.

Similarly, the Pilgrim festivals—which were surveyed in
chapter 17—can continue to serve as focal points in the religious calendar. Passover, which celebrates human freedom, can
function as a symbol of liberation, uniting the Jewish people
with their ancestors, who endured slavery and persecution. The
message of the Exodus continues to remind the Jewish nation
that justice and freedom will eventually prevail throughout the
world: remembering the deliverance of the ancient Israelites
from bondage, modern Jews can work together for the emancipation of those who are currently enslaved. The second Pilgrim
festival, *Shavuot,* affirms the religious stature of classical Jewish
sources—the symbol of the giving of the law on Mount Sinai
remains a potent reminder of the riches of the Jewish heritage.
Sukkot, too, has spiritual significance for the modern age. As a
sign of hope, it symbolizes the determination of the Jewish people to survive against all odds. In a post-Holocaust world, such
conviction is of vital importance: despite the terrible tragedies

of the twentieth century, *Sukkot* can serve to remind the Jewish people of the presence of the Divine in the life of the nation.

The High Holy Days, too, can continue to serve as the focus for reflection and inspiration. Chapter 18 highlighted the centrality of the moral law during these days of awe. Even though modern Jews have jettisoned the vast compendium of law found in the Bible and rabbinic sources, the community has held fast to the ethical insights of the tradition. Repeatedly during these holy days, the congregation confesses its sins and resolves to improve. Even if supplications to God have no impact, this does not imply that worship on Rosh Hashanah and Yom Kippur is meaningless. On the contrary, Rosh Hashanah and Yom Kippur can continue to recall Jews to an awareness of their ethical failings and the importance of the highest moral values in conducting daily life.

Days of Joy, too, can act as spiritual points of reference. As we observed in Chapter 19, *Purim* symbolizes the victory of the Jewish people over their enemies. As the Book of Esther relates, Haman's scheme against the Jews was foiled, and Jews were protected by King Ahasuerus. In allegorical terms, Haman—the defeated adversary of the Jewish nation—personifies evil tormentors of the Jews through the centuries. Similarly, the festival of Hanukkah celebrates the triumph of the Jewish people over foreign peoples who have sought to denigrate the Jewish religion. The central observance of Hanukkah is the kindling of the festival lamp which represents the triumph of light over darkness. These festivals can continue to remind Jewry of the possibilities of hope in the face of a hostile world. In addition, they can encourage the Jewish community to labor on behalf of the marginalized and exploited. Just as Jews were liberated from their enemies in ancient times, so modern Jewry can labor to free those who are presently enslaved.

Turning to the life-cycle events outlined in chapter 20, these various celebrations can serve as religious milestones in the lives of the adherents of the faith. Even if these observances are not perceived as divine commands, they can have spiritual meaning for contemporary Jews. The naming of a child, for example, is an occasion for reinforcing the family's link with previous generations. Redeeming the first-born is a reminder of the obligation of religious dedication and duty. Circumcision is an occasion for thanking God and reinforcing communal ties. Bar and bat mitzvah emphasize personal commitment to Judaism and the Jewish people. Similarly, the Jewish marriage ceremony emphasizes the bonds between the married couple and the Jewish community.

In the same spirit, home celebrations bind the individual Jewish family to the community. As we noted in chapter 21, the Jewish home is described as a *mikdash meat* (a minor sanctuary). In previous centuries, its religious elements recalled the Temple, menorah, and altar. Even though home observance varies widely amongst the different religious movements, there is a general recognition that worship in the home is of vital importance in establishing a Jewish way of life. Both husbands and wives occupy critically significant roles. The Jewish wife is the mainstay of the family, dedicating herself to the welfare of her husband and children. The sanctification of the home through home-based religious activities offers rich spiritual resources for the modern Jewish community. Although the nature of family life has dramatically changed with the altered status of women, the inclusion of homosexual couples, and the increase in single-parent families, home observance binds each member of the family to past generations and to the entire Jewish community.

Chapter 22 of this study focused on death and mourning. Despite the manifold practices in the Jewish community, there is a common core of observance. A new vision of Judaism for contemporary Jews should accept this wide variation. As we have seen, no longer do Jews live in isolated communities where they are bound by ancient law. Rather, the Jewish community is now divided into a number of sub-groups with conflicting ideologies. Given this diversity, it is imperative that Jewry adopts a spirit of tolerance and respect. In this way, mourners will be permitted to grieve in their own ways and to express gratitude for the lives of the deceased.

This volume thus reviews the tradition and calls for a fundamental change of religious perception. Rejecting the religious absolutism of the past, a vibrant philosophy of Judaism should be open to insights of the modern world. In previous centuries, Jews lived an isolated, inward-looking existence in which Jewish life was regulated by the legal heritage and supervised by rabbinic authorities. No longer is this the case. Since the Enlightenment, the ghetto walls have been torn down, and the coercive power of the rabbinical establishment has vanished. Today, Jews are free to determine for themselves which features of the Jewish heritage continue to retain spiritual significance. A vibrant philosophy of Judaism for the twenty-first century must acknowledge the universality of this central feature of the contemporary world.

As far as belief is concerned, this study has suggested the abandonment of those doctrinal aspects of the faith which are no longer viable. It has called for a Copernican shift in perception in which the traditional doctrine of God is set aside. In place of the absolutist claims of both the Bible and the rabbinic tradition, this new vision of Judaism acknowledges the inevitable subjectivity of religious perception. No longer is the Jewish concept of God pivotal; instead, there is a conscious awareness that the religious doctrines of Judaism stem from different periods in the evolution of the tradition and are shaped by human perception.

Similarly, this study calls for a reorientation of religious observance. From biblical times, Jews perceived themselves as bound by an eternal covenant which was sealed on Mount Sinai. The law, they believed, was divinely revealed, and sin was understood as a transgression of God's will. Today Orthodox Jews carry on this tradition, regarding themselves as the true heirs of Pharisaic Judaism. In the non-Orthodox world, on the other hand, deviations from the legal code have been justified by an appeal to the findings of biblical scholarship. This study similarly embraces such findings, but takes the further step in advocating the principle of personal liberty. A modern approach to Jewish practice, I believe, should acknowledge and respect the rights of individual Jews to determine for themselves which aspects of the tradition are religiously meaningful. Throughout the second half of this study, such individual decision-making has been continually affirmed.

In the Book of Genesis, Jacob is portrayed as wrestling with a messenger of God until dawn. Yet, when the messenger saw that he could not defeat Jacob, he pleaded to be released. Jacob, however, demanded a blessing. In reply, the messenger told him that his name would no longer be Jacob, but Israel. Jacob had struggled with God and prevailed. Through the ages, Jews have followed this same path. In every generation, they have wrestled with God, aiming to determine his nature and action in the world. Arguably, the true Israel can only prevail if it continues to wrestle with God. This study stands within this tradition of God-wrestling, seeking to discover in this process a viable form of the Jewish faith for the modern age.

Notes

Chapter 2: Divine Unity

1. *The Union Prayerbook,* I (Central Conference of American Rabbis, 1961), 101.

2. *Ibid.,* 120.

3. *Ibid.,* 150–51.

4. *Sifre* 329; *Yalkut* 946.

5. *Mekhilta, Ba-Hodesh,* 5.

6. *B. Talmud, Meg* 25a; Ber 33b.

7. *J. Talmud Taan,* 2:1.

8. Ex. R. 29:5.

9. Dan Cohn-Sherbok, *Jewish Mysticism: an Anthology* (Oneworld, 1995), 119.

302 THE VISION OF JUDAISM

10. *Ibid.,* 118–19

11. *Ibid.,* 121–22

Chapter 3: Omnipotence and Omniscience

1.   *The Union Prayerbook,* I (Central Conference of American Rabbis, 1961), 105.

2.   *Ibid.*

3.   *Ibid.,* 124.

4.   Saadiah Gaon, *Beliefs and Opinions* (Yale Univ Press, 1948), II, 13, 134.

5.   Moses Maimonides, *Guide for the Perplexed* (Hebrew Publishing Co., 1881), Part III, 59–61.

6.   Ezra ben Solomon, *Perush Al Shir Ha-Shirim* (Altona, 1764), 6a.

7.   Aquinas, *Summa Theologica,* vol. 5, 163–165.

8.   *Mishnah, Avot,* 3:19.

9.   Louis Jacobs, *Principles of the Jewish Faith* (Jason Aronson, 1988), 325.

10. *Ibid.,* 320–21

11. Steven Jacobs, *Rethinking Jewish Faith* (State University of New York Press, 1994), 119–22.

12. *Commentary to the Pentatevch,* vol. 2, 134.

Chapter 4: Creation

1.   *The Union Prayerbook,* II (Central Conference of American Rabbis, 1961), 44.

2.   *The Union Prayerbook,* I (Central Conference of American Rabbis, 1961), 93.

3.   S. *Singer,* Authorized Daily Prayer Book (London, 1962), 17.

4.   *Ibid.,* 10.

5.   *Ibid.,* 93.

6.   Maimonides, *Yad, Yesode Ha-Torah,* 1:1–3.

7.   *Genesis Rabbah,* 1:1.

8.   *Talmud, Hag,* 12a.

9.   *Genesis Rabbah,* 1:9.

10. *Genesis Rabbah* 10:3.

11. *Genesis Rabbah* 12:4.

12. *Genesis Rabbah* 9:2.

13. *Mishnah, Avot,* 6:11.

14. Dan Cohn-Sherbok, *Jewish Mysticism: An Anthology* (Oneworld, 1995), 119.

15. Louis Jacobs, *A Jewish Theology* (Darton Longman and Todd, 1973), 96.

16. Phineas Elijah b. Meir Hurwitz, *Sefer Ha-Berit,* Part I, *Maamar* 3 in Jacobs, *A Jewish Theology,* 99.

17. W. Gunther Plaut, *Judaism and the Scientific Spirit* (New York, 1962), 36–9.

18. Norman Lamm, "The Religious Implications of Extraterrestrial Life," *Tradition,* Vol. 7, No. 4–Vol. 8, No. 10, Winter 1965-Spring 1966 in Jacobs, *A Jewish Theology,* 106.

19. Jacobs, *A Jewish Theology,* 106–7.

20. Maimonides, *Yad, Yesode Ha-Torah,* 1, 1–3.

Chapter 5: Divine Providence

1. *The Union Prayer Book,* I (Central Conference of American Rabbis, 1940), 12.

2. *Ibid,* 12.

3. *Ibid.* 14–16.

4. *Ibid.,* 24.

5. *Union Haggadah* (Central Conference of American Rabbis, 1923), 28–31.

6. *Mishnah, Avot,* 3:19.

7. *Talmud, Hull.* 76.

8. *Guide for the Perplexed,* III, 134b.

9. Abraham Ibn Daud, *Emunah Ramah* (Frankfort Am-Main, 1982), 73–4.

10. Joseph Ergas, *Shomer Emunim,* in Jacobs, *A Jewish Theology* (Darton, Longman, and Todd, 1973) 115.

11. Phineas of Koretz, *Peer La-Yesharim,* No. 38.

12. Hayim of Sanz, *Divre Hayim* to *Mikketz,* in Louis Jacobs, *A Jewish Theology* (Jason Aronson, 1988), 115.

13. Tos Yom Tobh, in Jacobs, *Principles of the Jewish Faith,* 328.

14. Arthur A. Cohen, *Tremendum* in Dan Cohn-Sherbok, *Holocaust*

Theology: A Reader (Exeter University Press, 2002), 245.

15. Edward Feld, *The Spirit of Renewal* (Jewish Lights, 1994), 143.

16. Richard Rubenstein, *After Auschwitz*, in Dan Cohn-Sherbok, *Holocaust Theology* (Lamp, 1989), 82.

17. *Ibid.*

Chapter 6: Revelation and Inspiration

1. Dan Cohn-Sherbok, *Modern Judaism* (Macmillan, 1996), 83.

2. *Ibid.*, 85.

3. *Commentary to the Mishnah, Sanhedrin* 10:1.

4. *Singer's Prayerbook*, 41.

5. *Talmud, Ber.* 5a.

6. *Zohar*, III, 152a.

7. Joseph di Trani, *Mabit Bet Elohim*, Gate 3, Chapter 23, 93–7.

Chapter 7: Torah and Commandments

1. *Union Prayer Book*, I (Central Conference of American Rabbis, 1961), 12.

2. *Ibid.*, 22.

3. *Ibid.*, 53.

4. *Ibid.*, 94.

5. *Ibid.*, 94–5.

6. *Mishnah, Avot* 1:1.

Chapter 8: Sin, Repentance, and Forgiveness

1. *Union Prayer Book*, I (Central Conference of American Rabbis, 1961), 108.

2. *Union Prayer Book*, II (Central Conference of American Rabbis, 1961), 26.

3. *Ibid.*, 148–50.

4. *Ibid.*, 332–34.

5. *Gen. R.* 9:7.

6. *Yoma* 69b.

7.   *Kidd.* 30b.

8.   Moses Maimonides, *Mishneh Torah,* in Louis Jacobs, *A Jewish Theology,* (Darton, Longman, and Todd, 1973) 249.

9.   *Ibid.,* 249–250.

10.   *Shaare Teshuvah,* I, 10–50 in Jacobs, *A Jewish Theology,* 252.

11.   *Ibid.,* 255.

12.   *Mahzor for Rosh Hashanah and Yom Kippur* (The Rabbinical Assembly, 2000), 405.

13.   Pittsburgh Platform in Dan Cohn-Sherbok, *Modern Judaism* (Macmillan, 1996) 82–3.

14.   Columbus Platform in *Ibid.,* 85.

15.   San Francisco Platform in *Ibid.,* 93.

16.   *Mahzor for Rosh Hashanah and Yom Kippur* (Rabbinical Assembly, 2000), 377–371.

Chapter 9: Chosen People

1.   *Union Prayer Book,* I (Central Conference of American Rabbis, 1961), 93.

2.   *Ibid.,* 34.

3.   *Ibid.,* 53.

4.   *Ibid.,* 80.

5.   *Ibid.,* 134.

6.   *Union Prayer Book,* II (Central Conference of American Rabbis, 1961), 77.

7.   *Ibid.,* 238.

8.   Joseph Hertz, *Daily Prayer Book* (Bloch, 1948), 409.

9.   *The Book of Beliefs and Convictions* in D. Frank, O. Leaman, C. Manekin, *The Jewish Philosophy Reader* (Routledge, 2000), 171–72.

10.   Judah Halevi, *Kuzari* in Hans Lewy (ed), *Three Jewish Philosophers* (Macmillan, 1972), 33–35.

11.   CCAR Statement of Principles in *www.ccarnet.org/platforms/principles.*

Chapter 10: Promised Land

1.   Pittsburgh Platform in Dan Cohn-Sherbok, *Modern Judaism* (Macmillan,

1996), 83.

2.   Dan Cohn-Sherbok, *Israel: The History of an Idea* (Society for the Promotion of Christian Knowledge, 1992), 139.

3.   Columbus Platform in Dan Cohn-Sherbok, *Modern Judaism*, 85.

4.   *Union Prayerbook*, I, 68.

5.   Paul Mendes-Flohr, Jehuda Reinharz, eds., *The Jews in the Modern World* (Oxford University Press, 1995), 582.

6.   *Ibid.*, 629.

Chapter 11: Messiah

1.   Pittsburgh Platform in Dan Cohn-Sherbok, *Modern Judaism* (Macmillan, 1996), 83.

2.   *Union Prayer Book*, I, 101.

3.   *Ibid.*, 108.

4.   *Ibid.*, 162.

5.   *Ibid.*, 182.

Chapter 12: Afterlife

1.   Gunther Plaut (ed), *The Growth of Reform Judaism* (New York: 1965), 34d.

2.   *Rabbi's Manual* (Central Conference of American Rabbis, 1961), 68.

3.   *Ibid.*, 71.

4.   *Ibid.*, 74.

5.   *Ibid.*

6.   Ibid., 89.

7.   *Talmud, San.* 90b.

8.   A. Super, *Immortality in the Babylonian Talmud* (unpublished Ph.D. thesis, 1967), 191–93.

9.   L. Ginzberg, *The Lengends of the Jews* (Jewish Publication Society, 1968), II, 310–13.

10.   *Talmud, Shabb.*, 31a.

11.   *Talmud, Sanh*, 74a.

12.   J.H. Hertz, *Commentary to the Prayer Book*, 255.

13. Jacobs, *Principles of the Jewish Faith*, (Jason Aronson, 1988), 364.

14. *Ibid.*, 415.

15. K. Kohler, *Jewish Theology*, KTAV, 1968, 309.

16. Moses Maimonides, *Mishneh Torah, Teshuvah* 8.

Chapter 13: Jewish Community

1. In Dan Cohn-Sherbok, *Modern Judaism* (Macmillan, 1996), 84–6.

Chapter 14: Worship

1. *Rabbinic Manual* (Central Conference of American Rabbis, 1961), 11.

2. *Ibid.*, 15.

3. *Ibid.*, 23.

4. *Ibid.*, 26–27.

5. *Ibid.*, 46.

6. *Ibid.*, 56–57.

7. *Ibid.*, 71.

8. Steven Jacobs, *Rethinking Jewish Faith*, in Dan Cohn-Sherbok, *Holocaust Theology: A Reader* (Exeter Univ Press, 2002), 258.

Chapter 15: Education

1. *Mishnah, Avot* 5:21.

2. *Talmud, BB*, 21a.

Chapter 16: The Sabbath

1. *Union Prayer Book*, I (Central Conference of American Rabbis, 1966), 7.

2. *Ibid.*, 93.

3. *Ibid.*, 18.

4. *Ibid.*, 20.

5. *Ibid.*, 38.

6. *Ibid.*, 129.

7. *Mishnah.*

8. *A Prayerbook for Shabbat, Festivals, and Weekdays* (The Rabbinic Assembly, 1985), 701.

9. *Ibid.*, 703.

Chapter 17: Passover, Sukkot, and Shavuot

1. *Union Prayer Book*, I (Central Conference of American Rabbis, 1961), 230–31.

2. *Ibid.*, 234.

3. *Ibid.*, 236.

4. *Authorized Daily Prayer Book* (Bloch, 1984), 315.

Chapter 18: High Holy Days

1. *Union Prayerbook*, II (Central Conference of American Rabbis, 1961), 28.

2. *Ibid.*, 77.

3. *Ibid.*, 350.

4. *Mahzor for Rosh Hashanah and Yom Kippur* (Rabbinical Assembly, 2000), 353.

5. *Ibid.*, 379–81.

6. *Mahzor for Rosh Hashonah and Yom Kippur* (Rabbinical Assembly, 2000), 407–408.

7. *Gates of the Seasons* (Central Conference of American Rabbis, 1983).

Chapter 19: Days of Joy

1. *Union Prayer Book*, I (Central Conference of American Rabbis, 1961), 298.

2. *Ibid.*, 380–81.

3. *The Complete Artscroll Siddur* (Mesorah, 1997), 783–85.

4. *Ibid.*, 157.

5. *Ibid.*, 191.

Chapter 20: Life-Cycle Events

1. *Rabbinic Manual* (Central Conference of American Rabbis, 1961), 14.

2. *Ibid.*, 10.

3. *Ibid.*, 26–27.

4. *Ibid.*, 27.

Chapter 21: Home

1. *Rabbinic Manual* (Central Conference of American Rabbis, 1961), 50–53.

2. *Talmud, Kid.*, 30b.

3. Statement of Reform Judaism on Gays in *www.uahc.org/reform'rac/news/081298.html.*

Chapter 22: Death and Mourning

1. *Rabbinic Manual* (Central Conference of American Rabbis, 1961), 66.

2. *Ibid.*, 71.

3. *Ibid.*, 72.

4. *Ibid.*, 73.

5. *Ibid.*, 96.

Glossary

Afikoman: part of the middle *matzah*

Alenu: prayer at the end of a service

Amidah: the eighteen benedictions

Amorah: Palestinian sage

Ashkenazim: Jews originating in Eastern Europe

Ayn Sof: the Infinite

Bar Mitzvah: male adolescent ceremony

Bat Mitzvah: female adolescent ceremony

Bet Din: rabbinical court

Bimah: platform

Cohen: priest

Dayyan: judge

Exilarch: head of the Babylonian community

Gaon: head of a Babylonian academy

Gemara: rabbinic discussions on the Mishnah

Habad: Hasidic movement whose name is based on the initials of the words *hokhmah* (wisdom), *binah* (understanding), and *daat* (knowledge)

Haftarah: prophetic reading

Haggadah: Passover prayer book

Halakhah: Jewish law

Hallel: Psalms 113-118

Hanukkah: festival of lights

Haskalah: Jewish Enlightenment

Hasidism: mystical Jewish movement founded in the eighteenth century

Havdalah: service at the end of the Sabbath

Havurot: informal prayer groups

Heder: Jewish elementary school

Kabbalah: Jewish mysticism

Kaddish: prayer for the dead

Kallah: advanced rabbinic academy

Kashrut: dietary laws

Kiddush: sanctification prayer

Kippot: skullcap

Lulav: palm branch

Maariv: evening service

Maftir: reader of the Haftarah

Malkhuyyot: prayer dealing with God's rule

Marror: bitter herb

Midrash: rabbinic commentary on Scripture

Mikveh: ritual bath

Minyan: quorum of ten men

Mishnah: compendium of Oral Law

Mitzvah: commandment

Mohel: circumciser

Musaf: additional service

Nagid: head of Spanish or North African community

Noahide Laws: laws which must be observed by all persons

Omer: barley offering

Parnas: head of the community

Purim: feast of Esther

Rosh Hashanah: New Year

Seder: Passover ceremony at home

Sephardim: Jews originating in Spain or North Africa

Sefirot: Divine emanations

Selihot: penitential prayers

Shaharit: morning service

Shekhinah: Divine Presence

Shema: prayer

Shofar: ram's horn

Siddur: traditional prayer book

Sidrah: section of the Torah reading

Sifre: midrash on Exodus

Sitra Ahra: demonic realm

Tallit: prayer shawl

Talmud: compendium of law based on the Mishnah

Tanakh: Hebrew Bible

Tefillin: phylacteries

Tikkun: restoration of the world

Torah Miktav: written law

Tzimtzum: Divine contraction

Tzitzit: fringes

Yartzeit: anniversary of a death

Yeshivah: rabbinical academy

Yetzer Ha-Ra: evil inclination

Yetzer Tov: good inclination

Zemirot: Sabbath songs

Zohar: medieval mystical work.

Further Reading

Divine Unity

Buber, Martin. *I and Thou.* Scribner, 2000.

Cohn-Sherbok, Dan. *Holocaust Theology: A Reader.* Exeter University Press, 2002.

Hoffman, Joshua and Rosenkrantz, Cory. *The Divine Attributes.* Blackwell, 2002.

Jacobs, Louis. *Principles of the Jewish Faith.* Vallentine Mitchell. 1964.

Koltach, Alfred, ed., *What Jews Say about God.* Jonathan David, 1999.

Omnipotence and Omniscience

Birnbaum, David. *God and Evil.* KTAV, 1989.

Blumenthal, David. *Facing the Abusing God: A Theology of Protest.* Westminster: John Knox Press, 1993.

Jacobs, Louis. *A Jewish Theology.* Behrman House, 1973.

Kushner, Harold. *When Bad Things Happen to Good People.* Schocken, 2001.

Learner, Michael. *Jewish Renewal: A Path to Healing and Transformation.* HarperCollins, 1995.

Creation

Alter, Michael, ed., *What is the Purpose of Creation: A Jewish Anthology.* Jason Aronson, 1991.

Duchrow, Ulrich. *Shalom: Biblical Perspectives on Creation, Justice and Peace.* CCBI, 1989.

Norbert Samuelson. *Judaism and the Doctrine of Creation.* Cambridge University Press, 1994.

Schroeder, Gerald. *Genesis and the Big Bang: The Discovery of Harmony Between Modern Science and the Bible.* Bantam, 1991.

Wexelman, David. *The Jewish Concept of Reincarnation and Creation: Based on the Writings of Rabbi Chaim Vital.* Jason Aronson, 1998.

Divine Providence

Blumenthal, David. *The Banality of Good and Evil: Moral Lessons from the Shoah and Jewish Tradition.* Georgetown University Press, 1999.

Borowitz, Eugene. *Choices in Modern Jewish Thought.* Behrman House, 1983.

Friedlander, Albert, ed., *Out of the Whirlwind.* Schocken, 1988.

Jacobs, Steven. *Rethinking Jewish Faith.* State University of New York Press, 1994.

Raphael, Melissa. *The Female Face of God after Auschwitz.* Routledge, 2003.

Schulweis, Harold. *Evil and the Morality of God.* Hebrew Union College Press, 1994.

Revelation and Inspiration

Buber, Martin. *The Revelation and the Covenant.* Humanities Press International, 1988.

Halivni, David Weiss. *Revelation Restored,* Westview, 1997.

Jacobs, Louis. *Torah and Israel: Traditionalism Without Fundamentalism.* Hebrew Union College Press, 1997.

Kepnes, Steven; Ochs, Peter; Gibbs, Robert. *Reasoning After Revelation.* SCM, 2002.

Neusner, Jacob and Chilton, Bruce. *Revelation.* Trinity Press International, 1995.

Torah and Commandments

Caplan, Philip. *The Puzzle of the 613 Commandments and Why Bother?* Jason Aronson, 1996.

Cardozo, Nathan. *The Written and Oral Torah, A Comprehensive Introduction.* Jason Aronson, 1997.

Chill, Abraham. *The Mitzvot: The Commandments and Their Rationale.* Bloch, 1974.

Mikva, Rachel, ed., *Broken Tablets: Restoring the Ten Commandments and Ourselves.* Jewish Lights, 2001.

Sperling, Abraham. *Reasons for Jewish Customs and Traditions.* Bloch, 1975.

Sin, Repentance and Forgiveness

Cohen, Abraham. *Everyman's Talmud: The Major Teachings of the Rabbinic Sages.* Schocken, 1995.

Feldman, Daniel. *The Right and the Good: Halakhah and Human Relations.* Jason Aronson, 1999.

Kushner, Harold. *How Good Do We Have to Be: A New Understanding of Guilt and Forgiveness.* Little, Brown, 1996.

Sears, David. *Compassion for Humanity in the Jewish Tradition.* Jason Aronson, 1998.

Warshofsky, Mark. *Jewish Living: A Guide to Contemporary Reform Practice.* UAHC, 2000.

Chosen People

Almog, S.; Reinharz, Jehuda; Shapira, Anita, eds., *Zionism and Religion.* University Press of New England, 1998.

Frank, Daniel, ed., *People Apart: Chosenness and Ritual in Jewish Philosophical Thought.* State University of New York, 1993.

Gilman, Neil. *Shattered Fragments: Reconverting Theology for the Modern Man.* Jewish Publication Society, 1992.

Novak, David. *The Election of Israel: The Idea of the Chosen People.* Cambridge

University Press, 1995.

Wyschograd, Michael. *The Body of Faith: God and the People of Israel.* Jason Aronson, 1996.

Promised Land

Chapman, Colin. *Whose Promised Land?* Lion, 2002.

Cohn-Sherbok, Dan. *Israel: The History of an Idea.* SPCK, 1992.

Erlich, Avi. *Ancient Zionism: The Biblical Origins of the National Idea.* Free Press, 1994.

Finkelstein, Norman. *Image and Reality of the Israel-Palestine Conflict.* Verso, 2001.

Herzog, Chaim. *The Arab-Israeli Wars: War and Peace in the Middle East.* Vintage Books, 1983.

Messiah

Cohn-Sherbok, Dan. *The Jewish Messiah.* T and T Clark, 1997.

Gubbay, Lucien. *Quest for the Messiah.* Sussex, 1990.

Klausner, Jacob. *The Messianic Idea in History.* London, 1956.

Saperstein, Marc, ed., *Essential Papers on Messianic Movements and Personalities in Jewish History.* New York University Press, 1992.

Scholem, Gershom. *The Messianic Idea in Judaism.* New York, 1971.

Afterlife

Gershom, Yonassan. *Jewish Tales of Reincarnation.* Jason Aronson, 1999.

Jacobs, Louis. *A Jewish Theology.* Behrman House, 1973.

Pinson, Dov Ber. *Reincarnation and Judaism: The Journey of the Soul.* Jason Aronson, 1999.

Raphael, Simcha Paul. *Jewish Views of the Afterlife.* Jason Aronson, 1996.

Sonsino Rifat and Syme, Daniel. *What Happens After I Die: Jewish Views of Life after Death.* UAHC Press, 1990.

Jewish Community

Cohn-Sherbok, Dan. *Modern Judaism*. Macmillan, 1996.

Eleazar, Daniel and Geffen, Rela. *The Conservative Movement in Judaism*. State University of New York, 2000.

Helmreich, William. *The World of the Yeshiva: An Intimate Portrait of Orthodox Jewry*. KTAV, 2000.

Hirsch, Ammiel and Reinman, Yosef. *One People, Two Worlds: A Reform Rabbi and An Orthodox Rabbi Explore the Issues that Divide Them*. Schocken, 2002.

Raphael, Mark. *Profiles in American Judaism*. HarperCollins, 1988.

Worship

Donin, Hayim Halevy. *To Pray as a Jew: A Guide to the Prayer Book and the Synagogue Service*. Basic Books, 1991.

Hammer, Reuven. *Entering Jewish Prayer: A Guide to Personal Devotion and the Worship Service*. Schocken, 1995.

Kadish, Sharman. *Places of Worship: Synagogues*. Heinemann, 1999.

Levine, Joseph. *Rise and Be Seated: The Ups and Downs of Jewish Worship*. Jason Aronson, 2000.

Wagner, Jordan Lee. *The Synagogue Survival Kit*. Jason Aronson, 2001.

Education

Adron, Isa, ed., *A Congregation of Learners: Transforming the Synagogue into a Learning Community*. UAHC Press, 1995.

Goldman, Israel. *Lifelong Learning Among Jews: Adult Education in Judaism from Biblical Times to the Twentieth Century*. KTAV, 1975.

Neusner, Jacob. *Classical Judaism: Learning*. Peter Lang, 1993.

Ritterband, P. *Jewish Learning in American Universities*. Indiania University Press, 2002.

Rubin, Devorah. *Daughters of Destiny: Women Who Revolutionized Jewish Life and Torah Education*. Mesorah Publications, 1988.

The Sabbath

Cooper, David. *The Handbook of Jewish Meditaton Practices: A Guide for Enriching the Sabbath and Other Days of Your Life.* Jewish Lights, 2000.

Elkins, Dor Peretz, ed., *A Shabbat Reader: Universe of Cosmic Joy.* UAHC Press, 1998.

Heschel, Abraham Joshua. *The Sabbath.* Farrar Straus Giroux, 1975.

Isaacs, Ronald. *Every Person's Guide to Shabbat.* Jason Aronson, 1998.

Neuwith, Yehoshau. *Shemirath Shabbat: A Guide to the Practical Observance of Shabbat.* Volume 2. Feldheim, 1989.

Passover, Sukkot and Shavuot

Donin, Hayim. *To Be a Jew: A Guide to Jewish Observance in Contemporary Life.* Basic Books, 1991.

Goodman, Philip, ed., *Shavuot Anthology.* Jewish Publication Society, 1992.

Goodman, Philip, ed., *The Sukkot/Shimhat Torah Anthology.* Jewish Publication Society, 1992.

Isaacs, Ron. *Every Person's Guide to Shavuot.* Jason Aronson, 1999.

Schauss, Hayyim. *The Jewish Festivals: A Guide to Their History and Observance.* Schocken, 1996.

High Holy Days

Elkins, Dov Peretz, ed., *Moments of Transcendence: Inspirational Readings for Rosh Hashanah.* Jason Aronson, 1992.

Goodman, Philip, ed., *The Rosh Hashanah Anthology.* Jewish Publication Society, 1992.

Goodman, Philip, ed., *The Yom Kippur Anthology.* Jewish Publication Society, 1992.

Sorscher, Moshe; Auman, Kenneth; Sharfman, Solomon. *Companion Guide to the Rosh Hashanah Service: Featuring Selected Transliterations and Explanations of Prayers.* Judaica Press, 1998.

Scherman, Nosson, and Goldwurm, Hersh, eds., *Rosh Hashanah: Its Significance, Laws and Prayers.* Mesorah, 1989.

Days of Joy

Buxbaum, Yitzhak. *A Person is Like a Tree: A Sourcebook for Tu Beshvat.* Jason Aronson, 1999.

Elon, Ari; Hyman, Naomi; Waskow, Arthur, eds., *Trees, arth and Torah: A Tu'B'Shvat Anthology.* Jewish Publication Society, 1999.

Goodman, Philip, ed., *Purim Anthology.* Jewish Publication Society, 1988.

Randall, Ronnie. *Festival Cookbooks: Jewish Festivals Cookbook.* Hodder Wayland, 2001.

Schauss, Hayyim. *Jewish Festivals: From Their Beginnigs to Our Own Day.* UAHC Press, 1969.

Life-Cycle Events

Cardin, Nina Beth. *The Tapestry of Jewish Time: A Spiritual Guide to Holidays and Life-Cycle Events.* Behrman House, 2000.

David, Jo and Syme, Daniel. *The Book of the Jewish Life.* UAHC Press, 1997.

Geffen, Rela, ed., *Celebration and Renewal: Rites of Passage in Judaism.* Jewish Publication Society, 1993.

Goldman, Ari. *Being Jewish: The Spiritual and Cultural Practice of Judaism Today.* Simon and Schuster, 2000.

Greenberg, Melanie. *Blessings: Our Jewish Ceremonies.* Jewish Publication Society, 1995.

Home

Broner, E.M. *Bringing Home the Light: A Jewish Woman's Handbook of Rituals.* Council Oak Books, 1999.

Donin, Hayim. *To Be a Jew: A Guide to Jewish Obserance in Contemporary Life.* Basic Books, 1991.

Hoffman, Lawrence. *The Journey Home: Discovering the Deep Spiritual Wisdom of the Jewish Tradition.* Beacon Press, 2002.

Shire, Michael. *To Life! L'Chaim! Prayers and Blessings for the Jewish Home.* Francis Lincoln, 2000.

Syme, Daniel. *The Jewish Home: A Guide for Jewish Living.* UAHC Press, 1988.

Death and Mourning

Dorff, Elliot. *Matters of Life and Death.* Jewish Publication Society, 1998.

Grollman, Earl. *Living with Loss, Healing with Hope: A Jewish Perspective.* Beacon Press, 2000.

Lamm, Maurice. *The Jewish Way in Death and Mourning.* Jonathan David, 2000.

Palatnik, Lori. *Remember My Soul: A Guided Journey Through Shiva and the Thirty Days of Mourning for a Loved One.* Leviathan, 1998.

Reimer, Jack, ed., *Jewish Insights on Death and Mourning.* Syracuse University Press, 2002.

Index